RESEARCH HIGHLIGHTS IN SOCIAL WORK 46

Managing Sex Offender Risk

Research Highlights in Social Work

This topical series examines areas of particular interest to those in social and community work and related fields. Each book draws together different aspects of the subject, highlighting relevant research and drawing out implications for policy and practice. The project is under the editorial direction of Professor Joyce Lishman, Head of the School of Applied Social Studies at the Robert Gordon University.

Other books in the series

RESEARCH HIGHLIGHTS IN SOCIAL WORK 46

Managing Sex Offender Risk

Edited by Hazel Kemshall and Gill McIvor

Jessica Kingsley Publishers
London and Philadelphia

First published in the United Kingdom in 2004 by
Jessica Kingsley Publishers
116 Pentonville Road
London N1 9JB, England
and
400 Market Street, Suite 400
Philadelphia, PA 19106, USA
www.jkp.com

Copyright © 2004 Robert Gordon University, Research Highlights Advisory Group, School of Applied Social Studies

Library of Congress Cataloging in Publication Data
A CIP catalog record for this book is available from the Library of Congress

British Library Cataloguing in Publication Data
A CIP catalogue record for this book is available from the British Library

ISBN-10: 1 84310 197 1
ISBN-13: 978 1 84310 197 0

Printed and Bound in Great Britain by
Athenaeum Press, Gateshead, Tyne and Wear

Contents

Part Three   Community-based Risk Management
Strategies

Figures and Tables

CHAPTER ONE

Sex Offenders: Policy and Legislative Developments

Hazel Kemshall and Gill McIvor

Introduction

Concern with sex offenders, particularly paedophiles, has caught both public and media attention (Silverman and Wilson 2002). By the 1990s, sex offenders, most usually the spectre of the 'predatory paedophile', had come to dominate the penal agenda. Whilst the 1980s had seen heavy criticism of criminal justice agencies in the UK for a failure to take sexual crime, particularly against women, seriously (Worrall 1997), the 1990s saw a growing preoccupation with sex offending against children (Cowburn and Dominelli 2001). Although there has been a 100 per cent increase in notifiable sex offences between 1955 and 1999, sexual offences accounted for less than 1 per cent of the 37,492 notifiable offences recorded by the police between 1998 and 1999 in England and Wales (Cobley 2000; Home Office Statistical Bulletin 2000). In addition, detection and conviction rose in the 1980s and 1990s, and more sex offenders were imprisoned (Worrall 1997), with sentencing trends for sex offences moving in favour of custody (Hebenton and Thomas 1996). In Scotland, there was an overall increase in the number of offences involving rape, attempted rape, indecent assault and lewd and indecent behaviour between 1992 and 2001 (Scottish Executive 2002a). The number of persons proceeded against for sexual assaults or lewd and indecent behaviour was lower in 2001 than in 1991, but over the same period there was an increase in the proportion of those convicted of offences of this type who received a custodial sentence (Scottish Executive

2002b). Against this backdrop, sex offenders came to dominate the penal policy agenda of the 1990s, resulting in a 'criminal apartheid' approach towards them (Soothill and Francis 1997a, 1997b; Soothill, Francis and Ackerley 1998).

This development was fuelled by a series of high-profile cases and media panic about the growth of organized and pervasive paedophilia in society at large (for example 'satanic abuse' and the Butler-Schloss inquiry in Cleveland 1998 and the investigation into ritual abuse in Orkney in 1991; Scottish Office 1992). As Cobley has eloquently demonstrated, 'paedophile' has become a 'household word', as illustrated by her computer search of newspaper articles that revealed its use in '712 articles in six leading British newspapers' in the first quarter of 1998, 'whereas the word had only appeared 1,312 times in total in the four-year period between 1992 and 1995 (Cobley 2000, p.2). Against this climate, sex offending and paedophilia have become meshed (Soothill *et al.* 1998).

The concepts of the 'predatory paedophile' and 'stranger-danger' have been potent constructions, although the extent to which they are media-constructed 'moral panics' (Kitzinger 1999a, 1999b) or 'barometers of the state of the nation' has been hotly debated (Soothill and Soothill 1993, p.19; Wilczynski and Sinclair 1999, p.276). Kitzinger, for example, identifies the roots of the 'moral panic' in the mid-1980s' creation of the BBC's 'Childwatch' and the inception of 'Childline'. Certainly, the sex offender has been portrayed as particularly demonic with non-familial paedophiles constructed as 'Others' to be 'put under surveillance, punished, contained and constrained' (Young 1996, p. 9). Sanders and Lyon have described this as 'repetitive retribution' (1995) with a significant impact upon penal policy decisions (Muncie 1999).

Sex offending and paedophilia can also be understood as a manifestation of the 'new penology' and penal policy objectives driven by a rationale of risk across most of the Anglophone countries (Feeley and Simon 1992, 1994). Public concern with the harm resulting from sexual and violent offending is now undisputed (Scottish Executive 2000). The frequency and widespread nature of sexual offending have been reviewed by Finkelhor (1994), and Home Office statistics for England and Wales have established that males and females aged between 10 and 15 years are most at risk of indecent assault, with 66 male victimizations and 327 female victimizations per 100,000 of the population (Home Office 1998). The physical and psychological harm caused by sex offending has also been well documented (e.g. by the Social Work Services Inspectorate in Scotland: SWSI 1997), with its impact ranging from minimal physical harm to extensive abuse and psychological trauma (Scottish Executive 2001a). However, the MacLean Committee report on sexual and violent offending in Scotland attempted to place these concerns into context by noting the recidivism rates for serious violent and sexual crimes:

> In 1998, 50 people were imprisoned for four years or more for a sexual or violent crime, having previously (since 1989) received a similarly serious sentence for a sexual or violent crime. (Scottish Executive 2001b, p.5).

Similarly, Loucks (2002) found evidence that just over one-third of Scottish prisoners who had been sentenced for a serious violent or sexual offence posed a definite risk of further serious offending, although she also documents the difficulty involved in drawing conclusions about risk on the basis of the information that was available.

The cumulative effect of this growing preoccupation with the risks posed by sexual offenders (particularly paedophiles) has been the pursuit of both legislation and policy for the preventative sentencing and selective incapacitation of 'serious' sexual and violent offenders, and more robust systems for the monitoring and surveillance of such offenders in the community (Kemshall 2002).

Key trends

Three key trends can be discerned: selective incapacitation, preventative sentencing, and community risk management for high-risk offenders post-release or as part of community sentences. Selective incapacitation (Greenwood and Abrahamse 1982) was a response to burgeoning prison populations in all the Anglophone countries throughout the 1980s and 1990s (Flynn 1978), and reflected a desire to pursue a 'bifurcated' or twin-track approach to penal policy in which custody was reserved for the most 'dangerous, the most serious, and habitual recidivists' (Murray 1997). Selective incapacitation has not always operated in a rigorous manner, filtered by a 'populist punitiveness' (Bottoms 1995, p.40) that sought to extend the 'Three strikes and you're out' philosophy to a range of offences including property crime and burglary (Kemshall 2003). Violent and sexual offences were also targeted for special measures, and public protection was prioritized over proportionality. In England and Wales, preventative sentencing was introduced for those most likely to compromise public safety by s.2.2. (*b*) of the Criminal Justice Act 1991. The rationale was the prevention of serious harm to the public and the use of disproportionate sentencing to prevent future risky offending (Wasik and Taylor 1991) – a strategy of what Henham (2003, p.59) has called 'predictive confinement' (2003, p.59). Sex offenders were one key group targeted for this type of sentencing, although the criteria for determining 'dangerousness' and the uncertain nature of risk prediction as a basis for disproportionate sentencing have been heavily criticised (von Hirsch and Ashworth 1996; Wood 1988). The efficacy of such sentencing for both appropriately targeting the right offenders and reducing harmful offending has also been questioned (Pratt 1997).

The 1990s also saw the development of 'community risk management' for high-risk offenders in the community (Connelley and Williamson 2000). This approach emphasizes containment, surveillance and restriction, prioritizing risk management (defined as control and harm reduction) over rehabilitation (Kemshall 2003). Interventions and treatment programmes also gained momentum within a broader penal policy of correctional, cognitive-behavioural approaches to offenders (Holt 2000). Such programmes, delivered both in prison and in the community, aimed at risk reduction through changing both the cognitions and behaviours of sex offenders (Beech and Fisher, and Marshall, Serran and Moulden, this volume). Community management also comprised other special measures for sex offenders, in particular paedophiles, including special attention to prison release arrangements and the use of parole restrictions, and intensive monitoring and surveillance measures for those in the community (Scottish Executive 2001; Hebenton and Thomas 1996, 1997; Scottish Executive 2001; SWSI 1997, 2000).

By the turn of the century, sex offenders in England and Wales were subject to the following legislation:

- The Sex Offender Act 1997 provided for a sex offender register designed to monitor and track such offenders (see Thomas, this volume). These provisions also apply in Scotland (Scottish Executive 2000).

- Section 20 of the Crime and Disorder Act 1998 provided for a Sex Offender Order. A Sex Offender Order is available to a chief officer of police from a magistrates' court (sheriff court in Scotland) if there is reasonable cause to believe that the defendant 'has acted' in such a way that an order is necessary to protect the public from the offender. Offenders who are subject to these orders – which run for a minimum of five years and may have negative conditions or 'prohibitions' attached – are required to register under the Sex Offender Act 1997 within 14 days of the order being made. Breach of a Sex Offender Order can carry up to a five-year custodial penalty upon indictment.

- The Crime and Disorder Act also provided for extended periods of supervision on the grounds of protecting the public from serious harm and can be used for sex offenders who have served a determinate custodial sentence of any length. Supervision periods can be for up to ten years. Similar provisions were introduced in Scotland initially through s.210A of the Criminal Procedure (Scotland) Act 1995.

- Amendments under the Criminal Justice and Court Services Act 2000 require sex offenders in England and Wales to notify of foreign travel. There are increased penalties for non-registration and additional powers for photographing and finger-printing of offenders, well as a requirement to register within 72 hours.

- In November 2002, a further paper – *Protecting the Public* (Home Office 2002) – was issued by the Home Office for England and Wales:, 'Protecting the Public' (Home Office 2002) aimed at increasing the level of public protection. It proposes measures to tighten the sex offender register, improve monitoring of sex offenders in the community and build in safeguards against evasion of registration requirements (Social Services Parliamentary Monitor: 3). In particular, a new offence of grooming is proposed, as are measures to protect children from paedophiles using the Internet. (Social Services Parliamentary Monitor 2002).

In England and Wales, there is also a statutory provision for joint risk assessment and management by police and probation in ss.67 and 68 of the Criminal Justice and Court Services Act 2000 and the official creation of Multi-Agency Public Protection Panels (Maguire and Kemshall, this volume). In Scotland, arrangements for multi-agency risk assessment and management are less formalized and operate differently in different parts of the country (McIvor and Kemshall 2002).

In Scotland, a review by the SWSI of the management of sex offenders in the community was prompted by the murder of a ten-year-old boy by a convicted sex offender who was subject to social work supervision. The resulting report – *A Commitment to Protect* (SWSI 1997) – concluded that strategic and operational collaboration between the agencies involved in managing risk should be improved at national and local levels, and improvements should be made in the assessment and supervision of sex offenders. *A Commitment to Protect* also recommended the establishment of an Expert Panel on Sex Offending. The panel was established in 1998, chaired by Lady Cosgrove. Its report built upon the initial work of *A Commitment to Protect* by providing a framework and series of recommendations to improve the management of sex offenders. The recommendations of the Cosgrove Committee were largely accepted by the Scottish Executive (see www.scotland.gov.uk/library5/accr.pdf).

The MacLean Committee was subsequently established in 1999 to consider provision for the assessment and management of serious violent and sexual offenders. Amongst its recommendations was a proposal for a new sentence, *the Order for Lifelong Restriction (OLR)*, which was introduced in the Criminal Justice (Scotland) Act 2003. Offenders who have been convicted of a serious violent, sexual or life-endangering offence and who are assessed as high-risk will be made subject to an OLR by the court. The OLR will make the offender subject to measures – if necessary for the rest of his or her life – designed to ensure that the risk to the public is minimized. A risk management plan (RMP) will be prepared for each offender sentenced to an OLR. The plan will provide an assessment of the offender's risk, specify what measures will be taken to minimize that risk and detail the roles that each of the responsible bodies, such as social work departments, will play in managing that risk. The legislation also makes provision for the establishment of a Risk Management Authority (RMA) whose responsibilities will include ensuring that the RMP is drawn up and implemented properly. (Full details of the OLR can be found at http://www.scotland.gov.uk/library3/justice/svsom.pdf).

There have been significant implications for criminal justice personnel and social workers engaged with offenders. The significance to the probation service in England and Wales and the political importance of credible work with sex offenders were reflected in the Her Majesty's Inspectorate of Probation (HMIP) report *'Exercising Constant Vigilance: The Role of the Probation Service in Protecting the Public from Sex Offenders'* (HMIP 1998). Little distinction was made in the document between types of sex offences and levels of harm, and the emphasis upon sex offending work significantly outweighed its actual volume on the service caseload, where it comprised 3 per cent of probation supervision cases, and 9 per cent of the through-care caseload (HMIP 1998: 31). Intensive group work programmes were, however, devised (McEwan and Sullivan 1996), and sex offending was one area in which the probation service was at pains to demonstrate the effectiveness of its community management arrangements (Gocke 1995; Nash 1999).

In Scotland, central government concern about the effectiveness of sex offender risk management was evidenced in an inspection undertaken by the SWSI of sex offender cases supervised by eight local authorities. The inspection concluded that progress had been made in the assessment and supervision of sex offenders. Further progress was, however, deemed to be required to raise the quality of supervision and to improve the effectiveness of risk management by ensuring that it was informed by risk assessments and included structured offence-focused work with individuals and groups (SWSI 2000).

The effective community management of the predatory paedophile has presented a severe challenge: how to manage effectively in the community those with serious and potentially harmful behaviours and those who are also perceived as being 'beyond the pale' and unworthy of community integration. The sex offender register has been presented as a key mechanism in the management of such offenders (Home Office 2002; Plotnikoff and Woolfson 2000), although the impact of the register as a risk management and harm reduction tool has been disputed (Zevitz and Farkas 2002a, 2002b; Thomas, this volume).

The register has, however, provided a key impetus for multi-agency working on the management and treatment of sex offenders, although the effectiveness of such arrangements is variable (Maguire *et al.* 2001; see also Maguire, this volume). In Scotland, for example, effective risk management has, arguably, been undermined by the absence of shared approaches to risk assessment and its interpretation across different professional groups (McIvor and Kemshall 2002).

Arrangements for joint working on sex offenders was given impetus throughout the 1990s by the following key factors:

- high-profile cases, particularly those which contributed to the growing 'moral panic' surrounding paedophile rings, satanic abuse and 'stranger-danger' (Kitzinger 1999a, 1999b; Thompson 1998)

- individual cases that raised public awareness and discontent, particularly with release arrangements from prison and the perceived failure of community agencies to manage such offenders effectively (e.g. the cases of Sydney Cooke in England and Steven Leisk in Scotland)

- Home Office disquiet with the volume of 'serious incidents' within the probation service caseload, i.e. the number of offenders committing serious offences such as murder or rape while subject to supervision

- developments in America (and to a lesser extent in Canada) related to 'Megan's Law' (the disclosure of sex offender details to communities), 'tracking' systems to monitor the whereabouts of sex offenders in the community, and 'special measures' for those deemed to pose an unacceptable risk (Hebenton and Thomas 1997; Kanka 2000; Petrunik 2002)

- broader criminal justice policy to achieve 'joined-up' responses to crime, particularly through the Crime and Disorder Act 1998, and increased attempts to 'join up' and co-ordinate policy under the New Labour Government's modernization programme (Faulkner 2001).

The cumulative effect of these key factors was that the 1990s saw the establishment of public protection as a key objective of penal policy and legislation (Nash 1999). Violent, sexual and paedophilic offenders are now identified for special measures, including selective incarceration and community surveillance. This has also included those offenders whose antecedents, behavioural patterns, and personal characteristics indicate the potential for future harmful offending (Loucks 2002). This approach to 'dangerous' offenders, and most particularly sexual offenders, has been characterized as a 'community protection model' in which legislation prioritizes public protection through the use of mandatory, indeterminate and preventative sentencing. It has also signalled greater collaboration between criminal justice agencies and beyond (see Maguire, this volume), and raised significant issues about the disclosure of information about sex offenders across agencies (Scottish Executive 2001), as well as between agencies and the public (Thomas, this volume).

The impact on key agencies and those working with sex offenders

The MacLean Committee in Scotland acknowledged the difficulty in identifying the 'target group' for special measures, and, importantly, focused on the offender rather than offence type by emphasizing those whose 'antecedents or personal characteristics indicate that they are likely to present particularly high risks to the safety of the public'. (Scottish Executive 2000, p.4).

Although definitions of high risk are becoming more rigorous (see, for example, Scottish Executive 2000 and the definitions provided in the Home Office Offender Assessment System (OASys); Home Office 2001), the range of offence types and offenders potentially falling within such a category may be large. In addition, sexual offending can be difficult to define, and sex offenders are not a homogeneous group (Grubin 1998; SWSI 1997; Fisher and Beech, this volume; Kemshall, this volume; and Kendrick, this volume). *A Commitment to Protect* concerned itself with those whose sexual offending involves exploitation and/or assault, and emphasized the following categories: familial child sex abusers, non-familial child sex abusers, paedophiles, rapists and indecent exposers. Fisher and Beech (this volume) provide an extensive overview of adult male offending, Masson (this volume) and Kendrick (this volume) provide an examination of young sex offenders, and Kemshall (this volume) a review of female sexual offending. The clear implication for policy and practice is that sex offenders are not a homogeneous group, but present differing patterns of behaviour, different motivations for their behaviour, different reconviction rates and different treatment needs (Beech and Fisher this volume).

This presents significant difficulties for those agencies and staff required to identify and risk assess sex offenders. These can be briefly summarised as follows:

- There are difficulties in identifying those risky enough for special measures and avoiding net-widening. Identifying the 'potential' for committing offences of serious harm in the future can be very difficult, and, for some staff (and sentencers), morally repugnant (Henham 2003). This is particularly difficult when the presenting offence(s) would not be considered high-risk.

- Assessment tools and practices have tended not to distinguish between differing types of sex offenders, and transference to female and young offenders has been problematic. This situation has been exacerbated by the lack of reliable and user-friendly risk assessment tools for sex offending, and by delays by key agencies in adopting those available (McIvor and Kemshall 2002).

- Prediction remains problematic, although tools have been subject to constant refinement and improvement, and accuracy levels have been significantly improved (see Grubin, this volume). The present penal climate has, however, seen rather less concern with false positives than with false negatives.

- Staff and agencies are operating in a 'blame culture', in which accountability for the risk assessment and management of offenders, particularly sex offenders, is high (Kemshall 1998, 2003). This can result in defensive practice and the over-inflation of risks as workers and their agencies strive to avoid litigation and blame (Carson 1996).

- Different risk assessment tools have been adopted by different criminal justice and social work agencies, and tools are used in different contexts by different grades of staff with varying degrees of training and knowledge (McIvor and Kemshall 2002).

The growing preoccupation with assessing the risks posed by sex offenders has resulted in a broadening of the professional groups involved in the identification of those who may pose a significant risk of harm and the formalization of risk assessment procedures and risk management processes. For example, the introduction of the OLR in Scotland will place an onus upon the prosecution to identify cases that meet the initial criteria for such an order, while the risk assessment itself will be carried out by accredited practitioners using tools that have been accredited by the RMA. The RMA will also have responsibility for approving RMPs for those subject to ORLs. The development of risk management strategies has so far been hampered by those factors that impinge upon the quality and utility of risk assessments. It has also, however, been influenced by the policy context in which such work is undertaken, by the effectiveness of the available techniques for effecting behavioural change and by the difficulties inherent in facilitating the integration of sex offenders into hostile communities.

Risk management of sex offenders

This has proved to be a challenging area of work in a retributive and punitive penal climate. What Connelley and Williamson have labelled the 'community protection model' has come to dominate, with monitoring, tracking and surveillance seen as key risk management strategies (see Thomas, this volume). Treatment interventions have also received much attention, usually linked to particular criminal justice agencies such as the prison service, and probation (Scotland), and compulsorily delivered to sex offenders as part of supervision/punishment orders or, within prison, as part of parole eligibility. These programmes were given impetus (and funding) from policy-makers concerned to reduce sex offence recidivism and also to capitalize upon the growing 'What Works' literature on effective treatment programmes from the late 1970s onwards (see Marshall, Serran and Moulder, this volume). Beech and Fisher (this volume) describe how the rehabilitative treatment of sex offenders has become a big industry over the last 10 years, both in prison and community settings. The treatment ethos has been distinctive. Based on cognitive-behavioural treatment (CBT), it emphasizes changes in both the cognition and behaviours of sex offenders (see Marshall, Serran and Moulder, and Beech and Fisher, this volume). Although CBT with sex offenders has established a reputable track-record with adult male offenders, more recent evaluative work has acknowledged that certain categories of offender are less amenable to treatment, e.g. predatory paedophiles (Beech and Fisher this volume) or offenders with personality disorder (Marshall, Serran and Moulder, this volume), and the transferability of CBT to young offenders and female offenders has worked less well (Masson and Kemshall, this volume).

The more recent challenge for both research and practice has been how to adapt CBT to cover the diversity of offence types and motivations to sexually offend, and, *as importantly,* how to reintegrate the 'monsters in our midst' (Channel Four 1998) into the community. The latter has involved increased emphasis upon stable and, where appropriate, supportive accommodation (SWSI 1997), e.g. 'a half-way house' offering semi-secure and intensive treatment (comparable to the 'less restrictive alternative' operated by the Arizona Community and Protection Treatment Centre) (Scottish Executive 2000, p.60). There has also been an important re-integrative initiative rooted in faith-based communities in Canada and the USA: 'Circles of Support' (Petrunik 2002). In brief, the initiative recognizes that many sex offenders are social isolates, and a Circle of Support is provided in the community following release from prison/treatment centre or to support a community order. Such circles are made up of volunteers with whom the offender will have significant contact (e.g. church leaders and mentors). In addition to providing social support, the volunteers are trained to identify 'warning signals' of relapse (Ward, and Devilly, this volume) as well as to inform the statutory authorities should the offender's behaviour warrant it. There are currently two pilot schemes in the UK, and long-term evaluation is awaited.

The structure of the book

The book *Managing Sex Offender Risk* aims to present relevant research for the effective management of sex offenders. The focus is not solely restricted to intervention strategies and programmes, but encompasses a broad overview of the typologies and characteristics of sex offenders and sexual offending in Part One; a review of current intervention techniques in prison and the community in Part Two; and a broader view of multi-agency work and the community management of sex offenders in Part Three. All the chapters present relevant research, but also strive to highlight the implications for policy and practice. The book is aimed at a busy policy and practitioner audience as well as academics within the field; and, as such, the authors have attempted a tight focus rooted in contemporary empirical research.

References

Bottoms, A. (1995) 'The Politics and Philosophy of Sentencing.' In: C. Clarkson and R. Morgan (eds.) *The Politics of Sentencing.* Oxford: Clarendon Press.

Butler-Schloss, E. (1988) *Report of the Commission of Inquiry into Child Sexual Abuse in Cleveland.* Presented to the Secretary of State for Social Services by the Right Honorable Lord Butler-Schloss, DBE, Cm 412. London: HMSO.

Carson, D. (1996) 'Risking Legal Repercussions.' In H. Kemshall and J. Pritchard (eds) *Good Practice in Risk Assessment and Risk Management,* volume 1. London: Jessica Kingsley Publishers.

Channel Four (1998) *Monsters in our Midst: Community Perceptions of Sexual Offenders.* Channel Four, 8 January 1998.

Cobley, C. (2000) *Sex Offenders: Law, Policy and Practice.* Bristol: Jordans.

Connelley, C. and Williamson, S. (2000) *Review of the Research Literature on Serious Violent and Sexual Offenders.* Crime and Criminal Justice Research Findings No. 46. Edinburgh: Scottish Executive Research Council.

Cowburn, M. and Dominelli, L. (2001) 'Masking Hegemonic Masculinity: Reconstructing the Paedophile as the Dangerous Stranger.' *British Journal of Social Work 31,* 399–415

Faulkner, D. (2001) *Crime, State and Citizen: A Field Full of Folk.* Winchester: Waterside Press.

Feeley, M. and Simon, J. (1992) 'The New Penology: Notes on the Emerging Strategy for Corrections.' *Criminology 30,* 4, 449-475

Feeley, M. and Simon, J. (1994) 'Actuarial Justice: The Emerging New Criminal Law.' In D. Nelken (ed.) *The Futures of Criminology.* London: Sage.

Finkelhor, D. (1994) 'The International Epidemiology of Child Sexual Abuse.' *Child Abuse and Neglect 18,* 5, 409-417

Flynn, E. E. (1978) 'Classification for Risk and Supervision – a Preliminary Conceptualization.' In J. C. Freeman (ed) *Prisons Past and Future.* London: Heinemann.

Gocke, B. (1995) 'Working with People who Have Committed Sex Offences.' In B. Williams (ed) *Probation Values.* Birmingham: Venture Press.

Greenwood, P. and Abrahamse, A. (1982) *Selective Incapacitation.* Santa Monica, CA: RAND Corporation.

Grubin, D. (1998) *Sex Offending Against Children: Understanding the Risk.* Police Research Series Paper No. 99. London: Home Office.

Hebenton, B. and Thomas, T. (1996) 'Tracking Sex Offenders.' *Howard Journal 35,* 2, 97-112

Hebenton, B. and Thomas, T. (1997) *Keeping Track? Observations on Sex Offender Registers in the U.S.* Police Research Group Crime Detection and Prevention Paper No.83. London: Home Office.

Henham, R. (2003) 'The Policy and Practice of Protective Sentencing.' *Criminal Justice 3,* 1, 57-82

HMIP (Her Majesty's Inspectorate of Probation) (1998) *Exercising Constant Vigilance: The Role of the Probation Service in Protecting the Public from Sex Offenders.* Report of a Thematic Inspection. London: Home Office.

Holt, P. (2000) *Take-up and Roll-out: Contexts and Issues in the Implementation of Effective Practice in the Probation Service.* Community and Criminal Justice Unit Monograph No. 1. Leicester: De Montfort University.

Home Office (1998) *Aspects of Crime: Children as Victims 1996.* Compiled by the Crime and Criminal Justice Unit, Research and Statistics Directorate. London: Home Office.

Home Office (2001) *The Offender Assessment System: OASys.* London: Home Office.

Home Office (2002) *Protecting the Public.* Cm 5668. London: Home Office.

Home Office Statistical Bulletin 1/00 (2000) *Recorded Crime Statistics, England and Wales, October 1998 – September 1999.* London: Home Office.

Kanka, M. (2000) 'How Megan's Death Changed Us All: The Personal Story of a Mother and Anti-crime Advocate.' The Megan Nicole Kanka Foundation. Online: www.apbnews.com/safetycenter/family/kanka/sooo/03/28/kanka0328_0l.ht m. Accessed 28 March 2000

Kemshall, H. (1998) *Risk in Probation Practice.* Aldershot: Ashgate.

Kemshall, H. (2002) *Risk Assessment and Management of Serious Violent and Sexual Offenders: A Review of Current Issues.* Edinburgh: Scottish Executive Social Research, Crime and Criminal Justice.

Kemshall, H. (2003) *Understanding Risk in Criminal Justice.* Buckingham: Open University Press.

Kitzinger, J. (1999a) 'Researching Risk and the Media.' *Health, Risk and Society 1,* 55-70

Kitzinger, J. (1999b) 'The Ultimate Neighbour from Hell: Media Framing of Paedophiles.' In B. Franklin (ed) *Social Policy, Media and Misrepresentation.* London: Routledge.

Loucks, N. (2002) *Recidivism Among Serious Violent and Sexual Offenders.* Edinburgh: Scottish Executive Social Research.

Maguire, M., Kemshall, H., Noaks, L. and Wincup, E. (2001) 'Risk Management of Sexual and Violent Offenders: The Work of Public Protection Panels.' Police Research Series Paper No.139. London: Home Office.

McEwan., S. and Sullivan, J. (1996) 'Sex Offender Risk Assessment.' In H. Kemshall and J. Pritchard (eds) *Good Practice in Risk Assessment and Risk Management,* volume 1. London: Jessica Kingsley Publishers.

McIvor, G. and Kemshall, H., with Levy, G. (2002) *Serious Violent and Sexual Offenders: The Use of Risk Assessment Tools in Scotland.* Edinburgh: Scottish Executive Social Research, Crime and Criminal Justice.

Muncie, J. (1999) 'Exorcising Demons: Media, Politics and Criminal Justice.' In B. Franklin (ed) *Social Policy, The Media and Misrepresentation.* London: Routledge.

Murray, C. (1997) *Does Prison Work?* Choice in Welfare No. 38. London: Institute for Economic Affairs.

Nash, M. (1999) *Police, Probation and Protecting the Public.* London: Blackstone Press.

Petrunik, M. G. (2002) 'Managing Unacceptable Risk: Sex Offenders, Community Response, and Social Policy in the United States and Canada.' *International Journal of Offender Therapy and Comparative Criminology 46,* 4, 483-511.

Plotnikoff, J. and Woolfson, R. (2000) *Where Are They Now? An Evaluation of Sex Offender Registration in England and Wales.* London: Home Office.

Pratt, J. (1997) *Governing the Dangerous*. Sydney: Federation Press.

Sanders, C. R. and Lyon, E. (1995) 'Repetitive Retribution: Media Images and the Cultural Construction of Criminal Justice.' In J. Ferrell and C. Sanders (eds) *Cultural Criminology*. Boston, MA: NE University Press.

Scottish Executive (2000) *A Report on the Committee on Serious Violent and Sexual Offenders* (MacLean Report). Edinburgh: Scottish Executive.

Scottish Executive (2001) *Reducing the Risk: Improving the Response to Sex Offending. Report of the Expert Panel on Sex Offending* (Cosgrove Report). Edinburgh: Scottish Executive.

Scottish Executive (2001) *The Sex Offender Act 1997: Guidance for Agencies*. Edinburgh: Scottish Executive.

Scottish Executive (2002a) *Recorded Crime in Scotland, 2001*. Statistical Bulletin CrJ/2002/1. Edinburgh: Scottish Executive National Statistics.

Scottish Executive (2002b) *Criminal Proceedings in Scottish Courts, 2001*. Statistical Bulletin CrJ/2002/9. Edinburgh: Scottish Executive National Statistics.

Scottish Office (1992) *The Report of the Inquiry into the Removal of Children from Orkney in 1991* (Clyde Report). Edinburgh: HMSO.

Silverman, J. and Wilson, D. (2002) *Innocence Betrayed: Paedophilia, Media and Society*. Cambridge: Polity Press.

Social Services Parliamentary Monitor (2002) 'Plans to Strengthen Laws Covering Sex Offenders and Sex Offences.' *Social Services Parliamentary Monitor 92*, pp.3–4.

Soothill, K. and Francis, B. (1997a) 'Sexual Reconvictions and the Sex Offenders Act 1997. (Part One).' *New Law Journal*, 5 September, 1285–1286.

Soothill, K. and Francis, B. (1997b) 'Sexual Reconvictions and the Sex Offenders Act 1997. (Part Two).' *New Law Journal*, 12 September, 1324–1325.

Soothill, K. and Soothill, D. (1993) 'Prosecuting the Victim? A Study of the Reporting Barristers' Comments in Rape Cases.' *Howard Journal 32*, 12–24.

Soothill, K., Francis, B. and Ackerley, E. (1998) 'Paedophilia and Paedophiles.' *New Law Journal*, June 12, 882–883.

SWSI (Social Work Services Inspectorate) (1997) *A Commitment to Protect. Supervising Sex Offenders: Proposals for More Effective Practice*. Edinburgh: SWSI.

SWSI (Social Work Services Inspectorate) (2000) *Managing the Risk: An Inspection of the Management of Sex Offender Cases in the Community*. Edinburgh: SWSI.

Thompson, K. (1998) *Moral Panics*. London: Routledge.

Von Hirsch, A. and Ashworth, A. (1996) 'Protective Sentencing under Section 2 (2)b: The Criteria for Dangerousness.' *Criminal Law Review*, 175–183.

Wasik, M. and Taylor, R. D. (1991) *Blackstone's Guide to the Criminal Justice Act 1991*. Oxford: Blackstone Press.

Wilczynski, A. and Sinclair, K. (1999) 'Moral Tales: Representations of Child Abuse in the Quality and Tabloid Media.' *The Australian and New Zealand Journal of Criminology 32*, 3, 262–283.

Wood, D. (1988) 'Dangerous Offenders and the Morality of Protective Sentencing.' *Criminal Law Review*, 424–433.

Worrall, A. (1997) *Punishment in the Community: The Future of Criminal Justice*. London: Longman.

Young, A. (1996) *Imagining Crime: Textual Outlaws and Criminal Conversations.* London: Sage.

Zevitz, R. and Farkas, M. (2000a) 'Sex Offender Community Notification: Managing High Risk Criminals or Exacting Further Vengeance?' *Behavioural Sciences and the Law 18*, 2/3, 375–391.

Zevitz, R. and Farkas, M. (2000b) 'Sex Offender Community Notification: Examining the Importance of Neighbourhood Meetings.' *Behavioural Sciences and the Law 18*, 2/3, 393–408.

PART ONE

The Characteristics of Sexual Offenders

CHAPTER 2

Adult Male Sex Offenders

Dawn D. Fisher and Anthony R. Beech

Introduction

When describing adult male sex offenders, we are actually describing an extremely diverse group, ranging from what is commonly regarded as the less serious end of sexual offending, i.e. men who commit non-contact offences such as exposing themselves or making obscene telephone calls, through to men who have killed as part of a sexual assault. The aim of this chapter is to report what is currently known about a number of different types of sexual offender. This list is not totally exhaustive but outlines the most common 'types' of offender that somebody working in the field will come across.

While this chapter will focus on adult male sex offenders, it should be borne in mind that a third of all reported sexual offences are committed by the under-18 age group. Female sex offenders are currently known to be a small number of the overall population of sex offenders in prison and the community. Prison statistics for England and Wales 2001[1] report that female sex offenders make up about 0.5 per cent of sexual offenders in prison at that time (25 females compared with 4840 males), although it should be pointed out that the number of female offenders is much higher than these official figures suggest. Evidence for this statement is reported in a meta-analysis of eight victim surveys by Fergusson and Mullen (1999) where it was found

1   Prison statistics England and Wales 2001 available from the Home Office Stationery Office, London.

that, on average, 2.5 per cent of female victims and 21.3 per cent of male victims report that they were abused by female perpetrators.

The groups of adult male sex offenders that will be looked at in some depth are those who have committed the following types of offence:

- *Child abuse.* Men who abuse children are often classified according to their relationship with the victim (i.e. related or non-related) and the type of victim they target (i.e. male or female and age group). Offending may range from non-contact offences through to serious penetrative offences. The motivation may range from men having a primary sexual interest in children (paedophiles) to hebephiles, who offend against older-age children, often daughters or stepdaughters.

- *Rape.* Rape is defined here as an assault upon an adult usually involving, or with the intent to commit, penetrative sexual acts without the victim's permission. Men who commit such offences have varying motivations, which may be sexual, anger related, sadistic or a combination of any of these.

- *Sexual murder.* Men may murder their victim during the commission of a sexual offence. The motivation may vary from those who murder their victim to prevent disclosure of the sexual offence to those who find the murder arousing in itself.

- *Internet offences.* There is a relatively new type of sexual offender who has been charged/convicted of downloading illegal sexual material (usually child pornography) from the Internet. It is unclear at the present time whether there are different types of Internet offender. It would seem reasonable to assume that some Internet offenders are also 'hands-on' offenders, some have the motivation to offend sexually but have not done so yet, and others may be compulsively drawn to collecting indecent images of children but have no intention of engaging in contact offences.

- *Exhibitionism.* This type of sexual offence is classed as non-contact because the offender typically does not physically touch the victim but instead exposes his genitals from a distance. The motivation for such offences varies and influences the degree of risk of more serious contact offences presented by the offender.

As can be seen from these brief descriptions, there is a high level of heterogeneity and the distinct possibility of an individual crossing several different categories. This has led to attempts to develop classification systems for sex offenders that have not been wholly successful (see Fisher and Mair 1998 for a review of classification schemes). Many research studies and reviews of sexual offenders (see Laws and O'Donohue 1997) therefore resort to describing sex offenders by the types of offence they commit, i.e. rapists, child abusers, etc. We will therefore look at each of these types in more detail while acknowledging that there may be 'cross-over' groups in which offenders commit a range of illegal/non-consensual sexual behaviours.

Before looking at the specific groups of sex offenders outlined above, the prevalence of sex offenders in general will be considered. Prevalence can be estimated from a variety of sources of information, including report rates of offences, surveys of the general population that ask about sexual victimization experiences, and statistics regarding known (i.e. convicted) offenders.

Prevalence of sexual offences committed by adult males

The primary difficulty in identifying the extent of sexual offending is the fact that sexual offences are greatly under-reported, probably more so than any other type of offence. Moxon (2002) reports that 'only a small fraction of these offences are reported to the police and getting people to talk freely in interviews can be difficult'. This under-reporting is, however, unlikely to be uniform across all types of offending so can lead to biases in the types of offence that are reported and which lead to convictions. Generally speaking, the more serious the type of offence and the more distant the relationship between victim and offender, the more likely the offence is to be reported. Thus, offences carried out by a close relation are less likely to be reported than if the offender is a stranger or not well known to the victim (Myhill and Allen 2002).

In addition to the under-reporting of sexual offences, there is also the problem of sexual offences being difficult to prosecute satisfactorily and result in a conviction. The nature of sexual offending means that it is generally one person's word against another's, with no other evidence. There are often problems in using children or those with learning disabilities as witnesses, and victims may retract their statements because of fear or pressure from others. Prior, Glaser and Lynch (1997) report that, of those child abuse cases reported to the police, 56 per cent result in no further action, 35 per cent of perpetrators are charged and fewer than 10 per cent are convicted. Harris and Grace (1999) note that only 10 per cent of rape offences reported to the police end in the conviction and incarceration of the perpetrator.

Despite the problems of official statistics being under-estimates of the true extent of offending (Friendship *et al.* 2001) and possibly also representing a biased sample, they are the only definite information available. The latest Home Office figures record 45,700 sexual crimes out of a total of 5.8 million recorded crimes in the year ending September 2002 (Povey, Ellis and Nicholas 2003). Sex offences therefore currently account for about 8 in 1000 (just under 1%) of all recorded crimes. The reported level of sexual assault has more than doubled over the past 20 years, with just under 20,000 sexual offences reported in 1982. The total number of crimes reported in 1982 was slightly less than 3.3 million, so the rise of 175 per cent in all reported crime over the past 20 years is less than the 23 per cent rise in reported level of sexual offences (Home Office 2004).

The latest Home Office figures for 2001 report that the average population in custody was 62,650 (Councell and Olagundoye 2003). Of these inmates, 5039 (4840 adults and 199 juveniles) were sex offenders. Therefore, 8 per cent of the prison population are sexual offenders. In terms of the types of adult offender in prison, 2608 have committed rape offences. The rest have been convicted of a range of offences such as indecent assault, unlawful sexual intercourse, incest, gross indecency with a child, procuration and abduction. However, these may be misleading with regard to the specific offences for which offenders are convicted, as the use of plea-bargaining can mean that more serious charges are not pursued if the offender pleads guilty to lesser charges. This can result in offenders being recorded as having committed less serious offences than is the case.

Not all convicted sex offenders are sent to prison, instead being given a community sentence and coming under the jurisdiction of the probation service. The probation service is also responsible for the supervision and monitoring of sex offenders released from prison for periods of parole. In England and Wales, the probation service has undertaken to provide a group treatment programme for all sex offenders that meet the criteria for the programme. There are currently three programmes running nationally that the Correctional Services Panel has accredited.[2] The latest official figures are that the probation service was supervising 10,096 individuals either on a community sentence or in prison as of December 2000 (Middleton 2003). The number of sex offenders in prison in 2001 was 4040; these figures therefore suggest that slightly more sex offenders were in the community – either on probation orders or parole – than in prison at that time.

As for the overall number of convicted offenders in the general population, Marshall (1997) reports that, by the age of 40, 1 in 90 men born in England and Wales will have a conviction for a serious sexual offence.

Classification of sexual offenders

Up-to-date thinking about the offence process should be drawn from the work of Ward and Hudson (1998), who suggest that it is possible to classify rapists and child abusers according to one of four different routes to offending. These groups are defined by the individual offender's goal towards deviant sex (i.e. avoidant or approach) and the selection of strategies designed to achieve their goal (i.e. active or passive).

The *avoidant* goal offender is described as having a commitment to restraint as the overall goal is one of avoidance. However, self-regulation deficiencies, for example inadequate coping skills (under-regulation) or inappropriate strategies (misregulation), ultimately result in goal failure. Consequently, negative affective states and covert planning characterize the avoidant pathway. For the *approach* goal offender, positive affective states, explicit planning and the presence of distorted attitudes about victims and offending behaviour typify the process leading to offending.

Ward and Hudson (1998) further divide the approach and avoidant pathways into *active* and *passive*. The approach offender who is active is explicitly seeking opportunities to offend and actively setting up situations in which to offend. The approach-passive offender, however, while

2   For more information about this panel visit:
      www.homeoffice.gov.uk/pubapps/ppac1099.htm

motivated to offend, does so only when the opportunity presents itself (approach-automatic offender). With the avoidant offender, the active pathway is one in which the offender makes an effort to avoid offending, whereas the passive offender would prefer not to offend but does nothing to prevent himself.

We will now describe specific types of sexual offender. Within each of these sections, we will describe current thinking on types of each of these groups of sex offender.

Child abusers

The prevalence of sexual offences against children is alarming. Cawson *et al.* (2000), in a study of the prevalence of child maltreatment in the UK undertaken for the National Society for the Prevention of Cruelty to Children, reported that 16 per cent of girls and 7 per cent of boys have been sexually assaulted before the age of 13 years. In England, the latest figures for the incidence of children under 18 years of age placed on child protection registers is 23 children per 10,000 of the population aged under 18. Of these referrals, 10 per cent were considered to be at risk of sexual abuse (Department of Health 2002).

In the treatment of adult offenders against children, sex offenders are not a homogeneous group but are responsible for a wide range of different offence types committed for a variety of reasons. Attempts to develop a satis-factory classification system for all sex offenders have met with little success (Fisher and Mair 1998). The most common method of classifying child abusers is to classify them according to sex of victim and relationship to victim, but, as Bickley and Beech (2001) point out, there is a number of problems with these systems, particularly as classification by clinical or pragmatic description does not say very much about risk level or treatment need.

Beech (1998) has developed a method of classifying child abusers according to their level of problems on a battery of psychological measures. He identified two main types of child abuser, which he termed 'high' and 'low' deviancy.

High-deviancy child abusers

In terms of their psychological profile, these offenders are identified as having a high level of treatment need as measured by high levels of pro-offending attitudes and social adequacy problems. In terms of pro-offending attitudes, Fisher, Beech and Browne (1999) found that high-deviancy men had significantly higher levels of distorted attitudes towards children and sex (cognitive distortions) than non-offender controls. Here, they perceived children as sexually sophisticated and proactive with adults and as being unharmed by such contact. This group was also found to have significantly poorer empathy than non-offenders for the victims of sexual abuse. Other significant differences between high-deviancy men and non-offenders indicated that the former reported difficulty in forming intimate adult attachments while perceiving that their emotional needs (emotional identification) could be better met by interacting with children than adults. High-deviancy men were also found to be significantly more under-assertive and to have significantly lower levels of self-esteem than non-offenders. In the Ward and Hudson (1998) system, these men would generally be considered (at least before treatment) as approach goal offenders. The high-deviancy offender who employs specific strategies involving the grooming and control of victims would be considered as an approach explicit offender.

Low-deviancy child abusers

These offenders appear to have a lower level of treatment need than high-deviancy men in that although they (like high-deviancy men) show poor empathy for the victims of sexual assault, they do not evidence globalized cognitive distortions about children. In addition, they do not show the high levels of emotional identification with children seen in high-deviancy men. On the contrary, emotional identification with children in this group has been found to be significantly lower than in non-offender controls (Fisher *et al.* 1999), this probably being part of their denial about future risk to children. Fisher *et al.* found that this group again showed significantly higher levels of social adequacy problems than non-offenders, but this was not as marked as that found in high-deviancy men.

Not only did the psychometric responses differ between the two deviancy groups, but the groups also differed in terms of offence history. Beech (1998) found that the high-deviancy group, compared with the low-deviancy group, had significantly more victims, were more likely to have a previous conviction for a sexual offence, were more likely to have committed offences outside the family and were more likely to have committed offences against boys. Compared with high-deviancy offenders, low-deviancy offenders were more likely to have committed offences against girls within the family.

It could be argued that the high-deviancy/low-deviancy distinction is simply a renaming of distinctions previously articulated in the literature, e.g. fixated versus regressed (Groth 1978), preferential versus situational (Howells 1981), and high and low fixation (Knight and Prentky 1990). In response to such concerns, it should be noted that nearly a third of the men who would be identified as regressed/situational perpetrators in such classifications (and would by definition be treated as low risk) were found to be classified as high-deviancy in the Beech system.

Such a classification has been an influence on the development of treatment programmes in the UK as these two categories of offender obviously have different treatment needs. Beech, Fisher and Beckett (1999) report that high-deviancy child abusers require twice as many hours' treatment than low-deviancy child abusers to show a 'treatment effect'. Such a finding obviously has implications for treatment as it is important not to waste resources by either providing offenders with more input than they need, which may be counterproductive, or not having sufficient impact because the treatment is too short. This finding has fed into current treatment for sexual offenders in the Probation and Prison Services (Beech and Mann 2002).

Rape

Myhill and Allen (2002) reported on the British Crime Survey (1998, 2000) of sexual victimization in a sample of 6944 women aged between 16 and 59. The results showed that 4.9 per cent of women (an estimated 754,000 victims) reported being raped since the age of 16 and 9.7 per cent reported some form of sexual victimization since the age of 16 (including rape). Rape was defined as 'forced sexual intercourse (vaginal or anal penetration) but did not stipulate that penetration had to be penile. Women in the 16–24-year age range were most at risk, and women were most likely to be attacked by men they knew, current partners accounting for 45 per cent of the rapes and strangers only 8 per cent. Only 20 per cent of the rapes were reported to the police, and there was a bias in reporting according to the relationship with the offender. Stranger rapes were far more likely to be reported (36% of cases reported), whereas date rape was the least likely (8% of those reported).

The majority of the rapes occurred in domestic settings, and, overall, sexual attacks from partners and ex-partners were more than twice as likely to result in a physical injury to the victim. With regard specifically to rape, 74 per cent of women raped reported the use of physical force or violence, 37 per cent resulted in physical injury, of which 10 per cent reported 'severe' injury, i.e. cuts or broken bones. Sexual victimization from partners and ex-partners was also more likely to involve multiple attacks. Myhill and Allen (2002) suggest that 'sexual victimisation should be recognised as part of the domestic violence syndrome and its role in the cycle of violence should be explored further'.

Men who commit rape are a heterogeneous group. Myhill and Allen's (2002) results from the 1998 and 2000 British Crime Surveys show that women are the victims of partners, ex-partners, acquaintances, dates and much less often strangers. This pattern gives no clear idea of the characteristics of a typical rapist. Indeed, from these findings, the only clear fact regarding the characteristics of the perpetrator is that the victim will have generally known and been intimate with him at some point. As Marshall (2000) points out, 'these offenders are a good deal more like other people than most people would like to think'. Research evidence for this suggestion can be found in work by Malamuth (1981), who found that 35 per cent of a sample of US college males reported that they would be willing to rape if they were assured of not being punished.

Since the mid-1980s, the report rate for rape has steadily increased, but the conviction rate has significantly dropped. Thus, in 1985 there were 1842 rape offences recorded by the police with a conviction rate of 24 per cent, whereas in 1999 there were 7809 recorded offences and a conviction rate of just 8 per cent.

As for imprisoned rapists, Hudson and Ward (1997) note that they are typically very likely to be similar to the rest of the prison population in that they are generally of low socio-economic class, tend to have dropped out of school, show unstable employment in unskilled jobs and have similar psychiatric treatment rates and levels of social competence to those of other prisoners. The notable exception to this is assertiveness, which has been found to be markedly higher in rapists than other prison inmates (Stermac and Quinsey 1986). In fact, Marshall (2000) notes that rapists are characteristically unremarkable in any clinical or organic sense in that only 5–8 per cent of them suffer from psychosis or serious brain dysfunction, or have learning disabilities.

In comparison with other imprisoned sex offenders, i.e. child abusers, rapists tend to be younger, are more likely to be over-assertive (aggressive) than under-assertive (passive) and are more likely to have sustained a long-term relationship than child abusers (Hudson and Ward 1997). Hudson and Ward also note that rapists are less likely to have had physical health problems, half as likely to report having been sexually abused, but more likely to have been cruel to animals in their childhood compared with child abusers.

Again, like child abusers, it would appear that rapists are not a homogeneous group. In terms of typological approach, the best worked system that is both clinically and theoretically driven is probably the Massachusetts Treatment Center: revision 3 (MTC: R3) system for the classification of rapists, developed by Knight and Prentky (1990). This describes five main types of rapist:

1. *The opportunistic rapist.* This type of rapist could be seen as the approach-explicit offender described by Ward and Hudson (1998). Here, the offender has a number of pro-offending attitudes, including that there is nothing wrong with having coercive sex with women. The sexual assault committed by this type of rapist is an impulsive predatory act controlled more by situational circumstances (i.e. women being present at another crime) than by explicit sexual fantasy or anger.

2. *The non-sadistic sexual rapist.* Here, the rapist's motivations are sexual, driven by dominance needs or feelings of inadequacy. There will be a high level of sexual fantasy that precedes the offence(s). These fantasies will reflect sexual arousal, distorted attitudes about women and sex. Typically, there may be comparatively low levels of interpersonal aggression in this type of offender, the offender exhibiting just enough force to ensure compliance from the victim.

3. *The sadistic sexual rapist.* In this type of rapist there is a fusion of sex and aggression, i.e. anger is eroticized. Knight and Prentky note clinically that the frequent occurrence of erotic and destructive thoughts and fantasies is reported by the sadistic rapist.

4. *The vindictive rapist.* Here, women are the central and exclusive focus of these men's anger. There is little evidence of anger towards men. The sexual assault is marked by behaviours that are physically damaging and that are intended to degrade and humiliate their victim(s). There is no evidence, according to Knight and Prentky, that this anger is eroticized or that such men are preoccupied with sexual fantasies. The anger of the vindictive rapist may be so severe that it leads to violent behaviours that result in murder.

5. *The pervasively angry rapist.* This type of offender is hypothesized to be motivated by undifferentiated anger in all aspects of the offender's life (such offenders being equally likely to express their unmanageable aggression towards both men and women) (Knight 1999). These men, according to Knight, have long histories of antisocial behaviour in which rape is another expression of their anger and hostility.

As can be seen from this brief overview of the putative types of rapist, they would seem to have differing treatment needs. Some of the types (opportunistic/non-sadistic sexual) would obviously benefit from the type of therapy carried out in a typical cognitive-behavioural treatment programme for sexual offenders (as described by Beech and Fisher, this volume), in which distorted attitudes and social inadequacy problems are addressed in treatment. For other types of rapist (vindictive, pervasively angry or sadistic), however, this approach may not map on to the sorts of problem they have. In terms of examining the treatment provision for rapists, Polaschek and King (2002) note that this has received little attention compared with the treatment of child abusers. They further note that there is 'surprisingly little research on whether rapists can be effectively rehabilitated'.

In the literature, the descriptions of treatment for rapists are indistinguishable from the model typically used for child abusers, e.g. Marshall (2000), while the treatment of rapists in English and Welsh prisons consists of the same treatment that would be offered to child abusers. Some would, however, now argue that such programmes are too narrow for rapists, in that a typical sex offender treatment programme does not offer interventions that might be geared to some rapist problems such as impulsivity, antisocial cognitions and substance abuse problems (Polaschek and King 2002). It could be argued that it is possible to offer a number of programmes that would address their sexual and generally antisocial violent problems and their substance abuse problems, but as Polaschek and King again point out, this may be counterproductive in that conflicting messages may be sent out by different programmes. Second, the sheer amount of information given on such programmes may be difficult to retain. Finally, offenders may be exposed to irrelevant treatment targets that might undermine their motivation to engage in treatment.

Sexual murderers

Roberts and Grossman (1993), in a descriptive analysis of sexual homicide in Canada, cite that between 1974 and 1986 sexual homicides accounted for 4 per cent of all homicides recorded by the police. In the UK, as of March 2002, roughly 3500 men are serving a conviction for a murder or manslaughter. These prevalence rates would therefore account for 108–140 men being in prison for a sexually related murder. However, current estimates suggest that the figure in the UK is closer to 6 per cent as there are approximately 200 men within the prison system in the UK identified as having committed a murder with an apparent, or admitted, sexual motivation (Adam Carter, Lifer Unit, HM Prison Service, UK, personal communication, March 2001).

The classification of 'sexual murder' may, however, be very hard to achieve; Grubin (1994) notes that, as at the crime scene analysis level, forensic evidence for sexual motivation can be very difficult to discover as approximately one-third of female homicide victims are killed by someone with whom they are intimate. Therefore, evidence of sexual activity prior to death does not always indicate whether this was consensual or forced, particularly if the post mortem has not revealed any signs of violence. The victim of a murder cannot tell his or her version of the crime so, in terms of prevalence, it is possible that the number of sexual murders is higher than current knowledge indicates.

Most definitions emphasize that the killing is intentional and contains sexual behaviour. The intentional aspect of the killing can be open to debate, and so too can the sexual element. Clear evidence is sometimes available of sexual assault, either before or after death, and derived from forensic, or crime scene, evidence. In some crimes, however, the sexual element can be less obvious. The offender will sometimes admit to the killing but consistently deny any sexual motivation for his crime. If a sexual element is indicated, it may only be confirmed by the offender's openness in treatment (Clarke and Carter 2000).

As one aspect of work looking at the effectiveness of treatment for this group as part of a current Home Office research project, we suggest that sexual murderers can be categorized into the following:

- *Compulsive gynocide (compulsive killing of women).* Here, the offender is under extreme internal compulsion to kill (Revitch and Schlesinger 1989). The murder arises because the offender carries out his deviant/sadistic fantasies related to sex murder. This type of sexual murderer could be seen as a more extreme version of the sadistic rapist described above.

- *Sexual offence + murder without specific sexual element.* Here the killing is motivated by the offender's need to keep his victim quiet or to prevent detection during or after the commission of sexual assault. This type of sexual murderer may be seen as an approach goal offender who either impulsively kills or has planned to kill his victim to avoid detection.

- *Cathymic gynocide (grievance-motivated killing).* Here, the murder and associated sexual attack arises out of a strong build-up of violence arising from 'an unbearable state of tension, which is relieved through the violent attack itself' (Revitch and Schlessinger 1989). This tension arises from protracted conflict with another person(s) or circumstances usually unrelated to the murder victim. This type of sexual murderer could be seen as a more extreme version of the vindictive rapist described above.

It can be seen from this analysis that sexual murderers may have their own treatment needs over and above those seen in other sex offenders, but in terms of treatment it is only in the past five years that any specific work has taken place with this group.[3] However, this position has now changed, with between 50 and 60 per cent of identified sexual murderers having undertaken treatment for the sexual component of their offence (data from the Offender Behaviour Programmes Unit, HM Prison Service).

There is, however, a raft of issues when working with those who have murdered in a sexual context in that they may be resistant, in denial and extremely antagonistic about the possibility of undertaking any work concerning their offending behaviour (Milsom 1999); they would also, as noted above, appear to have their own unique treatment needs beyond those found in other sexual offenders.

Internet sexual offenders

An estimated 100 million individuals had access to the Internet in 2001, of whom 20 per cent each month visited sexually orientated sites (Cooper, Delmonico and Burg 2000). More recently, it has been estimated that 1 per cent (over 25 million) of Americans spend more than 40 hours per week engaged in online sexual activity (Cooper 2002). The use of the Internet for sexual purposes is therefore extremely widespread. Durkin and Bryant (1995), reporting on the criminal and deviant use of the Internet, suggest that such instant online gratification has the ability to provide reinforcement for sexual fantasies that would otherwise be extinguished. Although most of the 'adult-orientated' sites offer material that is no longer deemed illegal in

---

3   This is due to the fact that they will have not have been categorized (until recently) as sexual offenders. As there is no offence of sexual murder in the British legal system, all of these offenders will have been convicted of murder or manslaughter.

the UK, there is still a considerable number, apparently readily accessible with a credit card, that offer material of paedophilic or adult non-consensual sex. Quayle and Taylor (2002) note that people in fact now have access to the types of material that were previously available only at great expense and/or personal risk. In terms of the scale of the problem over the past few years, there has been a dramatic increase in the identified scale and prosecution of individuals who have carried out offences related to the Internet. In terms of looking at the types of offence that are committed in relation to the Internet involving the abuse of children, the Combating Paedophilic Information Networks in Europe Project, based at the University of Cork, Ireland, suggests that there are five categories of offence (Hammond 2002):

1. downloading child pornography

2. trading child pornography materials

3. distribution and production of child pornography materials

4. engagement with Internet seduction of children

5. contact offences leading on from Internet seduction of children.

As can be seen from this list, some of these categories involve (3 and 5) or can lead to (4) contact abuse. Categories 1 and 2 obviously encourage and promote the production of child pornography, but it is currently unclear whether all individuals viewing and downloading child pornography will necessarily commit contact sexual offences.

Carnes, Delmonico and Griffin (2001) suggest that people who have problematic behaviour with sex and the Internet tend to fall into three groups:

-   *The discovery group.* Individuals in this group begin using the Internet compulsively with no prior inappropriate sexual fantasies or behaviours. For this group, the Internet serves as the 'trigger' for problematic or compulsive use of the Internet (Cooper 2002).

-   *The predisposed group.* These are those who have had their first out-of-control sexual behaviour on the Internet after years of obsessing over unacted-upon sexual fantasies and urges. Here, the Internet serves as the 'fuel' that encourages problematic sexual behaviours to accelerate (Cooper 2002).

- *The lifelong sexually compulsive group.* These are individuals whose out-of-control sexual behaviour on the Internet is part of an ongoing severe sexual problem. For this group, Cooper (2002) notes that the Internet can: (a) be an extension of their behaviour and may be simply one more way to act out; (b) become a less risky way of acting out sexually problematic behaviours; (c) become a way of heightening arousal and adding new risk to already problematic behaviours.

For an individual who is currently committing sexual offences, this will act as both a potentiator for his offending and a way to justify and 'normalize' sexually deviant behaviour. Evidence for this is reported by Marshall (1988), who found that more than a third of child molesters reported being incited to commit an offence by exposure to pornographic material. More recently, Middleton (2003) has described how, in a polygraph examination of sexual offenders in the West Midlands Probation Area, 86 per cent of child abusers admitted using pornography as a precursor to offending. Further evidence to support this link comes from a survey of the US Postal Service in which it was found that 40 per cent of users of child pornography had previous convictions for child sexual offences, indicating a high number of previous offenders who used such material. Given the low rate of conviction for sexual offences, it may be that a significant proportion of the other 60 per cent who do not have convictions for sexual offences could also be hands-on abusers.

Is there, however, an argument for suggesting that the viewing of such material leads to contact sexual offences? Marshall (1988) cautions against describing such a direct link, suggesting instead that viewing pornography may accelerate a process already underway or may further justify an established set of antisocial beliefs. There could also be an argument that an Internet offender may have the predilection to be sexually attracted to children but may have enough internal inhibitions not actually to commit contact offences. The repeated viewing of such material could, however, lead to a weakening of this barrier to offending. Viewing such material could also lead to 'ironic effects'. An individual may not want to commit a sexual offence and may see a way of not doing this by fantasizing and masturbating to such material, which potentiates offending.

Exhibitionists

Individuals who expose their genitals to others, usually to women, have tended to be regarded as less serious sexual offenders and be thought to pose little risk of committing a contact offence. This has proved to be erroneous in that it is known that a significant number of contact sex offenders have previously exposed themselves before escalating in the seriousness of their sexual offending and many exhibitionists are involved in other forms of paraphilic behaviour (Abel *et al.* 1987). Clinical evidence also suggests that the functions of the behaviour reveal differing motives that impact on the risk presented by the individual. In an early study, Gebhard *et al.* (1965) reported that approximately 20 per cent of their sample committed later contact sexual offences and 10 per cent were described as 'actual or potential' rapists. Sugarman *et al.* (1994) examined the psychiatric records of 210 cases that had been assessed by the West Midlands Forensic Psychiatry Service and found that 26 per cent had a conviction for at least one contact sex offence. This included two offences of rape, three of attempted rape and 60 offences against children.

Exhibitionism appears to have an early onset, studies reporting an onset generally in the mid-teens (Abel and Rouleau 1990; Smukler and Schiebel 1975). Victims are primarily female, with exposure to males being rare (Murphy 1997). A large number of victims are also children or adolescents. MacDonald (1973) reported that 28 per cent of the victims were aged between 5 and 13 years.

It is likely that exhibitionism is a frequent behaviour. A survey of British nurses by Gittleson, Eacott and Mehta (1978) reported that 44 per cent had been exposed to outside of work, and Cox and MacMahon (1978) reported that 32 per cent of 405 female college students from four US universities had been exposed to. The rate of offending is also likely to be high, individual offenders often being convicted of multiple offences on many occasions.

The function of the behaviour can differ, some seeking some form of sexual contact and finding the situation of a woman seeing their genitals to be sexually arousing. Some may masturbate to this arousal at the time, whereas others masturbate later, in private. Some of these individuals have unrealistic beliefs about their victim and imagine that she may be attracted to them as a result of the exposure and want to have a sexual relationship with them. Other individuals seek to shock or frighten their victim and become aroused by the victim's fear. It is these individuals who are most likely to go on to commit serious contact offences, usually when the frightened expression of the victim is not sufficiently arousing. Rooth (1973) classified exhibitionists into two types, with type 1 being the 'inhibited, flaccid exposer' and type 2 being the 'sociopathic, erect exposer'.

It would be rare to find an exhibitionist in prison with no other contact sexual convictions. Thus, most treatment for this group would take place in community settings and consist of the same treatment offered to child abusers in the current accredited sex offender treatment programmes (Beech and Fisher, this volume).

Reconviction by types of sex offender

Reconviction studies are fraught with difficulty owing to the problems of under-reporting and securing conviction. Some are hampered by inadequate follow-up studies, whereas others may include all sex offenders together rather than considering specific types. Different types of offender do appear to have differing reconviction rates. High-frequency offenders such as exhibitionists have the highest reconviction rates, ranging from 41 to 71 per cent (Marshall and Barbaree 1990). With regard to child abusers, those who offend outside the family have higher reconviction rates (10–29% against girls, 13–40% against boys) than incest offenders (4–10%), while studies show that rapists' reconviction rates range from 7 to 35 per cent (Marshall and Barbaree 1990). It should be noted, however, that reconviction is only a proportion of recidivism, and the real recidivism rate is unknown.

Marshall and Barbaree (1990) attempted to identify the ratio of recidivism to reconviction and reported that the number of credible allegations to child protection agencies, added to the police recidivism data, would suggest that convictions should be multiplied by a factor of 2.4 for child abusers to give a more accurate level of offending. For exhibitionists, they suggested a factor of 2.8. More recently Falshaw, Friendship and Bates (2003) reported that the recidivism rate of a sample of 173 offenders who had been treated and/or assessed in the Thames Valley Project (a community-based treatment programme for sexual offenders) was 5.3 times the official rate of reconviction, as measured by the Offenders Index. Beech *et al.* (2002) reported that high-deviancy child abusers were over seven times more likely to be reconvicted for a sexual offence than low-deviancy child abusers. This study highlights the importance of identifying characteristics that predict risk of sexual reconviction.

Cross-over levels

A frequent question for those involved in risk prediction and child protection concerns the likelihood that someone who has been convicted for a particular type of sexual offence will present a risk to different types of victim. It should be borne in mind that if an individual has already crossed over, we know *de facto* that this person is of increased risk in that he has a wider number of potential victims, e.g. a child abuser offending against both boys and girls or both inside and outside the family.

In terms of hard data, Friendship and Thornton (2002) have reported the data on cross-over rates shown in Table 2.1.

Table 2.1 Sex of victim in index offence(s) by sex of victim in subsequent offences		
Victim in the index offence	*Rate of reconviction for a sexual offence against a male (%)*	*Rate of reconviction for a sexual offence against a female (%)*
Male aged 0–12	35	12
Female aged 0–12	3	16
Male aged 13–17	43	0
Female aged 13–17	1	10
Male aged 18+	23	0
Female aged 18+	1	19

Here, it can be noted that offenders who target male victims present more risk to females than those who offend against females present to males. Additionally, there is little cross-over between genders, with the exception of offenders who abuse young males, who pose almost the same level of risk to female children as men who have targeted female children.

Policy implications

The clear conclusion of this chapter is that sex offenders are not a homogenous group. The different types of adult male sex offender present differing patterns of behaviour, different motivations for their behaviour, different reconviction rates and different treatment needs. The implication of these differences is that each offender should be given a thorough assessment and offered treatment, which can take account of the specific treatment needs of the individual. The vast majority of treatment being offered by the prison and probation services currently places all types of offender within the same broad programme. Whether this is sufficient for all sex offenders or whether specific programmes will be required for different types of sex offender has yet to be established.

References

Abel, G. and Rouleau, J. (1990) 'The Nature and Extent of Sexual Assault.' In W.L. Marshall, D.R. Laws and H.E. Barbaree (eds) *Handbook of Sexual Assault: Issues, Theories and Treatment of the Offender.* New York: Plenum Press.

Abel, G., Becker, J. Cunningham-Rathner, J. and Rouleau, J. (1987) 'Self Reported Sex Crimes of 561 Non-incarcerated Paraphiliacs.' *Journal of Interpersonal Violence 2,* 3–25.

Beech, A.R. (1998) 'A Psychometric Typology of Child Abusers.' *International Journal of Offender Therapy and Comparative Criminology 42,* 319–339.

Beech, A.R. and Mann, R.E. (2002) 'Recent Developments in the Treatment of Sexual Offenders.' In J. McGuire (ed) *Offender Rehabilitation: Effective Programmes and Policies to Reduce Reoffending.* Chichester: Wiley.

Beech, A.R., Erikson, M., Friendship, C. and Hanson, R.K. (2002) 'Static and Dynamic Predictors of Reconviction.' *Sexual Abuse: A Journal of Research and Treatment 14,* 153–165.

Beech, A.R., Fisher, D. and Beckett, R.C. (1999) *An Evaluation of the Prison Sex Offender Treatment Programme. UK Home Office Occasional Report.* London: Home Office. Online: www.homeoffice.gov.uk/rds/pdfs/occ-step3.pdf

Bickley, J. and Beech, A.R. (2001) 'Classifying Child Abusers: Its Relevance to Theory and Clinical Practice.' *International Journal of Offender Therapy and Comparative Criminology 45,* 51–69.

Carnes, P., Delmonico, D.L. and Griffin, E. (2001) *In the Shadows of the Net.* Minnesota: Hazeldine.

Cawson, P., Wattam, C., Brooker, S. and Keely, G. (2000) *Child Maltreatment in the United Kingdom. A Study of the Prevalence of Child Abuse and Neglect.* London: NSPCC.

Clarke, J. and Carter, A.J. (2000) 'Relapse Prevention with Sexual Murderers.' In D.R. Laws, S.M. Hudson and T. Ward (eds) *Remaking Relapse Prevention with Sex Offenders.* Sage.

Cooper, A. (ed) (2002) *Sex and the Internet: A Guidebook for Clinicians.* New York: Brunner Routledge.

Cooper, A., Delmonico, D.L. and Burg, R. (2000) 'Cybersex Users, Abusers, and Compulsives: New Findings and Implications.' *Sexual Addictions and Compulsivity 7,* 5–29.

Councell, R. and Olagundoye, J. (2003) 'The Prison Population in 2001: A Statistical Review.' Home Office Research Findings No.195. London: Home Office. Online: www.homeoffice.gov.uk/rds/pdfs/r195.pdf

Cox, D.J. and MacMahon, B. (1978) 'Incidence of Male Exhibitionism in the United States as Reported by Victimised Female College Students.' *National Journal of Law and Psychiatry 1,* 453–457.

Department of Health (2002) *Children and Young Persons on Child Protection Registers, Year ending 31 March 2002.* London: Department of National Statistics. Online: www.doh.gov.uk/public/cpr2002.htm

Durkin, K.F. and Bryant, C.D. (1995) 'Log on to Sex: Some Notes on the Carnal Computer and Erotic Cyberspace as an Emerging Research Frontier.' *Deviant Behavior 16,* 179–200.

Falshaw, L, Friendship, C. and Bates, A. (2003) *Sexual Offenders – Measuring Reconviction, Reoffending and Recidivism.* Home Office Research Findings No. 183. London: Home Office. Online: www.homeoffice.gov.uk/rds/pdfs/r183.pdf

Fergusson, D.M. and Mullen, P.E. (1999) *Childhood Sexual Abuse: An Evidence-based Perspective.* Developmental Clinical Psychology and Psychiatry, volume 40. London: Sage.

Fisher, D. and Mair, G. (1998) *A Review of Classification Schemes for Sex Offenders.* Home Office Research Findings No. 78. London: Home Office. Online: www.homeoffice.gov.uk/rds/pdfs/r78.pdf

Fisher, D., Beech, A.R. and Browne, K.D. (1999) 'Comparison of Sex Offenders to Non-offenders on Selected Psychological Measures.' *International Journal of Offender Therapy and Comparative Criminology 43,* 473–491.

Friendship, C. and Thornton, D. (2002) 'Risk Assessment for Offenders.' In 'Treating the Adult Sex Offender, ' in K.D. Browne, H. Hanks, P. Stratton and C. Hamilton (eds) *The Prediction and Prevention of Child Abuse: A Handbook.* Chichester: Wiley.

Friendship, C., Thornton, D., Erikson, M. and Beech, A.R. (2001) 'Reconviction: A Critique and Comparison of Two Main Data Sources in England and Wales.' *Legal and Criminological Psychology 6,* 121–129.

Gebhard, P.H., Gagnon, J.H., Pomeroy, W.B. and Christenson, C.V. (1965) *Sex Offenders: An Analysis of Types.* London: Heinemann.

Gittleson, N.L., Eacott, S.E. and Mehta, B.M. (1978) 'Victims of Indecent Exposure.' *British Journal of Psychiatry 132,* 61–66.

Groth, A.N. (1978) 'Patterns of Sexual Assault Against Children and Adolescents.' In A.W. Burgess, A.N. Groth, L.L. Holstrom and S.M. Groi (eds) *Sexual Assault of Children and Adolescents*. Boston: Heath.

Grubin, D. (1994) 'Sexual Murder.' *British Journal of Psychiatry 165*, 624–629.

Hammond, S. (2002) *Development of a Cognitive Behavioural Therapy Module for People with a Sexual Interest in Children who also Exhibit Problematic Internet Use*. Pilot Manual, Copine Project. Cork: University College Cork.

Harris, J. and Grace, S. (1999) *A Question of Evidence: Investigating and Prosecuting Rape in the 1990s*. Home Office Research Study No.196. London: Home Office. Online: www.homeoffice.gov.uk/rds/pdfs/hors196.pdf.

Home Office (2004) *Recorded Crime Statistics 1898–2001*. Online: www.homeoffice.gov.uk/rds/pdfs/100years.xls.

Howells, K. (1981) 'Adult Sexual Interest in Children: Considerations Relevant to Theories of Etiology.' In M. Cook and K. Howells (eds) *Adult Sexual Interest in Children*. London: Academic Press.

Hudson, S. and Ward, T. (1997) 'Rape: Psychopathology and Theory.' In D.R. Laws and W. O'Donohue (eds) *Sexual Deviance: Theory, Assessment and Treatment*. New York: Guilford Press.

Knight, R. (1999) 'Validation of a Typology of Rapists.' *Journal of Interpersonal Violence 14*, 303–330.

Knight, R.A. and Prentky, R.A. (1990) 'Classifying Sexual Offenders: The Development and Corroboration of Taxonomic Models.' In W.L. Marshall, D.R. Laws and H.E. Barbaree (eds) *Handbook of Sexual Assault: Issues, Theories and Treatment of the Offender*. New York: Plenum Press.

Laws, D.R. and O'Donohue, W. (eds) (1997) *Sexual Deviance: Theory, Assessment and Treatment*. New York: Guilford Press.

MacDonald, J.M. (1973) *Indecent Exposure*. Springfield, IL: Charles C. Thomas.

Malamuth, N. (1981) 'Rape Proclivity Among Males.' *Journal of Social Issues 37*, 138–157.

Marshall, P. (1997) *The Prevalence of Convictions for Sexual Offending*. Home Office Research Findings No.55. London: Home Office. Online: www.homeoffice.gov.uk/rds/pdfs/r55.pdf

Marshall, W.L. (1988) 'The Use of Sexually Explicit Stimuli by Rapists, Child Molesters and Non-offenders.' *Journal of Sex Research 25*, 267–288.

Marshall, W.L. (2000) 'Adult Sexual Offenders Against Women.' In C.R. Hollin (ed) *Handbook of Offender Assessment and Treatment*. Chichester: Wiley.

Marshall, W.L. and Barbaree, H.E. (1990) 'Outcome of Comprehensive Treatment Programs.' In W.L. Marshall, D.R. Laws and H.E. Barbaree (eds) *Handbook of Sexual Assault: Issues, Theories and Treatment of the Offender*. New York: Plenum Press.

Middleton, D. (2003) 'Assessment of Individuals Convicted of Child Pornography Offences.' Probation Circular 14/2003.

Milsom, J. (1999) 'Sexual Murderers and Non-murdering Rapists: The Relationship that Emotional Loneliness Plays in Offence Type.' Unpublished MSc thesis, University of Leicester.

Moxon, D. (2002) 'Introduction.' In A. Myhill and J. Allen (eds) *Rape and Sexual Assault of Women: The Extent and Nature of the Problem*. Home Office Research Study No.237. London: Home Office. Online: www.homeoffice.gov.uk/rds/pdfs/hors237.pdf

Murphy, W.D. (1997) 'Exhibitionism: Psychopathology and Theory.' In D.R. Laws and W. O'Donohue (eds) *Sexual Deviance: Theory, Assessment and Treatment*. New York: Guilford Press.

Myhill, A. and Allen, J. (2002) *Rape and Sexual Assault of Women: The Extent and Nature of the Problem*. Home Office Research Study No.237. London: Home Office. Online: www.homeoffice.gov.uk/rds/pdfs/hors237.pdf

Polaschek, D. and King, L.L. (2002) 'Rehabilitating Rapists: Reconsidering the Issues.' *Australian Psychologist 37*, 215–221.

Povey, D., Ellis, C. and Nicholas, S. (2003) *Crime in England and Wales: Quarterly Update, January 2003*. London: National Statistics Office.

Prior, V., Glaser, D. and Lynch, M.A. (1997) 'Responding to Child Sexual Abuse: The Criminal Justice System.' *Child Abuse Review 6*, 128–140.

Quayle, E. and Taylor, M. (2002) 'Paedophiles, Pornography: Assessment Issues.' *British Journal of Social Work 32*, 863–875.

Revitch, E and Schlesinger, L.B. (1989) *Sex Murder and Sex Aggression: Phenomenology, Psychopathology, Psychodynamics and Prognosis*. Springfield, IL: Charles C. Thomas.

Roberts, J.V. and Grossman, M.G. (1993) 'Sexual Homicide in Canada: A Descriptive Analysis.' *Annals of Sex Research 6*, 5–25.

Rooth, G. (1973) 'Exhibitionism, Sexual Violence and Paedophilia.' *British Journal of Psychiatry 122*, 705–710.

Stermac, L.E. and Quinsey, V.L. (1986) 'Social Competence among Rapists.' *Behavioural Assessment 8*, 171–185.

Sugarman, P., Dumughn, C., Saad, K., Hinder, S. and Bluglass, R. (1994) 'Dangerousness in Exhibitionists.' *Journal of Forensic Psychiatry 5*, 287–296.

Smukler, A.J. and Schiebel, D. (1975) 'Personality Characteristics of Exhibitionists.' *Diseases of the Nervous System 36*, 600–603.

Ward, T. and Hudson, S.M. (1998) 'A Model of the Relapse Process in Sexual Offenders.' *Journal of Interpersonal Violence 13*, 700–725.

CHAPTER THREE

Female Sex Offenders

Hazel Kemshall

Introduction

Female sex offenders are considered a rarity, and until recently their offending was assessed through the filter of male models of sexual offending (Adshead, Howett and Mason 1994). The late 1980s saw the 'discovery' of the female sex offender (Elliot 1993), with the recognition that between 50 and 100 women each year sexually offend against children in England and Wales (Adshead *et al.* 1994). However, the recognition and identification of female sexual offending remains problematic, not least because we are 'reluctant to face any challenge to our socially constructed notions of the maternal and the feminine' (Crawford and Conn 1997, p.280). The 'discovery' of children sexually abused by women in day-care facilities in America in the 1980s (Adshead *et al.* 1994) and similar findings in Canada (Crawford and Conn 1997) initiated several studies into the incidence and prevalence of female sexual offending against children (Finkelhor and Russell 1984).

Recent research consistently indicates that female sex offenders make up about 0.5 per cent of all sexual offenders against children (Grayston and De Luca 1999; see also Fisher and Beech, this volume), although the 'true number' is thought to be higher (Faller 1995; Nathan and Ward 2002). Consequently, owing to the small numbers involved, the knowledge base tends to be derived from case studies rather than large-scale surveys or meta-analyses (Davin, Hislop and Dunbar 1999). Research and investigation into female sex offending has also been hindered by a general reluctance to accept that women sexually abuse (Valios 2002).

Hetherton (1999) has argued how cultural myths about women prevent both societal and individual recognition of the female sexual abuse of children. Idealized beliefs, particularly of the sanctity of motherhood, have resulted in a significant denial and minimization of female abuse (Saradjian 1996; Welldon 1988, 1995). Establishing the incidence of female sexual abuse is problematic for the following reasons (Allen 1990, 1991; Hetherton 1999; Wakefield and Under-Wager 1991):

- Differing notions of sexual abuse can result in the identification of differing incidence rates, and debates continue about what should or should not be included. Some definitions, for example, include women who knew about sexual offending by partners but who failed to report it (Kalders, Inkster and Britt 1997).

- Self-report victim studies can be unreliable, being based upon memory recall and the motivation to disclose retrospectively.

- Unrepresentative samples can produce skewed information on the incidence and type of female sexual offending. Some studies have used as few as ten women and others as many as 40 (Faller 1987; Wolfers 1993). Meta-analyses of such studies in order to produce offender profiles of female sexual offending can be flawed.

- There is under-reporting, particularly from male victims, of female abuse (Kasl 1990).

Throughout the 1990s, the 'males do and females don't' dichotomy was increasingly challenged (Allen 1991), with fierce debates between feminist organizations and academics on the one hand, and those attempting to promote the discussion and investigation of sexual abuse and offending by women on the other (Elliot 1993; Hetherton 1999). This has been a largely sterile debate focusing on whether sexual offending is an 'equal opportunity activity' (Cameron 1999, p.68). As Hetherton points out, this does not assist victims or those who work with them, and professionals are 'not immune to popular beliefs about female child sexual abuse' (1999, p.169). As Young puts it, now that the 'lid has been lifted off "the last taboo"…it is time to forget about politicising and concentrate on the essential task' (1993, p.108), i.e., the reduction in the number of potential victims and the provision of support services to both perpetrators and victims in need.

Characteristics of the female sexual offender: what is known

Most research has been into the female sexual abuse of children, hence this is the group most easily profiled. Within this, Hanks and Saradjian identify two main groups: 'those who abuse children; and those who abuse children in conjunction with others, usually males' (1992, p.vii). Within this, there are important sub-groups, essential to the most appropriate matching of intervention to abuse type (Hanks and Saradjian 1992, p.vii):

- Women who abuse their own children.

- Women abusing in conjunction with men.

- Women abusing as part of a married couple.

- Women abusing as part of a lesbian couple.

- Women abusing children with learning difficulties (mostly boys).

- Women who abuse adolescents, male and female.

(Hanks and Saradjian 1992: vii).

Details of each subcategory can be found in Hanks and Saradjian, but for the purposes of this chapter these sub-categories are useful in that they highlight the centrality of motivation, situational factors and power relationships in female abuse.

In addition, Hanks and Saradjian (1992, p.viii) found that three themes linked all these categories:

- Almost all were sexually abused as a child.

- Other forms of abuse, including emotional abuse, were present.

- Mothers who abuse their children frequently see the child as an extension of themselves.

Faller (1987), in a study of 40 women who sexually abused children, found other significant factors. The women victimized more than two children, including their own, often within what are termed 'polyincestuous family situations' in which 'there are at least two perpetrators and generally two or more victims' (Faller 1987, p.266). Such situations appear to place women at greater risk of becoming sexually abusive, although Faller is at pains to caution against the simplistic conclusion that this is merely the result of male dominance. Instead, intra-familial and polyincestuous cases were over-represented in her sample as the majority of cases were referred through child protection services investigating parental abuse. This highlights the perennial problem that only what is referred can be investigated and subsequently researched.

Others have contributed to the typology of female sex offending, with Matthews (1993) and Matthews, Matthews and Speltz (1991) being the most cited. Matthews' typology attempts to attribute levels of responsibility to the offender (Kalders, Inkster and Britt 1994, 1997). In brief, the highest level of responsibility is attributed to those who target adolescent boys and carry out abuse in the 'teacher/lover' role. Second, there are those who are predisposed to initiating abuse but whose own family backgrounds are seen as influential in their offending motivation. The final category is those female sex offenders who are coerced by a male.

Kalders *et al.* make the important point that typologies should capture motivations in order to be explanatory rather than merely descriptive. The typologies of both Matthews (1993) and Hanks and Saradjian (1992) meet this criterion.

Typologies have, however, been dependent upon small-scale studies and do require further empirical validation. Kalders *et al.* (1997) used a sample of 25 offenders from the New Zealand Police Computer Database who had been charged with sex offences against children between 1978 and 1994. The authors carried out a clinical analysis of eight cases from this original sample in order to develop appropriate typologies for assessment and treatment measures. Such small numbers make it difficult to validate the typologies. However, typologies can have a role in focusing assessment and in matching treatments to typology (Kalders *et al.* 1997; Saradjian 1996).

Investigation into the characteristics of female sex offending and typologies has continued, and studies such as those of Nathan and Ward (2002) and Kalders *et al.* (1997) have generally confirmed previous research, although there is some dispute about the significance of denial. Nathan and Ward (from a sample of 12 women) have added to the existing typologies women who offend with males but who are motivated by rejection and revenge, rather than coercion or fear. Nathan and Ward label these 'the male-accompanied: rejected/revengeful'.

The research work on validating, refining and extending the typology of female sexual offending is likely to continue. Recent research has emphasized the diversity of characteristics and motivations in female sexual offending (Atkinson 2000; Davin *et al.* 1999; Kalders *et al.* 1997; Nathan and Ward 2001, 2002). Typology and theory development requires more work, particularly to take account of diversity, and to develop what Nathan and Ward have called a 'richer classification' (2002, p.18).

Models of sex offending: the case for a gender-specific approach

Sex offending is not a homogeneous activity (Grubin 1998), and just as there is no stereotypical male offender/abuser, there is no typical female sexual offender (Young 1993). Female sex offenders are heterogeneous group reflecting a diverse range of offender characteristics and motivations. It is now accepted that male models of sex offending do not apply to women (Atkinson 2000). Consequently, it cannot be assumed that general theories and models derived from male sex offending can be uncritically transferred to female offenders (Adshead *et al.* 1994). As Young argues, it is not enough to see women as the 'desperate mimics' of men (1993, p.113), or 'all abusing women' as 'victims of patriarchal oppression' (1993, p.115).

Model One: the construction of a female pathology

This model links female sexual abusers to theories of female structural powerlessness in society (Wolfers 1993). The 'structured powerlessness of women' and the contrast between powerlessness in the public sphere and almost total power in the private sphere of motherhood is seen as integral to female sexual abuse. In brief, it is contended that women abuse in order to achieve control and power, but more importantly in order for *some* women to 'act out' their own internalized abusive experiences (Wolfers 1993, p.101). Female sexual abuse is not merely a perversion of the 'maternal instinct' (Welldon and Seamark 1996, p.45), instead, it is a by product of the structural powerlessness of women in patriarchal society. This powerlessness is compounded by drug dependency, victimization within polyincestuous settings and intergenerational abuse within extended families (Faller 1987; McCarty 1986).

There are, however, some limits to this model. Studies have been based on small samples. Wolfers' sample was 10 women (1992, 1993) and Faller's a little larger, at 40 (1987). In addition, such a model fails to adequately explain those female perpetrators who 'sexually abuse children without the involvement of a male partner' (e.g. alone or as part of a lesbian couple) (Allen 1991, p.13) and who are the prime instigators of abuse. The portrayal of female abusers as 'compliant victims' can be difficult to maintain and, as Cameron has argued with regard to Rosemary West, 'the relationship between what was done to her and what she did to others is not a straightforward matter' (1999, p.71). 'Cause-and-effect' relationships of this type are notoriously difficult to investigate, and simple determinism has been disputed (Cameron 1999). Kelly (1996) has noted the numerous methodological flaws in research trying to prove a correlation between being a victim and becoming a subsequent abuser, and has challenged the notion of a 'cycle of abuse'. Statistically, most victims (who are also girls) do not grow up to be abusers (Higgs, Canavan and Meyer 1992), and, as Kelly notes, there are different types of abuse, from emotional to severe sexual or physical abuse. Empirical knowledge about the type of abuse and victim typology that leads a victim to become an abuser is still at an early stage (Friedrich, Urquiza and Bielke 1989; Hindman 1989).

Grayston and De Luca (1999) found that whereas past victimization and trauma are strong risk factors for female sexual offending, some female offenders experience sexual fantasies and deviant sexual arousal, although it is not always clear how significant a motivating factor this is (Nathan and Ward 2002; Saradjian 1997). Women also abuse alone, and even where they offend with men, this is not always due to coercion or fear (Nathan and Ward 2002). Caution must, however, be exercised over generalized conclusions while sample sizes remain so small.

In broader terms, Cameron has argued for an important distinction between those 'women who do not have a meaningful choice – for example, battered women who kill…and implying that women as a subordinate group must inevitably lack agency, responsibility and will' (1999, p.76). The 1980s and 1990s also saw the development of the female pathology from early work that identified single factors such as early victimization or drug dependency as crucial factors (McCarty 1986), to later work that attempted to pursue a multi-factorial approach (Faller 1987; Wolfers 1993). The latter has been developed into an integrated approach with greater theoretical sophistication by Saradjian (1996).

Model Two: a holistic integrated framework

Saradjian has proposed a holistic integrated framework to explain female sexual offending. She bases this on 'an ethological approach to human motivation' (1996, p.187). In brief, the framework proposes a learning model of behaviour within which women learn from an early age how fundamental needs (such as sexual arousal) can be successfully met. This can include deviant behaviours, rooted in their direct experience or in modelling by significant others (e.g. adults who may have abused them), and through this women 'become conditioned to triggers associated with children/adolescents' (1996, p.201). In this way, sexual behaviour with children is both learnt and justified as an acceptable mechanism for meeting needs. Behaviour that meets needs is both rewarding and reinforcing, and hence repetitious. Saradjian contends that such behaviour is linked to feelings of 'well-being' and to the release of endogenous opioids and serotonin. The neuro-chemicals, the endogenous opioids, have been linked to the long-term management of stress and anxiety, often experienced by those female perpetrators who have themselves been the subject of long-term sexual abuse. Saradjian argues that this long-term release of endogenous opioids has resulted in a physiological dependency and proposes this as a key driver in the initiation of sexual acts with children.

Saradjian's model is important in that it attempts to integrate social, biological, and environmental factors into an explanatory framework of female sexual offending. The framework links cognitions, behaviours, experiences, environment and situational factors/triggers, and makes a significant contribution to explaining why and how female sexual offending occurs. It also helps to identify 'who', or at least those women who may have a predisposition to offend sexually against children. It should not, however, be assumed that all who have been the victim of abuse will go on to offend

(Higgs *et al.* 1992). The frequency of victimization, its severity, and subsequent access and proximity to children are seen as key variables in victims becoming abusers (Friedrich *et al.* 1989; Higgs *et al.* 1992), possibly owing to levels of trauma, learned behaviour and internalized models of acceptable behaviour (Saradjian 1996).

Assessment issues

Good assessment is the key to effective interventions (Saradjian 1996). Such assessments need to be underpinned by an empirical and theoretical knowledge of female sexual offending and those factors most likely to reduce the risk of sexually abusive behaviour (Saradjian 1996). This requires assessments to be grounded in empirical evidence, factual and targeted. Saradjian (1996, pp.203–4) has argued that assessments should:

- Give an opinion as to whether a woman is likely to have sexually abused a child or children.

- Consider the risk a woman who is known to have sexually abused a child or children has of re-offending.

- Consider the areas that need to be worked on in therapy to reduce the risk of re-offending, including most importantly the woman's motivation to change.

- Gain information from the perpetrator that may inform the therapy of the victim(s).

Assessments can, however, be significantly impaired by professional denial that women sexually offend, particularly against their own children (Hetherton 1999; Wolfers 1992). This can inadvertently reinforce the denial and minimization of perpetrators, a difficulty shared in common with their male counterparts (Beckett *et al.* 1994). As offender self-report and self-disclosure are the key sources of assessment information, denial and distortion can be highly problematic for the assessor. This requires well-developed interviewing skills rooted in sound theoretical models, informed by a research-based knowledge of female sexual offenders and appropriate training and support for the assessors. The latter is particularly important because, as Saradjian says:

When the assessor is so reliant on the self-report of the offender it is important to elicit as much co-operation as possible without developing a collusive relationship. (1996, p.205).

Assessment must also establish motivation to change and the type of intervention required.

Motivation to change

Motivation is a complex issue, although usage of the term in the addiction field has been largely restricted to assessing 'readiness to change' (Tober 1998; Miller and Rollnick 1991; Tober 1998). Tober argues for a broader definition of motivation:

> Motivation, whether in the biological, the cognitive or the behavioural sense, is best understood as the sum of drives and incentives surrounding a specific behaviour: the 'pushes and pulls'…that determine whether the behaviour will occur or not. (1998, p.187)

This suggests that understanding the motivation(s) to offend is an important precursor to understanding whether change is possible and how it might occur: literally an unpicking of the 'pushes and pulls'. There has, however, been extensive debate on whether motivation can be changed by therapeutic intervention and on the importance (or otherwise) of motivation to change behaviour (Logan, 1993; Tober 1998). In brief, it is contended that motivational change takes place when the costs of a behaviour are seen to outweigh the benefits (Prochaska and DiClemente 1984, 1986), a cost–benefit equation that may shift depending upon life circumstances or external events (such as arrest and imprisonment for the behaviour).

However, this cost–benefit model of change carries certain assumptions. It presumes that people can and do make rationally based cost–benefit calculations of their behaviour. The work of Bloor (1995) on HIV and intraveneous drug use has, however, revealed that although people may 'know' that the costs of their behaviours are outweighing the benefits, they often lack the opportunity or power to act otherwise. This can be a matter of services and of access to resources and to social networks of positive support. It can also be a matter of 'self-efficacy' (Annis and Davies 1989), whether the person believes that he or she can action change and has the skills to do so, and whether change will make a difference (Rollnick, Heather and Bell 1992). These issues have been seen as being particularly central to therapeutic interventions with female sex offenders (Saradjian 1996).

Motivational interviewing has been advocated as a key technique in promoting change (Miller and Rollnick 1991; Rollnick, Morgan and Heather 1996; Rollnick *et al.* 1992). The emphasis is upon enabling clients to define their own problem(s) and articulate their own intention to change. Tober outlines five steps in the motivational interviewing technique:

1. *'Bringing up the subject'*. This is an explanatory stage using open questions in order to begin the process of problem definition.

2. *'Description of the good things about' the behaviour of concern*. This stage establishes the reasons and motivations for the problematic behaviour(s).

3. *'Description of the less good things'*. This stage identifies the cost of the behaviour and enables the client to begin the process of weighing the balance.

4. *'Description of client concerns about the behaviour'*. This stage builds on client concerns expressed in the previous stage, and, importantly, seeks to personalize the negative consequences of behaviour of the type: 'This will happen to me if I continue to do this.'

5. *'Eliciting statement of intention to change'*. This final step is the most difficult. Is the client serious or merely stating what is expected? Criteria for real change are the level of knowledge and skill the client has to 'make it', belief in 'self-efficacy' and the required level of self-esteem.

(Adapted from Tober 1998, pp.190–191).

Motivational interviewing has been developed almost entirely in work with drug and alcohol addiction, and its appropriate and effective transfer to work with sex offenders should not necessarily be assumed. Achieving and maintaining change with sex offenders requires substantial work on re-moving denial and justificatory thinking patterns (Eldridge 1992; Saradjian 1996). Female sex offenders have been found to have the 'same kind of cog-nitive distortions, belief systems, justifications and transferences of blame that male offenders demonstrate' (Spencer 1999, p.28), hence motivational work needs to address this (Eldridge 1995). There are, however, significant gender differences that should be taken into account, not least that 'females are expected (by society) to be more vulnerable and passive, and as a consequence female offenders tend to rationalise from a victim stance' (Spencer 1999, p.28), and that female offenders have often exhibited high levels of trauma (Mathews, Hunter and Vuz 1997; Matthews 1998). This suggests that workers will have to balance offence-focused work with intensive therapeutic work on trauma.

Interventions

The aim of treatment interventions with female sex offenders has been well expressed by Wolfers:

> We need to challenge and confront the offending behaviour, enable women to understand what the triggers are which precipitate abusive acts and we need to build self-esteem and the ability to be assertive in non-abusive situations. (1992, p.13).

Cognitive-behavioural group-based interventions have a well-established track record with male sex offenders (see Beech and Fisher this volume, and Marshall, Serran and Moulden, this volume), although there has been a limited transference of this approach to female offenders. There have been exploratory programmes with women offenders, including in prison settings, but with a limited evaluation of treatment outcomes (Barnett, Corder and Jehu 1990; King 1989). Evaluations have been largely dependent upon 'evaluation sheets', 'cognition scales' and 'self-reports' (Barnett *et al.* 1990), with a lack of long-term recidivism studies owing to the small scale of intervention programmes for women.

The core components of such programmes (Barnett *et al.* 1990; King 1989) have been:

- a focus on the offence
- attention to cognitions and behaviours
- attention to disinhibitors (such as alcohol and drugs) and pre-disposing factors
- key situational or trigger factors

- an emphasis upon protective factors, rehearsing and role-playing alternatives

- the development of relapse prevention techniques

Early programmes, such as that pioneered by Barnett *et al.* (1990) at Styal prison, used a confrontational approach with compulsory attendance. The rationale for this was to challenge denial and, justifications, and to promote change. The effectiveness of an overtly confrontational approach has, however, been challenged by others such as Saradjian, who advocate a more empathic (although not collusive) relationship between worker and client/offender. Saradjian's approach is cast within a therapeutic approach to intervention, usually on a one-to-one basis in which the therapeutic relationship itself plays a key role in enabling female offenders to understand the choices they have made, decreasing denial and increasing responsibility, building self-esteem, and developing positive non-sexual and non-exploitative relationships. Work is individually targeted at the woman's pattern of offending and the development of both intellectual and emotional empathy with her victims. Relapse prevention is targeted at individual patterns of thinking and behaviours, and emphasizes self-risk management so that individual offenders can seek to manage their own risky behaviours (see also Ward and Devilly, this volume).

Conclusion and summary

Female sex offending is no longer the 'undiscovered country', and both the prevalence and type of offending are increasingly being recognized. Research has often relied upon small samples, so building up empirical knowledge and typologies of female sex offending has been slow. The process has also been hindered by gender stereotypes and cultural myths about motherhood and femininity. The 1990s saw, however, a considerable exploration of female sex offending and extensive attention to building theoretical models to facilitate assessment and interventions. These models are developing in sophistication and integration (see, for example, Saradjian 1996), and have a direct application to practitioners in the field.

Empirically grounded explanatory models also have a key role in informing assessment, both the assessment of 'capacity to change' and the most appropriate matching of interventions to individual behaviours. Caution has been expressed against the simple transfer of assessment and intervention techniques from male offenders to female offenders. In particular, issues of victimization and trauma have been highlighted as central issues for *some* women, and both assessment and intervention techniques need to reflect this.

Finally, investigation into the types and patterns of female sex offending is continuing, informed by both victim studies and perpetrator studies (Wolfers 1993), although further research into the characteristics and motivations of female offending that make it different from male offending is still required (Allen 1991). Nathan and Ward argue that 'any comprehensive theory of female sexual offending will need to contain distinct offence pathways, each associated with different motives and vulnerability factors' (2002, p.19). It is exactly this kind of empirical knowledge that is required to inform the cutting-edge clinical practice with female sexual offenders that is needed by both victims and perpetrators alike.

Acknowledgement

The author would like to thank Joseph Yates, PhD student at De Montfort University, Leicester, for conducting the initial literature search upon which this chapter is based. The contents of the chapter are entirely the responsibility of the author.

References

Adshead, G., Howlett, M. and Mason, F. (1994) 'Women who Sexually Abuse Children: The Undiscovered Country.' *Journal of Sexual Aggression 1*, 1, 45–56.

Allen, C. M. (1990) 'Women as Perpetrators of Child Sexual Abuse: Recognition Barriers.' In A. L. Horton, B. L Johnson, L. M. Rondry and D. Williams (eds) *The Incest Perpetrator: A Family Member No One Wants To Treat.* Newbury Park, CA: Sage.

Allen, C. M. (1991) *Women and Men who Sexually Abuse Children: A Comparative Analysis.* Vermont: Safer Society Press.

Annis, H. M. and Davies, C. S. (1989) 'Relapse Prevention.' In R. K. Hester and W. R. Miller (eds) *Handbook of Alcoholism Treatment Approaches.* New York: Plenum Press.

Atkinson, J. (2000) *Case Studies of Female Sex Offenders in the Correctional Service of Canada.* Toronto: Correctional Services.

Barnett, S., Corder, R. and Jehu, D. (1990) 'Group Work Treatment for Women Sex Offenders Against Children.' *Groupwork 3*, 2, 191–203.

Beckett, R., Beech, A., Fisher, D. and Fordham, A. S. (1994) *Community-based Treatment for Sex Offenders: An Evaluation of Seven Treatment Programmes*. A Report for the Home Office by the STEP Team. London: Home Office.

Bloor, M. (1995) *The Sociology of HIV Transmission*. London: Sage.

Cameron, D. (1999) 'Rosemary West: Motives and Meanings.' *Journal of Sexual Aggression* 4, 2, 68–80.

Crawford, C. and Conn, L. (1997) 'Female Sexual Abuse: Unrecognised Abuse and Ignored Victims.' *Journal of the British Association for Counselling 8*, 1, 278–280.

Davin, P. A., Hislop, J. C. R. and Dunbar, T. (1999) *Female Sexual Abusers*. Vermont: Safer Society Press.

Eldridge, H. (1995) 'Adult Female Perpetrators of Child Sexual Abuse: Patterns of Offending and Strategies for Effective Assessment and Intervention.' Appendix 2 of the response of the Lucy Faithfull Foundation to the *Working Together* consultation paper. Bordesley Hall, Alvechurch, Birmingham: Lucy Faithfull Foundation.

Elliot, M. (1993) *Female Sexual Abuse of Children: The Ultimate Taboo*. Harlow: Longman.

Faller, K. C. (1987) 'Women who Sexually Abuse Children.' *Violence And Victims 2*, 4, 263–276.

Faller, K. C. (1995) 'A Clinical Sample of Women who Have Sexually Abused Children.' *Journal of Sexual Abuse 4*, 13–20.

Finkelhor, D. and Russell, D. (1984) 'Women as Perpetrators.' In D. Finkelhor (ed) *Child Sexual Abuse*. New York: NY Free Press.

Friedrich, W., Urquiza, A. and, Bielke, R. (1989) 'Behaviour Problems in Sexually Abused Young Children.' *Journal of Pediatric Psychology 11*, 45–57.

Grayston, A. D. and De Luca, R. V. (1999) 'Female Perpetrators of Child Sexual Abuse: A Review of the Clinical and Empirical Literature.' *Aggression and Violent Behaviour 4*, 93–106.

Grubin, D. (1998) *Sex Ooffending Against Children: Understanding the Risk*. Police Research Series Paper No. 99. London: Home Office.

Hanks, H. and Saradjian, J. (1992) 'The Female Abuser.' *Community Care,* 25 June, vii–viii.

Hetherton, J. (1999) 'The Idealisation of Women: Its Role in the Minimisation of Child Sexual Abuse by Females.' *Child Abuse and Neglect 23*, 2, 161–174.

Higgs, D. C., Canavan, M. M. and Meyer, W. J. (1992) 'Moving from Defense to Offense: The Development of an Adolescent Female Sex Offending.' *Journal of Sex Research 29*, 1, 131–139.

Hindman, J. (1989) *Just Before Dawn*. Oregon: Alexandra Associates.

Kalders, A. S., Inkster, H. C. and Britt, E. F. (1994) *Female Child Sex Offenders in New Zealand*. Christchurch: Psychological Service, Department of Corrections.

Kalders, A. S., Inkster, H. C. and Britt, E. F. (1997) 'Females who Offend Sexually Against Children in New Zealand.' *Journal of Sexual Aggression 3*, 1, 15–29.

Kasl, C. D. (1990) 'Female Perpetrators of Sexual Abuse: A Feminist View.' In M. Hunter (ed) *The Sexually Abused Male*, volume 1. *Prevalence, Impact and Treatment*. Lexington MA: Lexington.

Kelly, L. (1996) 'Weasel Words.' *Trouble and Strife*, p.33.

King, J. (1989) 'A Recipe for Change.' *Community Care*, 27 April.

Logan, F. (1993) 'Animal Learning and Motivation and Addictive Drugs.' *Psychological Reports 73*, 291–306.

Mathews, R., Hunter, J.A. and Vuz, J. (1997) 'Juvenile Female Sexual Offenders: Clinical Characteristics and Treatment Issues.' *Sexual Abuse: A Journal of Research and Treatment 9*, 3, 187–189.

Matthews, J.K. (1993) 'Working with Female Sexual Abuse.' In M. Elliot (ed) *Female Sexual Abuse of Children: The Ultimate Taboo*. Harlow: Longman.

Matthews, J. K. (1998) 'An 11 Year Perspective of Working with Female Sexual Offenders.' In W. L. Marshall, Y. M. Fernandez, S. M. Hudson and T. Ward (eds) *Sourcebook of Treatment Programs for Sexual Offenders*. New York: Plenum Press.

Matthews, J. K., Matthews, R. and Speltz, K. (1991) 'Female Sexual Offenders: A Typology.' In M. Q. Patton (ed) *Family Sexual Abuse: Frontline Research and Evaluation*. California: Sage.

Miller, W. R. and Rollnick, S. (1991) *Motivational Interviewing: Preparing People for Change*. New York: Guilford Press.

Nathan, P. and Ward, T. (2001) 'Females who Sexually Abuse Children: Assessment and Treatment Issues.' *Psychiatry, Psychology and Law 8*, 8 1, 44–56.

Nathan, P. and Ward, T. (2002) 'Female Sex Offenders: Clinical and Demographic Factors.' *Journal of Sexual Aggression 8*, 1, 5–21.

Prochaska, J. O. and DiClemente, C. C. (1984) *The Trans-theoretical Approach: Crossing Traditional Boundaries of Therapy*. Homewood, IL: Dow Jones–Irwin.

Prochaska, J. O. and DiClemente, C. C. (1986) 'Towards a Comprehensive Model of Change.' In W. R. Miller and N. Heather (eds) *Treating Addictive Behaviours: Processes of Change*. New York: Plenum Press.

Rollnick, S., Heather, N. and Bell, A. (1992) 'Negotiating Behaviour Change in Medical Settings: The Development of Brief Motivational Interviewing.' *Journal of Mental Health 1*, 25–37.

Rollnick, S., Morgan, M. and Heather, N. (1996) 'Development of a Brief Scale to Measure Outcome Expectations of Reduced Consumption Among Excessive Drinkers.' *Addictive Behaviours 21*, 377–387.

Saradjian, J. (1996) *Women who Sexually Abuse Children: From Research to Clinical Practice*. Chichester: John Wiley.

Saradjian, J. (1997) 'Factors that Specifically Exacerbated the Trauma of Victims of Childhood Sexual Abuse by Maternal Perpetrators.' *Journal of Sexual Aggression 3*, 1, 3–14.

Spencer, A. (1999) *Working with Sex Offenders in Prison and Through Release to the Community: A Handbook*. London: Jessica Kingsley Publishers.

Tober, G. (1998) 'Learning Theory, Addiction, Counselling.' In K. Cigno and D. Bourn (eds) *Cognitive-behavioural Social Work in Practice*. Aldershot: Ashgate.

Wakefield, H. and Under-Wager, R. (1991) 'Female Child Sexual Abusers: A Critical Review of the Literature.' *Journal of Forensic Psychology 9*, 43–69.

Welldon, E. V. (1988) *Mother, Madonna, Whore: The Idealisation and Denigration of Motherhood*. London: Guildford Press.

Welldon, E. V. (1995) 'Female Perversions and Hysteria.' *British Journal of Psychotherapy 11*, 406–414.

Welldon, E. V. and Seamark, J. (1996) 'Female Sex Offenders.' *Prison Service Journal 107*, 39–47.

Wolfers, O. (1992) 'Same Abuse Different Parent.' *Social Work Today,*12 March, 12–13.

Wolfers, O. (1993) 'The Paradox of Women who Sexually Abuse Children.' In M. Elliot (ed) *The Female Abuse of Children: The Ultimate Taboo.* Chichester: Wiley.

Valios, N. (2002) 'Women Abuse.' *Community Care,*14–20 March, 28–29.

Young, V. (1993) 'Women Abusers: A Feminist Perspective.' In M. Elliot (ed) *The Female Abuse of Children: The Ultimate Taboo.* Chichester: Wiley.

CHAPTER 4

Young Sex Offenders

Helen Masson

Introduction

Concerns about children and young people who have sexually abused others have been on welfare professionals' agenda in the UK since the early 1990s, following the publication of the National Children's Home's *Report of the Committee of Enquiry into Children and Young People who Sexually Abuse Other Children* (NCH 1992) and the first, albeit brief, reference to how agencies should respond to abuse by children and young people in paragraph 5.24 in the second edition of *Working Together* (Department of Health 1991). In this chapter, the focus will be on young sex offenders, those over the age of criminal responsibility and convicted of a criminal offence, although it should be noted that the problem of sexual harm or abuse by young perpetrators covers a much wider age span (Erooga and Masson 1999). After a historical sketch outlining the history of the emergence of the problem of young sex offenders and an overview of the size of the problem, this chapter will consider the characteristics of young sex offenders, risk assessment and interventions with young sex offenders, and the current state of policy and practice in the UK.

Emergence of the problem of young sexual abusers: incidence and prevalence

The increased focus on child sexual abuse and on adult perpetrators of sexual abuse, discussed by Kemshall and McIvor in the first chapter of this volume, probably created a climate of professional and public sensitivity within which other 'discoveries' about the phenomenon of child sexual abuse were more likely. In relation to the emergence of the problem of sexual abuse by children and young people, however, particular factors appear to have been influential, including: the arrival of literature from the USA, where the problem had surfaced a decade earlier (see, for example, Ryan and Lane 1991, 1997); incidence and prevalence studies (see below); the concerns of front-line staff in field and residential work, in both statutory and voluntary settings, who were struggling to manage and develop adequate responses to these youngsters (NCH 1992); and the efforts of a small number of well-placed organizations and certain key individuals to raise awareness of the problem and put it on the agendas of government departments and welfare agencies. Notable among these organizations were the National Organisation for the Treatment of Abusers (NOTA), which was originally established as a support and training organization for professionals working with adult sex offenders, various voluntary sector children's organizations such as the National Children's Home and Barnardos, and at least one interested Social Services Inspector (now retired) in the Department of Health.

Incidence and prevalence studies

Any discussion of the incidence and prevalence of sexual abuse by young people is problematic. As the following analysis of official and research statistics indicates, even such 'objective' figures cover a multitude of ambiguities. An attempt is nevertheless made here to assess the current state of knowledge about the size of the problem of children and young people who sexually abuse others.

CRIMINAL STATISTICS

Criminal statistics for England and Wales for 2000 (Home Office 2001) give the recorded level of sexual offences as 37,311. This total comprises less than 1 per cent of all notifiable offences. It should also be noted that fewer than 1 per cent of these 37,311 offences were committed by females. Out of the total of recorded sexual offences, 5200 individuals were subsequently reprimanded or finally warned (if juvenile offenders) or cautioned (if adult) for a sexual offence, or were found guilty of a sexual offence in a court of law. (Interestingly, the 5200 cautions and convictions in 2000 represent a steadily decreasing annual number from the 10,700 recorded in 1988 and 1989.) Approximately 21 per cent (1100) of the 5200 were aged between 10 and 21 years of age. A total of 1300 of the 5200 cautioned or found guilty were reprimanded, finally warned or cautioned. Of these, approximately 15 per cent (200) were aged 12–14 years, 15 per cent (200) were aged 15–17 years and 7.5 per cent (100) were aged 18–20 years. In other words (predominantly male) children and young people aged between 10 and 21 years accounted for 38 per cent of all reprimands, final warnings and cautions for sexual offences. Of the approximately 3900 males who were found guilty in a court of a sexual offence, 2.5 per cent (100) were aged 12–4 years, 8 per cent (300) were aged 15–17 years, and 5 per cent (200) were aged between 18 and 20. Thus, a much smaller but significant percentage of young people (15 per cent) accounted for findings of guilt as a result of court process, compared with the percentage of young people accounting for reprimands and final warnings.

These official statistics are likely to represent just a small proportion of sexual abuse committed by children and young people, particularly as it is claimed (NCH 1992) that much abuse goes unreported or is not recognized or dealt with as such. Moreover, as a number of commentators have powerfully argued (see, for example, Cicourel 1967; May 1993; Scott 1990; Shipman 1981), such ostensibly reliable data are, in fact, highly problematic given the tortuous and socially situated processes through which they are generated and the confusing and inconsistent nature of the data themselves. Shipman comments:

> To Cicourel, official statistics of juvenile crime are made up in the same way as rumour is generated and transmitted. Vague and discontinuous pieces of information are transformed into ordered occurrences. (1981, p.122)

PREVALENCE STUDIES

Various other kinds of study have also attempted to estimate the extent of sexual abuse by young people. In a major retrospective study of adults concerning their experiences of abuse in childhood, Finkelhor (1979) found that 34 per cent of women and 39 per cent of men who recalled having a sexual encounter during their childhood with someone five or more years older than themselves reported that the older partner was aged between 10 and 19 years. Other studies (Ageton 1983; Fromuth, Jones and Burkhart 1991) suggest that about 3 per cent of all adolescent males have committed sexually abusive acts, while Abel *et al.* (1987) found that approximately 50 per cent of adult sex offenders they studied reported that they had had deviant sexual interests during their adolescent years.

Caution must always be applied when interpreting the results of such retrospective studies. For example, in the case of Abel *et al.*'s (1987) study, their findings have been misinterpreted as demonstrating high rates of adolescent sexual deviancy that get carried through into adulthood. It may instead be that many or indeed all adolescent males have deviant sexual interests but only a proportion act on those interests at the time or later in their lives (Beckett 1999). Research on this conjecture has yet to be conducted. Nevertheless, weighing up these kinds of statistical and research finding, overview reports (see, for example, Grubin 1998; Kelly, Regan and Burton 1991; NCH 1992; Openshaw *et al.* 1993) consistently conclude that between about 25 and 33 per cent of all alleged sexual abuse involves young (mainly adolescent) perpetrators.

Characteristics of young sex offenders

As criminal statistics seem to suggest, reported young sexual offenders are mostly males in their middle to late teenage years. Early literature, indeed, (for example, NCH 1992; Ryan and Lane 1991) focused almost exclusively on male adolescents, although more has now been written about young children (10 years and under) who are displaying sexually harmful behaviour (Butler and Elliott 1999; Johnson 1988, 1989, 1993; Rasmussen 2002). In this section, the focus remains on by far the largest category of young sexual abusers – adolescent males – with a further brief outline of the characteristics of adolescent female sexual abusers, before some final comments are offered on the need to attend to the diversity of young sex offender populations (see also Kendrick, this volume, for a review of the characteristics of young people who are sexually aggressive).

Male adolescent sexual abusers

It is argued in texts overviewing the terrain that are based on existing published studies (see, for example, Barbaree, Marshall and Hudson 1993; Grubin 1998; Morrison and Print 1995; Ryan and Lane 1997) that a generalized picture of male adolescent sexual abusers and their offences can be developed. The victims of such offenders are said to be usually younger by a number of years. They comprise both male and female children, and are often, as is the case with adult child molesters, known to the abuser, for example as a sibling or through a baby-sitting relationship, although, in cases of rape, the abusers are apparently less likely to know their victims. Although the full range of sexually abusive behaviours identified in respect of adult sex offenders is also perpetrated by such youngsters, Ryan and Lane suggest that:

> The modal offence scenario most likely involves a seven or eight-year-old victim, and more likely a female who is not related to the offender by blood or marriage. The behaviour is unwanted, involves genital touching and often penetration (over 60 per cent), and is accompanied by sufficient coercion or force to overcome the victim's resistance. (1997, p.7)

In terms of their characteristics, and as literature on adult sex offenders also indicates, young male sexual abusers are typically portrayed as having a number of social skills deficits, often being described as socially isolated, lacking dating skills and sexual knowledge, and experiencing high levels of social anxiety. These conclusions are based on a rapidly increasing number of studies, in both North America and the UK, including a study of 305 offenders aged 18 years or younger by Fehrenbach *et al.* (1986), a study of 161 young sex offenders aged under 19 years by Wasserman and Kappel (1985), studies of 24 and 29 young child molesters aged under 16 years by Awad, Saunders and Levene (1984) and Awad and Saunders (1989) respectively, a British study conducted by Manocha and Mezey (1998) of 51 adolescents, aged between 13 and 18 years, and a database of over 1600 adolescent sex offenders in North America that has been compiled by the National Adolescent Perpetrator Network (Ryan *et al.* 1996). Not surprisingly, this reported lack of social competence is seen as often resulting in low self-esteem and emotional loneliness. Some commentators point out, however, that low self-esteem may be a consequence of contemporary events, e.g. being apprehended and punished, although for others it may be a problem that is long-standing and chronic. Thus, Marshall (1989) has suggested that problems of early emotional attachment contribute to a failure to establish intimate relationships in later life and subsequent low self-esteem and emotional loneliness.

Young male sexual abusers, it is asserted, may well be doing poorly at school in terms of both behaviour and educational attainment (see, for example, a study by Kahn and Chambers 1991 of 221 adolescent sex offenders), and, as in studies of adult male sexual offenders, a relatively high proportion of them (between 25 and 60 per cent depending on the study cited) report having been victims of sexual abuse themselves (Bentovim and Williams 1998; Hackett 2002). A number of studies therefore also suggest that the families of such youngsters may have a number of difficulties in terms of their stability and intrafamilial dynamics (Ryan and Lane 1997).

Despite the fact that most research into young sexual abusers has focused on adolescent males, there are many aspects of this population that warrant further study. Existing empirical studies are often flawed in that they do not adequately compare adolescent sexual abusers with either nonabusing adolescents or, for example, violent and non-violent delinquents. In the case of those that do, the results are not clear-cut, some studies suggesting that many of the characteristics just described are also common in the backgrounds of other violent and non-violent juvenile delinquents (see, for example, Bischof, Stith and Whitney 1995; Ryan 1999), others proposing some significant differences (see, for comparison, Ford and Linney 1995; Katz 1990). As Barbaree *et al.* comment:

> In all likelihood, the population of juvenile sex offenders is every bit as heterogeneous as the population of adult sex offenders. (1993, p.16)

As in the case of adult sex offenders, some research has now begun to identify subgroups within the total population with a view to refining current assessment and treatment approaches. Thus, for example, Richardson *et al.* (1997) have reported on their study in England of 100 male adolescent sex offenders aged 11–18, whom they categorized into four groups on the basis of the age of their victims and the relationship between abuser and victim. They identified four groupings: a group of 31 child abusers (whose victims were 4 or more years younger than themselves); a group of 20 who abused their siblings; a group of 24 abusers who had assaulted same-aged or older victims; and a mixed group of 22 subjects. Interestingly, the researchers found that 41 per cent of the victims of the child group were male, about twice the rate of the mixed and incest groups. None of the peer group victims was male, and, indeed, the backgrounds of the 'peer group' were found to be most similar to those of adult rapists. It would appear that further research in this area is needed and may prove fruitful in distinguishing between different categories of male adolescent sexual abusers.

It should also be noted that there is only a very limited literature that highlights the particular issues related to young sex offenders from black and minority ethnic communities (Abassi and Jamal 2002), to young people who are homosexual (Hackett 2000) or to working with young people with learning difficulties (O'Callaghan 2001; Stermac and Sheridan 1993). It is probably safe to assume that, as research findings emerge, assessment and in-tervention programmes will have to be developed to cater for a range of young sex offender populations, in terms of both their characteristics and their levels of adjustment or maladjustment.

Female adolescent sexual abusers

In their overview of female youth who sexually abuse, Lane with Lobanov-Rostovsky (1997) comment on the very disturbed backgrounds of the young female abusers with whom they have worked, noting high levels of both sexual and physical victimization, problematic relationships with parents, family separation and problems at school and with peers in particular. However, they also comment that:

> Many of the developmental experiences are similar to those identified in the history of male youth, although they may be experienced differently by female youth based on gender, socialisation and role expectations. (1997, p.348)

They and others (see, for example, Blues, Moffatt and Telford 1999; Williams and Buehler 2002) suggest that young female sexual abusers may well benefit from the same kinds of treatment approach as young male sexual abusers, although they comment that issues of autonomy and the consequences of female socialization experiences (e.g. in relation to anger management) may well be useful additional foci.

Assessment and interventions with young sex offenders

It is important, at the outset, to state that there is increasing agreement that children and young people who have sexually offended should not be regarded as mini adult sex offenders (Calder 2002; Chaffin and Bonner 1998; Erooga and Masson 1999). It cannot be assumed, therefore, that research, models and methods designed for work with adult sex offenders are transferable to work with this group, although elements of them may well be of relevance. Young sex offenders are immature so work with them should be developmentally appropriate and designed to address not only their problematic behaviours, but also all their social, emotional, educational and other needs.

It is worth stressing this point as early thinking based, in part, on a misinterpretation of research findings (see, for example, the Abel *et al.* study 1987 cited above) led to a discourse suggesting that young sex offenders were different from other kinds of young offender. Thus, in contrast to their non-sexually offending peers, it was argued that they tended to grow not out of their behaviour but into it unless they were 'treated', if necessary compelled, via a court order under the Children Act 1989 or under criminal legislation (NCH 1992). What now seems clearer is that, like other young offenders, the majority of young sex offenders will not go on to re-offend and become adult sex offenders, even if not intervened with or, at most, offered brief intervention, although a small but significant proportion are at much higher risk of doing so. Will (1994), for example, reported on an American conference at which Jim Brieling from the National Institute of Mental Health was reviewing the available literature on the outcome of treatment programmes. Will commented in his write-up:

> Although there are only a handful of good studies in this area, most show that the re-offending rate is low at less than 10%. Now, while this could mean that treatment programmes are incredibly powerful, it is more likely that it means

that the vast majority of offenders taken on for treatment are not going to re-offend again regardless of whether they have treatment or not. (1994, p.52)

Becker (1998) also comments that the few robust recidivism studies that have been undertaken also indicate that recidivism rates are low. Weinrott (1996) examined 22 treatment studies, although the majority followed subjects up for under 5 years and none used untreated control groups. Bearing these limitations in mind, Weinrott nevertheless concluded that it appeared that relatively few adolescents were charged with subsequent sexual crimes, two-thirds of the studies reporting re-offence rates of less than 10 per cent. In addition, he concluded that adolescent sexual offenders also appeared to be less likely than other delinquents to re-offend non-sexually. Clearly, however, more research is needed in this area in order to try to identify those young sexual abusers who are at higher risk of recidivism, as other studies now attempt to do in relation to adult sex offenders (Grubin 1998). To date, such studies are in their relative infancy, and it is not possible to predict future dangerousness within the population with a great degree of certainty, although some useful pointers, such as the degree of impulsivity involved in an offence, are emerging (Miner 2002).

In a UK based study, Glasgow *et al.* (1994) looked at all children alleged to have sexually abused children in the city of Liverpool during a 12-month period. Interestingly, they found that:

> adolescents were more than twice as likely to be suspected of having sexually abused another child than any other comparable age band *in adulthood or childhood.* (1994, p.196, emphasis added)

As a consequence, they argue strongly for a more explicit developmental perspective on sexual offending across the lifespan, a perspective that seeks to understand different patterns of sexual behaviour at different points in the life cycle and the constellations of factors that might increase the risk of certain individuals exhibiting sexually abusive behaviour at a given period in their lives. Glasgow *et al.* hypothesize, for example, that in adolescence, as opposed to young adulthood:

> abuse is more likely to occur in susceptible individuals because of a combination of the intense sexual drive which characterises the period, together with

numerous opportunities to abuse offered by continuing membership of the world of childhood. (1994, p.207)

The assessment of young sex offenders

Within a context of appropriate uncertainty about the ability to predict the risk of future offending, there is nevertheless an emerging consensus among professionals engaged in this area of work that any young person who comes to the notice of an agency for sexually aggressive or abusive behaviour should be offered an initial assessment, with extended assessment in the case of young people who are judged to pose a greater risk to others or to themselves. Such assessments will normally address initial priorities, such as the level of immediate risk posed by the young person and the child protection needs of current and future potential victims, as well as, in the longer term, the strengths and deficits of the young person, set in the context of his overall developmental needs and in the context of the strengths and deficits evident in his or her family and wider environment (Epps 1997, 1999). Assessment should also ensure that there is a detailed focus on the young person's sexually offending or sexually aggressive behaviour, including its antecedents and consequences, and that the young person's sexual knowledge, attitudes and cognitions are well understood. Victim statements should be read, as should any reports already prepared on the young abuser and his or her behaviour. The end point of such assessment work should be the formulation of a plan of intervention, commensurate with the seriousness of the allegation or offence and with the levels of risk and vulnerability presented by the young person (Will 1999).

Space precludes a detailed discussion of the content and process of assessment of young sex offenders, but there is an increasing literature that is of relevance. In particular, the reader's attention is drawn to various chapters in Erooga and Masson (1999) and to Calder (2002). In a chapter in the latter volume, O'Callaghan (2002) outlines the assessment approach adopted by G-MAP, a well-regarded, independent provider based in the north-west of England that offers a range of services to young sexual abusers and offenders. In particular, O'Callaghan refers to the assessment model developed by Print, Morrison and Henniker (2001), which draws on outcome and recidivism research in this area and combines the offence-specific focus of the ASSET national assessment framework used by Youth Offending Teams (YOTs) (Home Office 2000b) with the much broader *Framework for the Assessment of Children in Need and their Families* (DH 2000), which focuses on children's developmental needs, parental or carer capacity and environmental factors.

Interventions with young sex offenders

At the start of the twenty-first century, there now seems to be an increasing consensus about the goals of intervention. Thus, a primary focus is placed on community safety, the need to reduce offending and further victimization of others. In this context YOTs, established in England and Wales as a result of the Crime and Disorder Act 1998, have been given the lead responsibility for juvenile sexual offenders, although, as will be discussed shortly, inter-agency collaboration in relation to assessment and intervention with young people is essential in this area of work. Equally important are goals that focus on helping the young people to accept responsibility for their offending behaviour and to develop strategies and coping skills to avoid future offending, promote the holistic development of the young person, address the young person's own victimization where this is an issue, and, wherever possible, strengthen the family and social supports available to the young person (Erooga and Masson 1999; Hackett 2001; O'Callaghan 2002; see also Kendrick, this volume, for a more detailed discussion of interventions with young people who are sexually aggressive).

Adult sex offender treatment has developed considerably over the past decade, with an increasing focus on nationally accredited and evaluated programmes, usually based within probation services and prisons (Allam and Browne 1998; Mann and Thornton 1998). In contrast, the development of intervention programmes and placement provision for young sex offenders has been much more piecemeal, what development there has been often being dependent on the enthusiasm of a few dedicated professionals or locally inspired partnerships involving the statutory, voluntary and private sectors (HM Inspectorate of Probation 1998; Masson 1997/1998).

Similarly, there is no current countrywide database of available services, or any clear picture of staffing, resources, underpinning theoretical approaches or outcomes, although a survey in the UK and the Republic of Ireland, jointly funded by NOTA, the National Society for the Prevention of Cruelty to Children (NSPCC) and the Youth Justice Bureau (YJB), is currently underway, aimed at mapping what services exist and what they comprise (Hackett, Masson and Philips 2004; see Kendrick, this volume, for the situation in Scotland). What research into service provision there has been in this area pertains to the USA. Thus, for example, Ryan and Lane (1997) reported on a 1994 national survey conducted by the Safer Society (Freeman-Longo *et al.* 1995) that gathered information about the treatment approaches of 1784 programmes for child, adolescent and adult sex offenders in the USA. Of the respondents, 281 (41%) indicated they used a cognitive-behavioural model, 247 (36%) identified relapse prevention as their model of choice, whereas the remaining 156 respondents identified psycho-educational (14%), psychotherapeutic (5%), family systems (2%), sexual addictive (1%) and psychoanalytical (1%) approaches respectively. In the UK, an eclectic approach to intervention with young people and their carers appears to be in evidence, at least anecdotally, although with a similar emphasis, in relation to offence-specific work, on sexual abuse cycles and cognitive-behavioural work, covering such aspects as minimization, denial and projection of blame, cognitive distortions, deviant sexual arousal, victim empathy and victim awareness, rape-prone attitudes and beliefs, and relapse prevention strategies (Calder 2002; Erooga and Masson 1999; Lane 1997).

Nevertheless, as has already been emphasized, equal weight is placed on the need to attend to the whole of the young person's needs and those of his or her wider network. When discussing factors associated with the development of sexually abusive behaviour in children and young people in the late 1980s, Becker (1988) proposed a model including a broad range of factors that may contribute to the development of sexually abusive behaviour and therefore give pointers for the focus of intervention strategies:

- at an individual level: social isolation and attachment deficits, impulse conduct disorder, limited cognitive abilities and a history of physical and/or sexual abuse

- familial factors: carers who engage in coercive sexual behaviour, family belief systems supportive of such behaviour and carers who have poor interpersonal skills and lack empathy

- societal factors: a society that is supportive of coercive (male) sexual behaviour, a society that supports the sexualization of children and peer groups who behave in antisocial ways.

It is certainly the case that current intervention programmes now seem to agree on the importance of developing programmes that allow for systemic and personalized packages of care to meet the differing risks posed by and needs of young sex offenders (see, for example, Longo 2002; O'Callaghan 2002; Swenson *et al.* 1998), even though, in the UK, such programmes are as yet relatively thin on the ground.

For those young people who have committed serious crimes or who are judged to be in need of placement away from their family (Bankes, Daniels and Quartly 1999), the position is currently rather bleak. A very small number of specialist, often private, residential establishments exist in the UK (see, for example, Clarke 2002; Kendrick and Mair 2002), but, in general, most young sexual offenders who are placed in local authority accommodation or in young offenders' institutions find themselves in institutions that are ill equipped to respond to their needs or manage the risk they may present to other residents or inmates (Boswell 1995; Farmer and Pollock 1998; Green and Masson 2002; Littlechild and Masson 2002).

The current state of policy and practice in the UK

Since the late 1990s, the complexities of responding to children and young people who have sexually abused have considerably increased, particularly in England and Wales, in the context of major policy and legislative changes within both the child welfare/protection system and the criminal/youth justice system.

Thus the refocusing debate in the mid-to-late 1990s (Audit Commission 1995; DH 1995) heralded the emergence of a less interventionist, family-support-focused approach to child welfare, symbolized by the publication of the third edition of *Working Together to Safeguard Children* (DH 1999), in which the language of risk has been largely replaced by the language of need, and the *Framework for the Assessment of Children in Need and their Families*

(DH 2000). In *Working Together* (DH 1999), paragraphs 6.31–6.37, which address the problem of abuse by children and young people, state that Area Child Protection Committees and YOTs must work together to develop co-ordinated approaches to young sexual abusers in order to ensure that there is a clear operational framework in place within which assessment, decision-making and case management take place. All such youngsters should be assessed, consideration being given to appropriate educational and accommodation arrangements, and, in the case of young abusers who are themselves victims of abuse, a child protection case conference should be held. Emphasis is placed on the need for all the relevant agencies (e.g. social services, YOTs, health, education and psychological and psychiatric services such as child and adolescent mental health teams) to collaborate in the assessment and management of cases.

The youth justice system has simultaneously also been subject to a major and ongoing overhaul since the mid-to-late 1990s, an overhaul prompted by the publication of various Audit Commission reports (1996, 1998) and the Home Office's White Paper *No More Excuses* (1997). This signalled a much tougher approach to youth crime, based on a retributive punishment-orientated approach to offending and faster tracking from arrest to sentencing, with the provisions of the Crime and Disorder Act 1998 and subsequent legislation being described by Muncie and others as evidence of institutional intolerance to young people (Anderson 1999; Bell 1999; Goldson 1997; Muncie 1999). At the same time, in response to public anxiety and media outcries about adult paedophiles, the Sex Offender Act 1997 was passed, which, in addition to containing the pre-existing arrangements for Schedule 1 status, also introduced requirements for registering with the police, all of which apply, in somewhat modified form, to young sex offenders.

The net result is that, in England and Wales at least, young sexual abusers, who often have both care and control needs, have to be managed within child welfare and youth crime systems of response that are increasingly divergent in terms of their ideological bases, organizational arrangements, staffing and respective resources. The possible reasons for this seemingly systemic inability to respond to young people except in ways that reduce them to either innocent victims or depraved young hooligans are discussed elsewhere (Masson and Morrison 1999), and space precludes a detailed discussion here. This state of affairs is, however, further compounded by the fact that there has for many years been little dialogue and 'joined-up thinking' between relevant government departments, in particular the DH, and the Home Office in respect of their responsibilities to young people and their behaviour. In local areas, agencies and organizations have consequently been left to try to make sense of and integrate and implement policies that do not fit together easily.

In Scotland, there currently appears to be, in contrast, a much more integrated system of response to children in trouble and children in need. A central feature of the Scottish legal system is that children over the age of criminal responsibility who commit offences are regarded as being in need of care in the same way as children who are the victims of abuse or criminal offences. Thus, apart from those charged with and prosecuted for the most serious offences, all young offenders under the age of 16 are processed via Scotland's unique Children's Hearing system rather than through the criminal justice system. Even serious young offenders who are prosecuted may have their cases remitted to the Children's Hearing for disposal, or the court may seek advice from the Children's Hearing.

The Children's Hearing system came into being in 1971, following the implementation of the Social Work (Scotland) Act 1968 and in response to the recommendations of the Kilbrandon Committee, which reported in 1964 (Scottish Home and Health Department and Scottish Education Department 1964). Cases are referred to the Reporter, who then has a duty to investigate and decide whether no further action is required, whether the child should be referred to the local social work department for informal support or whether to arrange for a Children's Hearing, a lay tribunal composed of three members, because it is felt the child is in need of compulsory measures of supervision. The grounds on which a child may be brought before a Children's Hearing are set down in the Children (Scotland) Act 1995. In respect of young sex offenders, paragraphs 6.6–6.9 of the Scottish Office's interagency child protection guidance (Scottish Office 1998) outline the process for investigating, assessing and managing cases of abuse by a young person, a process very similar to that followed in England

and Wales, although set in the context of Scotland's Children's Hearing system.

In recent years, however, youth justice has been an emerging concept in Scotland. In 1999, a review of youth crime was initiated in response to concerns about persistent young offenders, which resulted in an Advisory Group Report *It's a Criminal Waste: Stop Crime Now* (Advisory Group on Youth Crime 2000) and a response by the Scottish Executive (Scottish Office 2000), which largely accepted the Advisory Group's various recommendations for increasing the extent and effectiveness of options currently available to Children's Hearings and the courts. Among various measures being introduced or proposed, some local authorities have set up pilot multi-agency youth justice teams, working with 14–18-year-olds. If this piloting and other changes to the current system lead to the further development of separate systems for dealing with young offenders, young people who have sexually abused others may find themselves in a similar position to those in the rest of the UK.

Recent developments in relation to young sex offenders

Despite the rather gloomy picture just presented, at least as far as England and Wales are concerned, there do appear to be some recent developments that are worthy of mention. Within the helpful context of a growing consensus that these youngsters are *not* necessarily the adult paedophiles of the future, and aside from the good work that is undoubtedly going on at local level, the following national developments would seem to hold out some hope for the future. First, an interdepartmental group (including the DH, Home Office and Department for Education and Skills), jointly convened by the YJB and the Home Office, was established in mid-2002, with the task of reporting to ministers in the spring of 2003 on policies and services for juvenile sexual offenders; this raises the possibility of more co-ordinated responses being enacted at the central government level that may benefit local areas.

The efforts of the YJB on various fronts are also to be commended, including their joint funding of the mapping survey referred to earlier (Hackett *et al.* 2004) and their funding of six development projects specifically working with young people who have sexually abused, for example, the AIM project in Greater Manchester, which has close links with G-MAP. The AIM project was established in 1999, following a successful bid by ten YOTs and other professionals in Greater Manchester for three-year funding, which has now been extended. The project has established interagency policies and procedures for use in the locality (including negotiating extended police bail periods so that initial assessments can be completed), provides training for practitioners and managers and has developed various models of assessment for use with the under-10s, adolescents, parents and carers, and intellectually disabled young people, models that focus on both strengths in a young person's situation as well as areas of concern.

Some hope may also be placed in the possibility of legislative reform in relation to sexual offences that takes into account the very particular needs of different ages of young sex offenders – 10–14-year-olds, 14–17- year-olds and 17–25-year-olds – following the recent consultation exercise entitled *Setting the Boundaries: Reforming the Law on Sex Offences* (Home Office 2000a).

Recent publications have also served to highlight the problems with the current systems of response, and make recommendations with regard to the future. These publications include *Childhood Lost* (Bridge Child Care Development Service 2001), a serious case review of Dominic McGilligan, an 18-year-old with a history of sexual offending who had just left residential care when he raped and murdered an 11-year-old boy in 1998, and *I Think I Might Need Some More Help with this Problem* (Lovell 2002), an NSPCC published report and recommendations on responding to children and young people who have sexually abused.

Conclusion

Responding to young sex offenders is complex work. This is not only because of the many possible factors that may contribute to any given young person's offending behaviour, but also because of the, as yet, modest and somewhat inconclusive findings of research into predicting risk, the outcomes of management and intervention approaches and the relative infancy of service development in the UK. In England and Wales specifically, poorly integrated child welfare and youth crime systems further compound the efforts of practitioners who wish to develop provision for this group of young people.

What does, however, seem to be generally agreed is that young sex offenders are not mini adult sex offenders, that the majority will not reoffend and that, with a careful assessment of risk and need and appropriate child-centred and offence-specific services, most should be enabled to get back on track in terms of a normal course of development towards adulthood. A small proportion of more disturbed young people, often with serious deficits in their social support networks, may nevertheless be at higher risk of repeat offending and will need careful interagency management involving the provision of tailor-made assessment and intervention packages of care.

References

Abassi, K. and Jamal, S. (2002) 'South Asian Adolescent Sex Offenders: Effective Assessment and Intervention Work.' In M. Calder (ed) *Young People who Sexually Abuse.* Lyme Regis: Russell House Publishing.

Abel, G., Becker, J., Cunningham-Rathner, J. and Rouleau, J. (1987) 'Self Reported Sex Crimes of 561 Non-incarcerated Paraphiliacs.' *Journal of Interpersonal Violence 2,* 6, 3–25.

Advisory Group on Youth Crime (2000) *It's a Criminal Waste: Stop Youth Crime Now.* London: Stationery Office.

Ageton, S. (1983) *Sexual Assault Among Adolescents.* Lexington, MA: Lexington Books.

Allam, J. and Browne, K. (1998) 'Evaluating Community-based Treatment Programmes for Men who Sexually Abuse.' *Child Abuse Review 7,* 13–29.

Anderson, B. (1999) 'Youth Crime and the Politics of Prevention.' In B. Goldson (ed) *Youth Justice: Contemporary Policy and Practice.* London: Ashgate.

Audit Commission (1995) *Seen but Not Heard: Co-ordinating Child Health And Social Services for Children in Need.* London: Audit Commission.

Audit Commission (1996) *Misspent Youth: Young People and Crime.* London: Audit Commission.

Audit Commission (1998) *Misspent Youth '98: The Challenge for Youth Justice.* London: Audit Commission.

Awad, G. and Saunders, E. (1989) 'Male Adolescent Sexual Assaulters.' *Journal of Interpersonal Violence 6,* 446–460.

Awad, G., Saunders, E. and Levene, J. (1984) 'A Clinical Study of Male Adolescent Sex Offenders.' *International Journal of Offender Therapy and Comparative Criminology 28,* 105–116.

Bankes, N., Daniels, K. and Quartly, C. (1999) 'Placement Provision and Placement Decisions: Resources and Processes.' In M. Erooga and H. Masson (eds) *Children and Young People Who Sexually Abuse Others. Challenges and Responses.* London: Routledge.

Barbaree, H.E., Marshall, W.L. and Hudson, S.M. (eds) (1993) *The Juvenile Sex Offender.* London: Guildford Press.

Becker, J. (1988) Cited in Bentovim, A. and Williams, B. (1998) 'Children and Adolescents: Victims who Become Perpetrators.' *Advances in Psychiatric Treatment 4,* 101–117.

Becker, J. (1998) 'What We Know About the Characteristics and Treatment of Adolescents who Have Committed Sexual Offenses.' *Child Maltreatment 3,* 4, 317–329.

Beckett, R. (1999) 'Evaluation of Adolescent Sexual Abusers.' In M. Erooga and H. Masson (eds) *Children and Young People who Sexually Abuse Others: Challenges and Responses.* London: Routledge.

Bell, C. (1999) 'Appealing for Justice for Children and Young People: A Critical Analysis of the Crime and Disorder Bill 1998.' In B. Goldson (ed) *Youth Justice: Contemporary Policy and Practice.* London: Ashgate.

Bentovim, A. and Williams, B. (1998) 'Children and Adolescents: Victims who Become Perpetrators.' *Advances in Psychiatric Treatment 4,* 101–117.

Bischof, G., Stith, S. and Whitney, M. (1995) 'Family Environments of Adolescent Sex Offenders and Other Juvenile Delinquents.' *Adolescence 30,* 117, 157–170.

Blues, A., Moffatt, C. and Telford, P. (1999) 'Work with Adolescent Females who Sexually Abuse – Similarities and Differences.' In M. Erooga and H. Masson (eds) *Children and Young People Who Sexually Abuse Others: Challenges and Responses.* London: Routledge.

Boswell, G. (1995) *Violent Victims.* London: Prince's Trust.

Bridge Child Care Development Service (2001) *Childhood Lost.* London: Bridge Child Care Development Service.

Butler, L. and Elliott, C. (1999) 'Stop and Think: Changing Sexually Aggressive Behaviour in Young Children.' In M. Erooga and H. Masson (eds) *Children and Young People who Sexually Abuse Others: Challenges and Responses.* London: Routledge.

Calder, M. (ed) (2002) *Young People who Sexually Abuse.* Lyme Regis: Russell House Publishing.

Chaffin, M. and Bonner, B. (1998) '"Don't Shoot, We're Your Children." Have we Gone Too Far in our Response to Adolescent Sexual Abusers and Children with Sexual Behavior Problems.' *Child Maltreatment 3,* 4, 314–316.

Cicourel, A.V. (1967) *The Social Organisation of Juvenile Justice.* London: Wiley.

Clarke, P. (2002) 'Therapeutic Communities: A Model for Effective Intervention with Teenagers Known to Have Perpetrated Sexual Abuse.' In M. Calder (ed) *Young People who Sexually Abuse.* Lyme Regis: Russell House Publishing.

DH (Department of Health) (1991) *Working Together Under the Children Act 1989 – A Guide to Arrangements for Interagency Co-operation for the Protection of Children from Abuse.* London: HMSO.

DH (Department of Health) (1995) *Messages from Research.* London: HMSO.

DH (Department of Health) (1999) *Working Together To Safeguard Children: A Guide to Inter-agency Working To Safeguard and Promote the Welfare of Children.* London: Stationery Office.

DH (Department of Health) (2000) *Framework for the Assessment of Children in Need and their Families.* London: DH.

Epps, K. (1997) 'Managing Risk.' In M. Hoghughi, with Bhate, S. and Graham, F. (eds) *Working with Sexually Abusive Adolescents.* London: Sage.

Epps, K. (1999) 'Looking After Young Sexual Abusers: Child Protection, Risk Management and Risk Reduction.' In M. Erooga and H. Masson (eds)*Children and Young People who Sexually Abuse Others: Challenges and Responses.* London: Routledge.

Erooga, M. and Masson, H. (eds) (1999) *Children and Young People who Sexually Abuse Others: Challenges and Responses.* London: Routledge.

Farmer, E. and Pollock, S. (1998) *Sexually Abused and Abusing Children in Substitute Care.* Chichester: Wiley.

Fehrenbach, P.A., Smith, W., Monastersky, C. and Deisher, R.W. (1986) 'Adolescent Sexual Offenders: Offender and Offence Characteristics.' *American Journal of Orthopsychiatry 56*, 225–233.

Finkelhor, D. (1979) *Sexually Victimised Children.* New York: Free Press.

Ford, M. and Linney, J. (1995) 'Comparative Analysis of Juvenile Sexual Offenders, Violent Nonsexual Offenders and Status Offenders.' *Journal of Interpersonal Violence 10*, 1, 56–70.

Freeman-Longo, R., Bird, S., Stevenson, W. and Fiske, J. (1995) *1994 Nationwide Survey of Treatment Programs and Models: Serving Abuse Reactive Children, Adolescent and Adult Sex Offenders.* Brandon, VT: Safer Society Press.

Fromuth, M.E., Jones, C.W. and Burkhart, B.R. (1991) 'Hidden Child Molestation: An Investigation of Perpetrators in a Non-clinical Sample.' *Journal of Interpersonal Violence 6*, 3, 376–384.

Glasgow, D., Horne, L., Calam, R. and Cox, A. (1994) 'Evidence, Incidence, Gender and Age in Sexual Abuse of Children Perpetrated by Children: Towards a Developmental Analysis of Child Sexual Abuse.' *Child Abuse Review 3*, 196–210.

Goldson, B. (1997) 'Children, Crime, Policy and Practice: Neither Welfare nor Justice.'*Children and Society 11*, 77–88.

Green, L. and Masson, H. (2002) 'Adolescents who Sexually Abuse and Residential Accommodation: Issues of Risk and Vulnerability.' *British Journal of Social Work 32*, 149–168.

Grubin, D. (1998) *Sex Offending Against Children: Understanding the Risk.* Police Research Series Paper No.99. London: Home Office.

Hackett, S. (2000) 'Sexual Aggression, Diversity and the Challenge of Anti-oppressive Practice.' *Journal of Sexual Aggression 5*, 1, 4–20.

Hackett, S. (2001) *Facing the Future. A Guide for Parents of Young People who Have Sexually Abused.* Lyme Regis: Russell House Publishing.

Hackett, S. (2002) 'Abused and Abusing: Work with Young People who Have a Dual Sexual Abuse Experience.' In M. Calder (ed) *Young People who Sexually Abuse.* Lyme Regis: Russell House Publishing.

Hackett, S., Masson, H. and Phillips, S. (2004) 'Mapping and Exploring Services for Young People who Sexually Abuse.' Work in progress funded by NOTA, NSPCC and YJB.

Her Majesty's Inspectorate of Probation (1998) *Exercising Constant Vigilance: The Role of the Probation Service in Protecting the Public from Sex Offenders.* London: Home Office.

Home Office (1997) *No More Excuses: A New Approach to Tackling Youth Crime In England and Wales.* Cm 3809. London: Stationery Office.

Home Office (2000a) *Setting the Boundaries. Reforming the Law on Sex Offences.* London: Home Office.

Home Office (2000b) *The ASSET form.* London: Youth Justice Board.

Home Office (2001) *Criminal Statistics for England and Wales 2000.* Cm 5312. London: Home Office.

Johnson, T.C. (1988) 'Child Perpetrators – Children who Molest Other Children: Preliminary Findings.' *Child Abuse and Neglect 12,* 219–229.

Johnson, T.C. (1989) 'Female Child Perpetrators: Children who Molest Other Children.' *Child Abuse and Neglect 13,* 571–585.

Johnson, T.C. (1993) 'Assessment of Sexual Behaviour Problems in Preschool-aged and Latency-aged Children.' *Child and Adolescent Psychiatric Clinics of North America 2,* 431–449.

Kahn, T.J. and Chambers, H. (1991) 'Assessing Reoffence Risk with Juvenile Sexual Offenders.' *Child Welfare 70,* 3, 333–345.

Katz, R. (1990) 'Psychosocial Adjustment in Adolescent Child Molesters.' *Child Abuse and Neglect 14,* 567–575.

Kelly, L., Regan, L. and Burton, S. (1991) *An Exploratory Study of the Prevalence of Sexual Abuse in a Sample of 16 to 21 Year Olds.* London: Child Abuse Studies Unit, Polytechnic of North London.

Kendrick, A. and Mair, R. (2002) 'Developing Focused Care: A Residential Unit for Sexually Aggressive Young Men.' In M. Calder (ed) *Young People who Sexually Abuse.* Lyme Regis: Russell House Publishing.

Lane, S. (1997) 'The Sexual Abuse Cycle.' In G. Ryan and S. Lane (eds) *Juvenile Sexual Offending. Causes, Consequences and Corrections,* 2nd edn. San Fransisco: Jossey-Bass.

Lane, S. with Lobanov-Rostovsky, C. (1997) 'Special Populations: Children, Females, the Developmentally Disabled, and Violent Youth.' In G. Ryan and S. Lane, *Juvenile Sexual Offending. Causes, Consequences and Corrections,* 2nd edn. San Francisco: Jossey-Bass.

Littlechild, B. and Masson, H. (2002) 'Young People who Have Sexually Abused. Law and Provision.' *ChildRight* July/August: 16–18.

Longo, R. (2002) 'A Holistic Approach to Treating Young People who Sexually Abuse.' In M. Calder (ed) *Young People Who Sexually Abuse.* Lyme Regis: Russell House Publishing.

Lovell, E. (2002) *'I think I Might Need Some More Help with This Problem.' Responding to Children and Young People who Display Sexually Harmful Behaviour.* London: NSPCC.

Mann, R. and Thornton, D. (1998) 'The Evolution of a Multi-site Offender Treatment Programme.' In W. Marshall, Y. Fernandez, S. Hudson and T. Ward (eds) *Sourcebook of Treatment Programs for Sexual Offenders*. New York: Plenum Press.

Manocha, K. and Mezey, G. (1998) 'British Adolescents who Sexually Abuse: A Descriptive Study.' *Journal of Forensic Psychiatry 9*, 3, 588–608.

Marshall, W.L. (1989) 'Invited Essay: Intimacy, Loneliness and Sexual Offenders.' *Behaviour Research and Therapy 27*, 491–503.

Masson, H. (1997/1998) 'Issues in Relation to Children and Young People who Sexually Abuse Other Children: A Survey of Practitioners' Views.' *Journal of Sexual Aggression 3*, 2, 101–118.

Masson, H. and Morrison, T. (1999) 'Young Sexual Abusers: Conceptual Frameworks, Issues and Imperatives.' *Children and Society 13*, 203–215.

May, T. (1993) *Social Research. Issues, Methods and Process*. Buckingham: Open University.

Miner (2002) 'Factors Associated with Recidivism in Juvenile Sexual Offenders: A Study of Serious Offenders.' In M. Calder (ed) *Young People who Sexually Abuse*. Lyme Regis: Russell House Publishing.

Morrison, T. and Print, B. (1995) *Adolescent Sexual Abusers: An Overview*. London: NOTA Whiting & Birch.

Muncie, J. (1999) 'Institutionalised Intolerance: Youth Justice and the 1998 Crime and Disorder Act.' *Critical Social Policy 19*, 2, 147–175.

NCH (National Children's Home) (1992) *The Report of the Committee of Enquiry into Children and Young People who Sexually Abuse Other Children*. London: NCH.

O'Callaghan, D. (2001) *A Framework for Undertaking Initial Assessments of Young People with Intellectual Disabilities who Present Problematic/Harmful Sexual Behaviours*. Manchester: G-MAP/AIM Project.

O'Callaghan, D. (2002) 'Providing a Research Informed Service for Young People who Sexually Abuse.' In M. Calder (ed) *Young People who Sexually Abuse*. Lyme Regis: Russell House Publishing.

Openshaw, D., Graves, R., Erickson, S. *et al.*(1993) 'Youthful Sexual Offenders: A Comprehensive Bibliography of Scholarly References, 1970–1992.' *Family Relations 42*, 222–226.

Print, B., Morrison, T. and Henniker, J. (2001) 'An Inter-agency Assessment Framework for Young People who Sexually Abuse: Principles, Processes and Practicalities.' In M. Calder (ed) *Juveniles and Children who Sexually Abuse: Frameworks for Assessment*, 2nd edn. Lyme Regis: Russell House Publishing.

Rasmussen, L. (2002) 'An Integrated Systemic Approach to Intervention with Children with Sexually Abusive Behaviour Problems.' In M. Calder (ed) *Young People who Sexually Abuse*. Lyme Regis: Russell House Publishing.

Richardson, G., Kelly, T., Bhate, S. and Graham, F. (1997) 'Group Differences in Abuser and Abuse Characteristics in a British Sample of Sexually Abusive Adolescents.' *Sexual Abuse, A Journal of Research and Treatment 9*, 239–257.

Ryan, G. (1999) 'Treatment of Sexually Abusive Youth: The Evolving Consensus.' *Journal of Interpersonal Violence 14*, 4, 422–436.

Ryan, G. and Lane, S. (eds) (1991) *Juvenile Sexual Offending. Causes, Consequences and Corrections*. Lexington, MA: Lexington Books.

Ryan, G. and Lane, S. (eds) (1997) *Juvenile Sexual Offending. Causes,Consequences and Corrections*, 2nd edn. San Fransisco: Jossey-Bass.

Ryan, G., Miyoshi, T., Metzner, J., Krugman, R. and Fryer, G. (1996) 'Trends in a National Sample of Sexually Abusive Youths.' *Journal of the American Academy of Child and Adolescent Psychiatry 35*, 17–25.

Scott, J. (1990) *A Matter of Record: Documentary Sources in Social Research*. Oxford: Polity Press/Blackwell.

Scottish Home and Health Department and Scottish Education Department (1964) *Report of the Committee on Children and Young Persons, Scotland (1964)* (Kilbrandon Report). Cm 3065. HMSO.

Scottish Office (1998) *Protecting Children – a Shared Responsibility. Guidance on Inter-agency Co-operation*. Edinburgh: Scottish Office.

Scottish Office (2000) *Scottish Executive's Response to the Advisory Group Report on the Youth Crime Review*. Stationery Office.

Shipman, M. (1981) *The Limitations of Social Research*, 2nd edn. London: Longman.

Stermac, L. and Sheridan, P. (1993) 'The Developmentally Disabled Adolescent Sex Offender.' In H.E. Barbaree, W.L. Marshall and S.M. Hudson (eds) *The Juvenile Sex Offender*. Guildford: Guildford Press.

Swenson, C., Henggeler, S., Schoenwald, S., Kaufman, K. and Randall, J. (1998) 'Changing the Social Ecologies of Adolescent Sexual Offenders: Implications of the Success of Multisystemic Therapy in Treating Serious Antisocial Behaviour in Adolescents.' *Child Maltreatment 3*, 4, 330–338.

Wasserman, J. and Kappel, S. (1985) *Adolescent Sex Offenders in Vermont*. Burlington, VT: Vermont Department of Health.

Weinrott, M. (1996) *Juvenile Sexual Aggression: A Critical Review*. Boulder, CO: Institute of Behavioural Science, University of Colorado.

Will, D. (1994) 'Impressions of the Tenth National Training Conference of the National Adolescent Perpetrator Network, Denver, Colorado, February 1994.' *NOTANews*, June, 50–53.

Will, D. (1999) 'Assessment Issues.' In M. Erooga and H. Masson (eds) *Children And Young People who Sexually Abuse Others: Challenges and Responses*. London: Routledge.

Williams, D. and Buehler, M. (2002) 'A Proposal for Comprehensive Community-based Treatment of Female Juvenile Sex Offenders.' In M.Calder (ed) *Young People who Sexually Abuse*. Lyme Regis: Russell House Publishing.

PART TWO

Assessment and Effective Interventions

CHAPTER 5

The Risk Assessment of Sex Offenders

Don Grubin

Introduction

The assessment of most sex offenders usually starts with a risk assessment. Increasingly, however, risk assessment formulations have expanded to mean more than a simple determination of how dangerous a sex offender might be – as well as establishing level of risk, they now encapsulate the assessment process more generally, providing the basis for the identification of treatment needs and the development of supervision plans. The emergence of risk assessment as the bedrock of sex offender evaluation is a consequence of the influence of the 'What Works' literature on current approaches to sex offender management, with its emphasis on clearly defined outcome measures, in particular a reduction in re-offending, by which to judge success and allocate resources. Gone are the days when insight and understanding were the primary goals of assessment.

Using risk assessment as a template for sex offender evaluation undoubtedly sharpens the assessment process, providing a focus on which to base decisions about treatment need, treatment targets and other interventions. But risk assessment is not straightforward, either conceptually or procedurally. A failure to recognize its various nuances can lead not only to mistakes in management, but also to legal challenge.

Consider the following two cases. Case One is that of a 38-year-old man due to be released from prison following a conviction for the indecent assault and rape of a young girl. His victim was a neighbour for whom he baby-sat over a four-year period, the offences starting when she was aged 9 and continuing until his arrest three years later when she was 12. He also baby-sat for other families, and although in retrospect some of his behaviours in relation to these families gave rise to concern, no other charges were brought against him. This was his first sex offence conviction, but he had a number of previous convictions for theft-related offences, and one for assault. He refused to take part in any sex offender-related treatment in prison as he consistently denied his guilt, in spite of strong evidence to the contrary.

Case Two is that of a 28-year-old man being assessed following his seventh conviction for indecent exposure, although he is known to have in fact exposed himself on hundreds of occasions. His offending always follows a common pattern: he approaches well-dressed young women in public parks and similar places, attracts their attention and then exposes himself while masturbating. He never approaches his victims or says anything to them, and on the few occasions when he has been confronted he runs off. He reports that he offends at times of stress. Apart from indecent exposure, he has no other sex offences convictions. He has received treatment in the past from a psychiatrist, from which he was said to have benefited, and he has been dealt with by the courts with fines, probation orders and short prison sentences.

When asked to determine the risk represented by these two offenders, the tendency is to respond with terms such as 'high' or 'very high' in the first instance, and a range from 'low' to 'medium' to 'high' in the second. However, regardless of the likelihood of the child molester re-offending, most assessors would be willing to bet the mortgage that the indecent exposer will do so – in other words, he has a higher likelihood of re-offending, and of re-offending more frequently, than the child molester. Why then the discrepancy in determining risk?

When analysing the basis of these risk assessments, it usually becomes apparent that the variation arises less from the way in which the assessments have been carried out, and more from the different meanings of risk used by assessors, and sometimes by the same assessor between the two cases. Confusion over the meaning of risk also lies at the root of much of the controversy regarding the uses of actuarial or clinical approaches to assessment.

The meaning of risk

When assessing a sex offender, at least four different types of risk need to be considered (Janus and Meehl 1997, citing Brooks):

1. likelihood of offending

2. imminence of offending

3. consequences of offending

4. frequency of offending.

Although these different meanings seem clear, it is easy to slip between them unawares. As in the two cases referred to above, it is not uncommon for the risk of further offending (likelihood) to become subtly blurred with the risk of harm (consequences) associated with potential re-offending; the greater harm associated with the offences of the child molester tends to make this the focus of risk in his case and hence the basis of comparison between him and the indecent exposer. When considering the indecent exposer in isolation, however, assessors more readily rate his risk as very high, concentrating on the risk of re-offending without being distracted by the consequences of re-offending.

In practice, when decisions about management need to be taken, considerations of immediacy (imminence) and profligacy (frequency) also bubble to the surface – an offender who has a high risk of re-offending soon is of more concern than one who has a high risk of re-offending some time in the future. A determination of immediacy, and to a lesser extent frequency, can be the deciding factor between custodial versus community management.

Assessing these different types of risk clearly requires different approaches. At the very least, factors that relate to one may be less relevant to another, but in addition the tools and techniques employed will need to vary depending on their strengths and attributes. It also needs to be recognized that variables relating to the risks associated with *re-offending* are not necessarily the same as those which relate to *offending* in the first place: much of what we know about risk comes from studies of men who already have a conviction for sex offending, and one must be cautious in generalizing to individuals whose fantasies or behaviours may cause concern but who have not actually committed an offence. Thus, different approaches may also be necessary depending on whether one is concerned about an individual's offending potential (which may be the case in mental health settings) as opposed to his re-offending potential (more common in the criminal justice world).

Defining what type of risk is being assessed, and recognizing that an individual may represent a different level of risk in respect of each of these, is the first step in getting the risk assessment right. When requested to provide a risk assessment as in the cases above, one should therefore always ask, 'Risk of what?', and 'Why do you want to know?'

The meaning of level of risk

When describing risk, terms such as 'low', 'medium', 'high' and 'very high' are invariably employed, but what do these terms mean? In some cases, they are used simply to indicate a subjective belief: an offender who is a 'medium' risk of re-offending (focusing on the *likelihood* of re-offending for the purposes of discussion) is a greater risk than someone rated 'low', but not as great a risk as someone rated 'high'. In other cases, an association is made with terms such as 'possible', 'probable', 'likely', 'more likely than not' and similar expressions. The lack of precision inherent in these elastic concepts makes them ripe for challenge, however, and difficult to defend (Edwards, Elwyn and Mulley 2002): one person's 'likely' is another person's 'probable'. This has led to attempts to quantify risk: if one can state that the risk of re-offending is 60 per cent, for example, it can be left to others to determine whether this should be considered to be medium, high, very high, probable or highly likely.

But even with quantification, what might a '60 per cent risk of re-offending' mean? Again, it may simply be a measure of subjective belief, a pseudonumber used to indicate relative risk, another way of saying 'more likely than not'. Alternatively, it could mean that, in certain circumstances, a particular individual has a 60 per cent chance of re-offending, equivalent to a weather forecaster predicting the chances of rain tomorrow. In this case, less than 100 per cent certainty is caused by the limited amount of information available, with the assumption that more information will lead to a more accurate prediction. Such detailed data are not, however, available about human beings, neither in the sense of knowing all the key bits of information, nor in understanding the laws that govern human behaviour (indeed, the extent to which this amount of information is potentially available about the climate is unclear). In such cases, more information does not usually improve accuracy – only one's certainty in the accuracy of the prediction.

Another meaning of the term '60 per cent risk' is that, over time, 6 out of 10 individuals with characteristics similar to this individual will re-offend. Thus, the probability statement '60 per cent risk' does not relate specifically to him but to the *class* of offenders to which he belongs. A statement in this form not only has real meaning in quantitative terms, but it is also testable.

Risk assessment versus risk prediction

The weather forecaster referred to above makes use of many repeated observations and measurements to arrive at the statement that there is a 60 per cent chance of rain tomorrow, which in effect means, 'In these circumstances, it rains 6 out of 10 times'. Testing the accuracy of this statement, however, does not depend on whether or not it actually rains tomorrow – after all, the forecaster is also saying that when circumstances are as they are, it does not rain 4 times out of 10. It is only over the longer term that accuracy can be judged, when a sufficient number of instances are available with which to compare the forecast. Thus, the forecaster is not in fact predicting whether or not it will rain tomorrow in the sense of it will or it won't (if this were the case, the forecast would need to be for a 100 per cent chance of rain), but is instead providing a probability estimate from which one can make decisions depending on how averse one is to getting wet – is the risk sufficient to warrant taking one's raincoat?

The situation is the same when one is making an assessment of the likelihood of a sex offender offending or re-offending. A 60 per cent chance of re-offending, for example, is a prediction not about a particular individual but about the class of individuals to which he belongs. This provides useful information with which one can start a risk assessment as it identifies the individual as being a member of a group that, as a whole, is of higher risk. The assessment is not wrong if he does not re-offend (or for that matter right if he does); it is wrong only if significantly fewer (or more) than 60 per cent of the group re-offend. It is no different from identifying a 20-year-old marketing executive in his new Ferrari as a higher-risk driver: even if he does not crash his car, it is not wrong to label him as high risk, and the cautious passenger will probably choose to travel with a 50-year-old Volvo owner.

Estimating likelihood of offending is therefore only the first step in risk assessment, risk management and treatment decisions. It is in effect a screening exercise that filters individuals into groups of greater or lesser risk. Once this has been done, each individual can then be evaluated in more detail, with those in the higher-risk groups being given greater priority depending on other factors such as risk of harm, frequency of offending and imminence of offending. The aim for those designing risk assessments is therefore to make the groups as homogeneous as possible in terms of the outcome measure of re-offending, and to ensure that individuals in higher-risk groups are in fact more likely to re-offend than those in lower-risk groups.

The importance of distinguishing between making a prediction about an individual as opposed to the group to which he belongs becomes clear when one considers the misunderstanding sometimes associated with a determination that an offender has a '50 per cent chance of re-offending'. A casual, but wrong, interpretation treats the statement as a prediction about the person, suggesting that there is a 50–50 risk of his re-offending, and one might as well flip a coin when deciding what to do about him. This apparent randomness disappears, however, when one recognizes that the statement really means that one in two people like him will re-offend, as opposed to, for example, the case of another offender, in which one in five similar individuals will re- offend. One is not making a prediction that either will re-offend; instead one is quantifying the extent to which the risk represented by one is greater (or less) than the risk of the other, which is dependent on the base rate of re-offending for the groups to which they belong.

The process of risk assessment

This approach to risk assessment can be compared with how one might determine the risk and subsequent management of an individual in relation to the possibility of his suffering a myocardial infarction. A person with a strong family history of heart disease, for example with a number of immediate relatives who have died at a young age from myocardial infarction, would be said to have a high *long-term* risk of having a myocardial infarction himself. There is not much that can be done about this risk, which is static and unchanging. Once aware of the risk, however, more attention can be paid to other factors that have a bearing on it, such as raised blood pressure or a high blood cholesterol level (which may turn out to be the mediators of the disease). These are things that can be influenced by treatment and can be viewed as stable but changeable risk factors. Similarly, there is another set of factors that has a more immediate impact on his risk of myocardial infarction, such as smoking and stress, which will be of greater concern in his case than they might be for someone with no family history of heart disease whose blood pressure is normal. Factors such as smoking and stress fluctuate over short periods of time and can be influenced immediately through intervention. These can be thought of as acute risk factors. The individual's current risk depends on the interplay between these three types of risk factor (Figure 5.1).

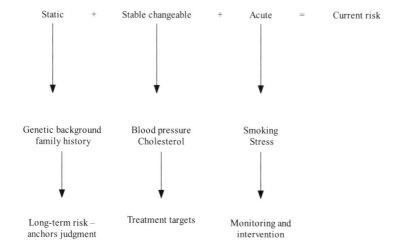

Figure 5.1 Risk assessment and management in myocardial infarction.

Risk assessment in sex offenders can be thought of in a similar manner (Figure 5.2). Static factors based on history can give an estimate of long-term risk to inform decisions about the likelihood of offending over the longer term. A subsequent consideration of risk factors that change over time, some of which are stable (relating to, for example, personality characteristics, attitudes and sex drive), others which change more rapidly (such as living circumstances or victim acquisition behaviours), allows for a more specific assessment of the immediacy of risk, the consequences of offending and whether any offending is likely to be frequently repeated or occasional. By differentiating risk factors that are amenable to treatment, and those which need to be monitored regularly, decisions can be made about treatment and management, with the aim of reducing risk. In the sex offender literature, these more changeable characteristics are usually referred to as dynamic risk factors.

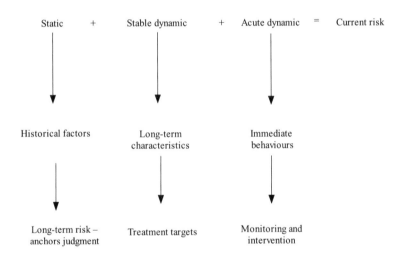

Figure 5.2 Risk assessment and management in sex offenders.

Combining estimates of long-term static risk with assessments of dynamic factors that take into account changes in circumstances and different aspects of risk is necessary for a comprehensive risk assessment. The result is what might be called an integrated risk management strategy, regardless of whether it is applied to a patient at risk of a heart attack or a sex offender at risk of re-offending. But having disentangled these various aspects of risk assessment, how is the assessment itself to be achieved?

Actuarial versus clinical assessment

Approaches to the determination of risk in violent as well as sexual offenders often polarize into debates about the merits or otherwise of actuarial versus clinical types of assessment (Dolan and Doyle 2000). Proponents of actuarial techniques argue that, because they focus on factors known to be associated with reconviction and avoid the distraction of things that do not, they are consistently shown to be better predictors of recidivism than are clinical methods, the latter performing only slightly better than chance (Hanson and Bussire 1998). For the champions of clinical assessment, however, it is precisely these so-called distractions that provide the necessary colour that allows meaningful conclusions to be drawn about the individual under consideration. For example, while the presence of the single variable 'sex offence conviction' increased the likelihood of a future conviction for a sex offence by a factor of seven in a four-year follow-up of all offenders released in one year from the English prison system (Marshall 1994), it remained the case that 93 per cent of those with a sex offence conviction were not reconvicted over this period (Grubin 1997). In general, clinical assessments tend to be good at identifying individuals at low risk but are over-inclusive in their determination of who is high risk; actuarial assessments, however, which give great weight to an individual's past convictions, tend to underestimate risk in first-time offenders, finding it difficult to discriminate between those who will go on to recidivate from those who will not.

Based on the considerations raised in the previous sections of this chapter, it should by now be clear that the proponents of actuarial and clinical assessments are talking at cross-purposes to each other. This becomes especially apparent when one considers so-called medium-risk groups; the majority of offenders tend to be found here, and although their re-offending rates are lower, in absolute terms they represent a large number of new offences. Where does one go once an offender has been labelled 'medium risk'? The two types of assessment each have a contribution to make to an overall assessment of risk, provided that their application is limited to those aspects of the assessment for which they are appropriate.

Actuarial techniques address only a single issue: the likelihood of re-offending over a set period of time. They tend to be based on historical (i.e. static), present or absent, unchanging or slow-to-change variables (e.g. age or number of convictions), which are relatively easy to collect for a large number of individuals. These variables are defined and scored in specified ways and then combined according to predetermined rules. The choice of variables, scoring conventions and subsequent algorithms is based on the outcome of studies involving a large number of offenders, in a manner similar to the way in which risk is determined in insurance settings; in other words, actuarial assessment is a statistically based method of determining outcome for groups of individuals. In theory, it leaves no room for subjective bias, in terms of either the variables chosen for analysis or the weight given to each – insurance premiums are not determined by the mood of the person taking your details on the end of the phone or by whether that person likes you or not.

What is sometimes overlooked is that clinical assessment is based on the same principle of using data from the past to estimate the probability of behaviour in the future, except that the data set relied on in this case is a looser collection of cases known to the assessor and thus varies depending on the person doing the assessment. In addition, because definitions and rules are poorly, if at all, specified, it is open to bias by particularly prominent factors or memorable cases.

The essential difference between actuarial and clinical approaches is that the latter is inductive in nature, whereas the former is deductive. Inductive reasoning is based on making inferences from specific cases (i.e. moving from the specific to the general), causing it to be highly dependent on the experience of the individual. In contrast, deductive inferences start from general principles and then make statements in specific cases: e.g. if one starts from the premise that all swans are white, then if an animal is a swan one can conclude it will be white, regardless of the experience of the observer. In the case of sex offenders, actuarial techniques look at groups of offenders to reach conclusions about specific individuals. When deductive processes are used, however, one is of course wholly dependent on the validity of the assumptions that underlie the rules of the system.

Clinical risk assessment is criticized for being unstructured, biased, lacking in consistency (particularly in the weight given to specific factors by different assessors), inductive, difficult to challenge and impossible to quantify. It is thus not well suited to the first stage in the risk assessment process – the determination of long-term risk. Actuarial assessment, however, has nothing to say about imminence, consequences or frequency of offending, the components of the subsequent stages of risk assessment (although, as discussed below, Hanson and colleagues in Canada have been testing whether dynamic risk can also be subjected to actuarial forms of assessment). It is also blind to idiosyncratic factors that may be particularly relevant in a specific individual. As such, a robust risk assessment will depend on the successful combination of the two approaches, with neither existing in isolation.

Actuarial instruments

A number of actuarial and quasi-actuarial instruments have been developed, although few have passed into general use. All tend to tap into two domains, one related to general criminality (i.e. the factors that predict re-offending generally, such as young age and past number of convictions), the other to sexual deviance (Hanson and Thornton 2000). As such, they make use of similar variables, although they differ in the numbers of variables involved and the weighting that each variable is given.

Actuarial instruments can only apply to populations similar to those from which they were developed. Because of the relatively large number needed to create an actuarial scale, actuarial instruments are, in the sex offender world, available only for adult male sex offenders. As yet, there are no such scales for female sex offenders or sex offenders under the age of 18, although in the case of younger offenders two instruments are currently in development: the Juvenile Sex Offender Assessment Protocol (J-SOAP; Prentky *et al.* 2000) and the Estimate of Risk of Adolescent Sex Offender Recidivism (ERASOR), for which published information is limited. Similarly, because relevant research has involved sex offenders (i.e. individuals who already have at least one sex offence conviction), there are no scales with which to determine the risk of sexual offending in non-sex offenders.

Most use is made of actuarial instruments in North America, where they play a particular, albeit controversial, role in determining likelihood of re-offending in relation to civil commitment laws (Janus and Meehl 1987), and they are likely to have a similar function in relation to the preventative detention of individuals labelled as having a 'dangerous severe personality disorder'. Although their objective nature and quantifiable outcome make them, in theory, well suited for this task, evidence with which to validate them is in practice sparse. Although the scales referred to below have been evaluated in a range of studies, published peer-reviewed research is in short supply, much of the work appearing in the form of conference presentations or Internet websites. Having said this, it must still be remembered that, unlike clinical opinion in individual cases, actuarial scales are testable, even if they have not yet been fully tested. The most widely used of the North American instruments are listed below.

The *Minnesota Sex Offender Screening Tool – Revised* (MnSOST-R) is based on 16 variables, some of which are more difficult to ascertain than others, such as items relating to substance use, employment and progress in treatment (Epperson 2000). Offenders scoring in the higher categories are reported to have a reconviction rate of over 60 per cent (although with fairly wide confidence intervals). Good predictive validity is claimed by the developers (r in the range 0.35–0.45, receiver operator characteristics (ROC)[1] area values ranging from 0.73 to 0.78), with similar results for rapists and child molesters. When tested on a sample from outside

---

1   Receiver operator characteristics (ROCs) are a good measure of predictive accuracy when the base rate of the relevant outcome measure is relatively low. They are reported in terms of the area under the curve (AUC). An ROC area of 0.5 indicates a performance no better than chance, whereas an area approaching 1 signifies near-perfect prediction. In practice, an

Minnesota, however, its performance was less good (Barbaree *et al.* 2001), and further independent validation is urgently needed.

Rapid Risk Assessment for Sexual Offence Recidivism (RRASOR) (Hanson 1997) is a brief (four-item) screening instrument that was probably the most widely used actuarial assessment in North America until it was supplanted by Static-99. The latter is, as discussed below, an amalgam of RRASOR and the UK instrument Structured Anchored Clinical Judgement (SACJ) (Hanson and Thornton 2000). RRASOR evolved from a large meta-analysis looking at over 160 variables associated with sex offender reconviction (Hanson and Bussière 1998); these, after a series of statistical operations, dissolved down to the four in the scale: age, past sex offences, having unrelated victims and having male victims. It places offenders in one of six groups, with a steady, near-linear increase in the rate of re-offending between groups: in the developmental sample, the two highest risk groups contained 7 per cent of the sample, with ten-year reconviction rates of about 49 per cent and 73 per cent respectively. Moderate predictive accuracy was reported by Hanson and Thornton (2000) in a study involving over 1200 offenders from three Canadian and one UK samples who were followed up for a period of 4–23 years ($r = 0.28$, ROC area = 0.68). Similar results have been described in a Swedish sample (Sjostedt and Langstrom 2001) followed up for just less than four years ($r = 0.22$, ROC area = 0.72). Interestingly, Barbaree *et al.'s* 2001 study, in which the MnSOST-R fared badly, reported in contrast especially good findings with respect to RRASOR (ROC area = 0.77).

The *Sex Offender Risk Appraisal Guide* (SORAG) is a 15-item scale intended to assess both violent and sexual recidivism (Quinsey *et al.* 1998). Its developmental sample came from a high secure psychiatric hospital, and it requires information regarding personality disorder, substance use and childhood behavioural problems. The tool produces nine risk groups with a

---

ROC area of 0.60 or more is usually considered to represent a moderate effect size, whereas one of 0.75 or greater represents a large effect size (Mossman, 1994). In terms of sex offender outcome, the greater the AUC, the more likely it is that a randomly selected re-offender will come from a higher-risk group than a randomly selected individual who has not re-offended.

linear increase in recidivism between them, the lowest number being in the highest-risk group. Studies have reported a wide range of predictive accuracy (with ROC areas ranging from 0.67 to 0.81), although it appears to co-relate particularly well with violent (as opposed to sexual) recidivism (Barbaree *et al.* 2001).

Static-99 is an actuarial instrument that was created in 1999 by combining the scales of two existing instruments: RRASOR (referred to above) and the SACJ (which was at the time routinely used in the English prison system), on the basis that RRASOR focused on items related to sexual deviance, whereas the SACJ also emphasized non-sexual criminal history (Hanson and Thornton 2000). Static-99 contains ten variables, only two (age and not having lived in a co-habiting relationship for more than two years) not being related to offending history. It results in seven risk groups; in the development sample, the highest-risk group, with a sexual recidivism rate of 52% over 15 years, contains 12% of the population. When compared directly with RRASOR and SACJ in a Canadian and British sample of over 1200 offenders (Hanson and Thornton 2000), Static-99 performed better than both, although the statistical significance is not altogether clear as there appeared to be some overlap in confidence intervals (for Static-99, $r = 0.33$, ROC area $= 0.71$, although the ROC area varied from 0.63 to 0.89 in the four different groups from which the sample was composed). In a Swedish sample (Sjostedt and Langstrom 2001), Static-99 performed even better (ROC area $= 0.76$).

Although not strictly speaking actuarial instruments, the *Sexual Violence Risk-20* (SVR-20) (Boer *et al.* 1997) and the *Risk for Sexual Violence Protocol* (RSVP) being developed by Laws and colleagues, are also worth considering when reviewing actuarial approaches. The SVR-20 and RSVP are designed to provide what the authors refer to as 'structured professional judgement'. These tools are intended not to provide risk scores but to ensure that risk assessment is 'conducted according to explicit guidelines that are grounded in the scientific literature' (Boer *et al.* 1997, p.6). Although terms such as 'low', 'medium' and 'high' rather than specific numbers, are used, they are anchored on known base rates of re-offending to give them meaning. It has yet to be demonstrated, however, that structured risk assessments such as these perform any better than traditional actuarial scales, although data related to the HCR-20 (SVR-20's violence assessment sister) suggest that this latter tool performs well in identifying violent recidivists (Dolan and Doyle 2000).

None of the instruments referred to above is used to any extent in the UK. Here, a single instrument, *Risk Matrix 2000* (RM2000) is generally employed by the prison, probation and police services. RM 2000 is in effect a revision of the SACJ protocol referred to above, which was never published but is described in Grubin (1998) and Hanson and Thornton (2000); the revision was intended to improve predictive accuracy, make the tool simpler to use and provide a prediction of violent as well as sexual re-offending (Thornton *et al.* in press). RM 2000 (Sex) is a seven-item scale that allocates offenders to low-, medium-, high- and very high-risk groups with re-offending rates in the region of 10 per cent, 20 per cent, 40 per cent and 60 per cent respectively, the very high-risk group containing 13 per cent of the development sample. According to Thornton *et al.* (in press), the RM 2000 is reported to have much greater predictive accuracy than the SACJ (ROC areas of 0.75 and over).

What all these instruments do well is to identify a small group of offenders who will have a high rate of re-offending. Their reasonably good specificity means that attention can be focused on a group of individuals who are genuinely high risk. The sensitivity of these instruments is, however, less good – a significant number of offenders in the lower-risk groups also re-offend. Although this does not mean that such individuals have been wrongly classified (lower-risk drivers are still involved in accidents), one must clearly avoid equating lower risk with no risk. It is worth noting that although those who criticize the use of actuarial scales usually do so because of their fear that some offenders may be wrongly labelled as high risk, the weak sensitivity of the scales in fact means that those who seek to use them to guarantee public safety should be more concerned – more of those who will re-offend are missed than are identified as high risk (see also Sjostedt and Langstrom 2001).

It is also worth noting that actuarial instruments, which are dependent on follow-up data from large cohorts of offenders, are by their very nature dated even before they are used. One cannot simply assume that the sex offenders on whom the scales are based, convicted in the 1980s and released in the early 1990s, are similar to the sex offenders of the twenty-first century. This has become particularly pertinent with the emergence of sex offenders whose crimes relate to the Internet, for whom very different factors may be predictive of not only re-offending, but also risk of harm.

In spite of these caveats, and the need for further validation, the actuarial instruments referred to above are almost certainly sufficiently robust to be used in the first stage of risk assessment – the determination of long-term risk. At that point, their utility comes to an end.

Assessment of dynamic risk

Although actuarial risk assessment provides a baseline that can anchor judgement about risk, it is the beginning rather than the end of the risk assessment/risk management process. Because they are empirically derived, variables that are important to the actuarial calculation do not come with theoretical explanations of why they are important: we know, for example, that a history of sex offence convictions is predictive of re-offending, but not why. Similarly, although youth is a predictor of re-offending, it is also the case that sex offences committed by older men may indicate entrenched pathology not present in their younger counterparts and unlikely to change, suggesting that older rather than younger offenders are more likely to re-offend (Grubin and Wingate 1996). Because actuarial assessment is aetiologically blind, dynamic variables can help to determine the relevance of static factors in specific cases, allowing a more sophisticated assessment of risk to be carried out.

It is thus necessary to build on actuarial risk assessment if it is to be applied in any meaningful way. In assessing risk of potential harm, imminence and frequency, more clinically based assessments come into their own; these types of risk vary over time and require ongoing evaluation, focusing on so-called dynamic risk factors. Hanson and Harris (2000) have pointed out that dynamic risk factors can themselves be divided into two types: those which are relatively stable, such as an offender's attitudes, his ability to form relationships and his capacity to 'regulate' himself in respect of sexual and more general behaviour; and 'acute' factors that change more rapidly, such as an offender's co-operation with supervision, his level of hostility and his access to victims (see Figures 5.1 and 5.2 above).

Researchers have been attempting to develop instruments that can identify and measure dynamic factors that will allow a quantification of dynamic risk in a manner similar to actuarial tools. In addition to procedures making use of 'structured professional judgement' referred to above (SVR-20 and RSVP), which are in effect a combination of actuarial and clinical-type assessment variables, three other approaches are worth mentioning.

First, psychometric testing has been advocated as a means of identifying stable dynamic risk factors indicative of either an increase or a reduction in risk as measured on actuarial scales. The most advanced of this type of approach is perhaps that developed by the STEP team in the UK (Beech *et al.* 2002). As part of an evaluation of sex offender treatment programmes in both prison and the community, the STEP team asked offenders to complete a large battery of psychometric tests. The team have identified what they refer to as a 'deviant' or 'untreated profile' in child molesters that they claim is associated with re-offending. This profile is produced by combining the results of a number of these tests: men with an 'untreated profile' display low social competence, have victim empathy deficits and show high levels of cognitive distortions, emotional loneliness and emotional congruence with children. In addition, offenders with such a profile require significantly longer in treatment before progress is made. Because of the low and slow rate of re-offending in their study sample, the number on which they base their claims is small.

A second approach is to consider aspects of psychological functioning known to be related to offending behaviour. An example of this is the Structured Risk Assessment (SRA) framework described by Thornton (2002). Although too complex to describe in any detail here, it focuses on four domains of functioning: sexual interests and arousal, cognitions (in particular cognitive distortions related to sexual offending), emotional regulation and self-management skills, with a judgement made about the extent to which difficulties in each of these domains both contribute to offending and are prevalent more generally in the psychological life of the offender.

Third, behavioural rating scales can be constructed that enable an assessor to look for and score repeatedly over time dynamic factors associated with re-offending. This approach is being developed by Hanson and Harris (2000), who are now, based on a retrospective review of dynamic factors linked to re-offending in sex offenders on probation, evaluating in a prospective trial the extent to which these factors can be used to produce a systematic evaluation of dynamic risk. The areas on which they have focused are general and sexual self-regulation, important social influences, intimacy deficits, co-operation with supervision and emotional 'collapse'. It is rare for risk assessment tools to be tested prospectively in this manner, and the results are awaited with anticipation.

Conclusion

Neither actuarial nor clinical techniques on their own are capable of providing a meaningful assessment of risk. The former are empirically driven but inflexible, whereas the latter lack an anchor and have a tendency to be blown by distracting winds. It is only when the two are integrated in a systematic manner that risk assessment becomes robust, transparent and defensible.

But even the most careful of assessments can be derailed by external considerations. Personal feelings about an offender whom one has treated, for example, can lead to either an over- or an under-estimation of risk, depending on whether these feelings are positive or negative in nature. There can also be political pressure to override the findings of actuarial assessment, particularly in cases where 'everyone knows' that an individual is dangerous even though he scores low on assessment tools. Whether 'clinical override' in such situations is appropriate will depend on how issues of public protection are balanced against those of the rights of the individual. The structure imposed by systematic assessment, however, at least ensures that considerations such as these are brought out into the open, particularly in jurisdictions that allow for the preventative detention of dangerous offenders.

References

Barbaree, H.E., Seto, M.C., Langton, C. and Peacock, E. (2001) 'Evaulating the Predictive Accuracy of Six Risk Assessment Instruments for Adult Sex Offenders.' *Criminal Justice and Behavior 28*, 490–521.

Beech, A., Friendship, C., Erikson, M. and Hanson, R.K. (2002) 'The Relationship Between Static and Dynamic Risk Factors and Reconviction in a Sample of U.K. Child Abusers.' *Sexual Abuse: A Journal of Research and Treatment 14*, 155–167.

Boer, D.P., Hart, S.D., Kropp, P.R. and Webster, C.D. (1997) *Manual for The Sexual Violence Risk–20: Professional Guidelines for Assessing Risk of Sexual Violence*. British Columbia Institute Against Family Violence. Burnaby, British Columbia: Mental Health, Law & Policy Institute, Simon Fraser University.

Dolan, M. and Doyle, C. (2000) 'Violence Risk Prediction: Clinical and Actuarial Measures and the Role of the Psychopathy Checklist.' *British Journal of Psychiatry 177*, 303–311.

Edwards, A., Elwyn, G. and Mulley, A. (2002) 'Explaining Risks: Turning Numerical Data into Meaningful Pictures.' *British Medical Journal 324*, 827–830.

Epperson, D.L. (2000) 'Cross Validation of the Minnesota Sex Offender Screening Tool – Revised (MnSOST-R). Online: www.129.186.143.73/faculty/epperson/ATSA2000/ index.htm

Grubin, D. (1997) 'Predictors of Risk in Serious Sex Offenders.' *British Journal of Psychiatry 170* (suppl. 32), 17–21.

Grubin, D. (1998) *Sex Offending Against Children: Understanding the Risk*. Police Research Series Paper No. 99. London: Home Office.

Grubin, D. and Wingate, S. (1996) 'Sexual Offence Recidivism: Prediction Versus Understanding.' *Criminal Behaviour and Mental Health 6*, 349–359.

Hanson, R.K. (1997) *The Development of a Brief Actuarial Risk Scale for Sexual Offense Recidivism*. User Report 97–04. Ottawa: Department of the Solicitor General of Canada.

Hanson, R.K. and Bussière, M.T. (1998) 'Predicting Relapse: A Meta-analysis of Sexual Offender Recidivism Studies.' *Journal of Consulting and Clinical Psychology 66*, 348–362.

Hanson, R.K. and Harris, A.J.R. (2000) 'Where Should We Intervene? Dynamic Predictors of Sex Offense Recidivism.' *Criminal Justice and Behavior 27*, 6–35.

Hanson, R.K. and Thornton, D. (2000) 'Improving Risk Assessments for Sex Offenders: A Comparison of Three Actuarial Scales.' *Law and Human Behavior 24*, 119–136.

Janus, E.S. and Meehl, P.E. (1997) 'Assessing the Legal Standard for Predictions of Dangerousness in Sex Offender Commitment Proceedings.' *Psychology, Public Policy and Law 3*, 33–64.

Marshall, P. (1994) *Reconviction of Imprisoned Sex Offenders*. Home Office Research and Statistics Department Research Bulletin No. 36. London: Home Office.

Mossman, D. (1994) 'Assessing Predictions of Violence: Being Accurate About Accuracy.' *Journal of Consulting and Clinical Psychology 62*, 783–792.

Prentky, R.A., Harris, B., Frizzell, K. and Righthand, S. (2000) 'An Actuarial Procedure for Assessing Risk with Juvenile Sex Offenders.' *Sexual Abuse: A Journal of Research and Treatment 12*, 71–93.

Quinsey, V.L., Harris, G.T., Rice, M.E. and Cormier, C.A. (1998) *Violent Offenders: Appraising and Managing Risk.* Washington DC: American Psychological Association.

Sjostedt, G. and Langstrom, N. (2001) 'Actuarial Assessment of Sex Offender Recidivism Risk: A Cross-validation of the RRASOR and the Static-99 in Sweden.' *Law and Human Behavior 25*, 629–645.

Thornton, D. (2002) 'Constructing and Testing a Framework for Dynamic Risk Assessment.' *Sexual Abuse: A Journal of Research and Treatment 14*, 139–153.

Thornton, D., Mann, R., Webster, S. *et al.* (in press) 'Distinguishing and Combining Risks for Sexual and Violent Recidivism.' In R. Prentky, E. Janus, M. Seto and A.W. Burgess (eds) 'Understanding and Managing Sexually Coercive Behavior.' *Annals of the New York Academy of Sciences.*

CHAPTER 6

Effective Intervention with Sexual Offenders

Bill Marshall, Gerris Serran
and Heather Moulden

Introduction

Considering the devastating consequences of sexual offending on the victims and their families (Koss and Harvey 1991), determining the most effective approach to sexual offender treatment is critical in order to reduce future risk of re-offending. Treatment programmes for sexual offenders have proliferated over the years (Burton and Smith-Darden 2001) and have evolved to become much more comprehensive in nature (Marshall, Anderson and Fernandez 1999). Despite this growth in the number of programmes, there are numerous challenges to the implementation and support of treatment, including legislation, the media and public attitudes towards treatment (Gordon and Hover 1999). In the USA, for example, some jurisdictions have eliminated prison-based programmes (e.g. Virginia and California) or do not offer treatment (e.g. Arizona and Idaho) and focus solely on punishment (e.g. a life sentence in Washington State after two felony offences). Within the field, some researchers and policy-makers continue to question whether treatment reduces recidivism. Despite these challenges, exciting progress has been made in areas related to motivation, therapeutic process and the knowledge of risk factors that can be addressed during treatment (see Hanson and Harris 2000; Marshall *et al.* 2002; Serran, *et al.* 2003). In addition, a recent meta-analysis (Hanson *et al.* 2002) and an evaluation of treatment effect sizes (Marshall and McGuire 2003) have revealed benefits for treatment, a more detailed examination of these results indicating the types of sexual offender who appear to show the best responses to treatment (Hanson *et al.* 2002).

Creating the context for effective intervention

Creating a supportive environment is integral to running effective treatment programmes, particularly in institutions. Numerous challenges exist to creating a supportive environment, e.g. the client's fear of being identified as a sexual offender, a lack of support from staff and budget cutbacks. Sexual offenders in a mixed prison are often afraid of being identified and hassled, which increases their anxiety about, and limits their effective participation in, treatment. The optimal solution is to devote a prison (or prisons) to the housing of solely sexual offenders (as has occurred in Scotland; see McIvor *et al.* 1997). If this is not feasible, one of two alternatives should be adopted: (1) confining sexual offenders to a separate area within an integrated prison; or (2) developing other strategies such as holding sessions in a private area and keeping the profile of the programme as minimally visible as possible.

Within integrated prisons, it is necessary to adopt a firm 'no hassling' policy, with immediate consequences for non-sexual offenders should they attempt to intimidate or harass sexual offenders. For this to work, the role of all staff becomes essential to creating an optimal environment. Staff should be made aware of the details of the programme and should undergo training in order to understand the nature of sexual offending and the goals of the treatment providers. Staff members can provide support and encouragement, and reinforce appropriate behaviour outside the group sessions. In this respect, the environment needs to be supportively challenging but not collusive, in order to help promote change while enhancing self-esteem.

Unfortunately, institutions all too often adopt a punitive approach toward sexual offenders, and some administrators and researchers argue that treatment is a waste of time and resources. Creating public awareness can promote support and understanding of the goals of treatment providers; in particular, using the media constructively can increase understanding and reduce myths about sexual offenders. Working in conjunction with parole or probation officers, family members and others involved in the offender's case provides both awareness and support. Cost–benefit analyses (Marshall 1992; Prentky and Burgess 1990) reveal that treatment not only reduces future offending against innocent victims, but also saves tax-payers a considerable amount of money. It is thus incumbent upon prison administrators, and others who can provide funding for treatment, to set aside any unfounded biases and support treatment programmes.

Issues related to effective intervention

Andrews and Bonta (1998) have described the principles of effective correctional treatment (risk, need and responsivity), based on a series of meta-analyses on the effects of treatment on recidivism in general criminal populations. According to the research on these principles, correctional treatment is most effective when it targets higher-risk offenders and factors directly related to criminal behaviour and is delivered in a manner consistent with the learning and personality style of the offender. Although minimal research has focused on the applicability of these principles to sexual offenders, a consideration of these issues should improve interventions. For example, conducting lengthy, intensive treatment with lower-risk offenders is not cost-efficient and might even prove detrimental (Andrews *et al.* 1990). New research on dynamic, or changeable, risk factors for sexual offenders can identify targets for intervention in order to reduce recidivism. In addition, flexibility during treatment allows the therapist to work with offenders at different levels of commitment and functioning.

The principles of effective intervention with general offenders that have been highlighted by Gendreau (1996) can be applied to sexual offending clients. Gendreau argues that services should vary in intensity (depending on risk level) and be behaviourally orientated (i.e. based on the principles of operant conditioning). According to this view, the use of positive reinforcement (such as material goods, activities or attention, praise and approval) accelerates learning. Other techniques, including modelling, graduated practice, roleplaying and training in problem-solving and moral reasoning (Andrews and Bonta 1998), are beneficial with criminal offenders, including sexual offenders.

Issues such as the characteristics of the therapist, offender and programme, as well as the therapist's interpersonal skills, are also important for effective intervention. Treatment programmes must be delivered in such a way as to facilitate the learning of new skills (e.g. interactive discussions rather than lecturing or education), and the offender should be given the opportunity to practise new strategies. More traditional treatment approaches, such as psychodynamic or non-directive therapy, have not been effective with either offenders in general (Andrews *et al.* 1990) or sexual offenders in particular (Furby, Weinrott and Blackshaw 1989). Punishment has also been examined as a strategy with offenders and is most likely to be applied if they are behaving in what is thought to be a resistant manner. Gendreau *et al.* (1993) conducted a preliminary meta-analysis examining the use of punishment with offenders and found that it increased recidivism. Punishment only works when escape is impossible, when punishment is applied immediately and at maximum intensity, and when it is applied at the earliest point in the deviant response chain and at every occurrence of deviant behaviour (McGuire 2002). This knowledge paves the way for developing effective interventions with sexual offender populations.

Treatment approaches

Treatment approaches have developed and expanded over time. Prior to 1970, the approach to assessment and treatment with sexual offenders included psychoanalytic therapy (Allen 1980; Conn 1949) or traditional group psychotherapy (Grossman 1985; Mathis 1980) and limited behavioural therapy (Bond and Evans 1967). Early behaviourists thought that simply reducing sexual interest in deviant acts would result in a reduction in offending (Bond and Evans 1967). Procedures such as aversion therapy (Abel, Levis and Clancy 1970), covert sensitization (Cautela 1967), orgasmic reconditioning (Marquis 1970) and satiation therapy (Marshall 1979) provided methods to reduce deviant sexual arousal and increase the attractiveness of prosocial sexual activities. Over the past few decades, more multifaceted programmes have been developed incorporating a wide range of factors, including attitudes, relationship skills, coping strategies and interpersonal factors (Abel, Rouleau and Cunningham-Rathner 1986; Becker and Kaplan 1993; Laws 1989; Maletzky 1991; Marques 1988; Marshall *et al.* 1999; Pithers 1990). Sexual offender treatment has evolved rapidly since the 1980s and has been guided both by theory and research. Current programmes are cognitive-behavioural in orientation and target a wide range of criminogenic needs (e.g. attitudes tolerant of sexual assault, lifestyle, impulsivity and deviant sexual interests) by teaching relevant skills in a way that matches the offenders' learning styles. Cognitive-behavioural group therapy appears to be the treatment of choice, although the way in which treatment is delivered appears to influence the degree of change evident with treatment (Serran *et al.*, 2003). In the following sections, we will describe this approach to treatment, along with some of the most common treatment targets.

Structure of current treatment programmes

In the Ontario Region of Correctional Service of Canada, an approach to the optimal allocation of resources has been developed for the treatment of sexual offenders. All sexual offenders entering the system are comprehensively assessed, on the basis of which they are allocated to a prison where their needs can be most effectively met. Those with psychiatric disorders are sent to an institution that specializes in dealing with these offenders. The high-risk/high-needs offenders transfer to a prison for extensive and intensive treatment. After successfully completing this programme, these offenders then move to a lower-security prison where they participate in further treatment before transfer to a minimum-security institution to begin a gradual release programme. Once they are released to the community, these high-risk offenders are placed in a half-way house where they are carefully monitored and participate in further treatment in a community programme.

Moderate-risk offenders transfer from the assessment institution to a prison where the programmes are designed to meet their needs and the needs of those cascading from higher-needs programmes. After effective treatment, the moderate-risk offenders may be transferred to minimum security for further treatment or release to the community, where they enter a treatment programme. Low-risk offenders move from the assessment institution to lower security, where they enter a less intensive programme prior to release. These low-risk offenders are rarely required to participate in further treatment when released from prison. A similar strategy exists within HM Prison Service in England and Wales, with the addition of a specialized programme by which the needs of lower intellectually functioning offenders can be met.

Treatment is typically offered in a group format with between six and nine participants, and one or two therapists in a group. Group therapy is seen to be more cost-efficient, and the offenders play an essential role in challenging other group members. Other sexual offenders are often perceived as more credible than the therapist so that their challenges appear to be quite effective. Furthermore, when offenders challenge one another, they often use personal experiences to illustrate their point, which is useful not only to the offender being challenged, but also to the challenger. The use of personal experience in challenging others helps group participants better to understand their own offending. Another benefit of group treatment is the opportunity for vicarious learning, such that when one member is challenged, the other group members have the opportunity to consider their own thoughts and behaviours and adjust them accordingly. The same is perhaps even more true during the skills training components. Last, in a prison setting, group members interact outside the therapy room. They are therefore in a position to monitor and challenge one another's behaviour outside of treatment, thus adding to the generalizability of the skills they are acquiring in treatment.

Groups typically meet between two and five times each week for approximately 2.5 hours each session, higher-intensity programmes meeting more frequently and lower-intensity programmes less frequently. Ideally, two therapists facilitate the therapy session, and under optimal conditions a male and female therapist co-facilitate. Some programmes (often called 'rolling' programmes) are open-ended, which allows for continuous intake, and each offender spends as long in treatment as is necessary to achieve the programme's goals. This approach differs from closed programmes, in which all participants start and finish at the same time and each topic is addressed as a module. In open-ended groups, participants are at different stages of treatment, and more senior members are able to model appropriate behaviour. These more senior participants are provided the opportunity to demonstrate their new skills in treatment by helping junior group members. Their role in the group allows them to practise newly acquired skills and be rewarded for using those skills effectively, both of which increase self-esteem and self-efficacy, and further entrench their new skills. Open-ended approaches also allow greater flexibility. For example, not all clients require the same time and attention for all issues addressed in treatment, nor do they all work at the same speed or in the same way. Open-ended pro-grammes allow offenders and therapists collaboratively to define treatment targets that are specific to the needs of each group member.

Comprehensive assessments guide effective intervention and provide a basis for evaluating treatment. Assessment targets typically include sexual behaviour, social functioning, life history, cognitive processes, personality, substance abuse, physical problems and risk-related issues. Interviews, self-report questionnaires, physiological procedures and external sources of information (e.g. police reports, victim statements and court records) provide pertinent information.

Risk assessment is an important part of clinical practice, and in recent years a series of actuarial measures have been developed (Hanson 2000; see also Grubin, this volume). The problem with actuarial risk assessment, however, is that these instruments concentrate on 'static' or unchangeable factors, whereas treatment attempts to modify changeable characteristics. Hanson and Harris (2000) have begun an extensive project to identify the contribution of dynamic factors such as attachments, attitudes supporting sexual abuse, sexual entitlement, minimizing risk, self-regulation and manipulativeness. Additional factors include substance misuse, lack of empathy, sexual preoccupation and an antisocial lifestyle. The identification of the role of these factors will both improve treatment comprehensiveness and provide a basis for modifying actuarially based risk assessment as a result of treatment gains.

Treatment content

Sexual offending is not an isolated behaviour but one that is enacted based on the experiences of a particular individual. In order better to understand the context and factors that contribute to the commission of a sexual offence, offenders in Ontario are required to write an autobiography. In this exercise, they are asked to identify events, feelings and relationships they feel are relevant to their offending. An offender may, for example, describe difficult social relationships as a child and adolescent, which then contributed to feelings of loneliness and difficulties with intimacy in adult interactions. The background and present aspects of the offender's life are explored as they relate to his offences. This systematic approach to highlighting and integrating the contributing factors not only helps the therapist to identify the offence pathway, but also provides the offender with a better understanding of his own behaviour, thus instilling a sense of responsibility and the ability to manage his behaviour in the future. The factors identified in this process are also considered risk factors, such that if they present again, the offender will be at a potentially higher risk of re-offending than if they are not present. It is not enough, however, simply to identify a given risk factor such as alcohol use; instead, the offender must understand what role alcohol use played in his offending. In identifying such risk factors, the offender is able to devise a plan (relapse prevention plan) to manage his behaviour more appropriately in the future by both avoiding high-risk factors and developing more healthy and fulfilling activities. Last, anyone learning new skills needs to feel supported and requires both encouragement and challenging. To this end, each offender must create a list of individuals (friends, family or professionals) and organizations that will provide specific types of support.

Treatment targets

Cognitive distortions

Although the idea that distorted cognitions (i.e. attitudes, beliefs and perceptions) play a role in sexual offending appeared at the beginning of the modern era of sexual offender treatment, it was not until Abel, Becker and Cunningham-Rathner (1984) published their views on the role of cognitive distortions that therapists and researchers began to approach these issues more systematically. Ward (2000) has conceptualized cognitive distortions as 'implicit theories', which involve the interpretation and distortion of information so that it is consistent with the beliefs people have about themselves and their world. For sexual offenders, 'implicit theories' of particular concern are those which are self-serving or offence-supportive, such as beliefs about women and children, or particular victims. Cognitive distortions serve to diminish the responsibility of the offender, minimize the harm he has done and justify continued offending without guilt. These distortions can also include categorical denial or minimizations of the forcefulness, intrusiveness or extent of offending. Research suggests that rapists hold negative views about women, endorse violence against women and accept rape myths, whereas child molesters view children as desiring sex with adults and as sexually responsive (Bumby 1996; Hanson, Gizzarelli and Scott 1994; Hayashino, Wurtele and Klebe 1995; Marolla and Scully 1986; Marshall and Moulden 2001; Stermac and Segal 1989). In cases where distortions are evident, Murphy (1990) suggests that a cognitive restructuring approach is the most appropriate way to modify these views. This involves providing clients with:

- a rationale for the role that cognitions play in maintaining their deviant behaviour
- corrective information and education
- assistance in identifying their specific distortions
- challenges to these distortions.

There is evidence from several programmes that these procedures are effective in modifying cognitive distortions (Murphy and Carich 2001) and, similarly, that denial and minimizations can be overcome (Barbaree 1991; Brake and Shannon 1997; Marshall 1994b; Schlank and Shaw 1996). Schank and Shaw (1996), for example, provide a pre-treatment programme aimed at overcoming denial by enhancing victim empathy and identifying relapse prevention strategies, both of which are seen as blocks to accepting responsibility. Marshall *et al.* (2001a), on the other hand, have developed a specific full treatment programme for categorical deniers that covers all the topics addressed in the treatment of admitters except that denial is not challenged. Although the latter programme seems to be a sensible approach for those sexual offenders who refuse any treatment aimed at overcoming their denial, no evidence on its efficacy has yet been provided.

Empathy

Evidence (Fernandez 2002) supports the contention that sexual offenders are not deficient in empathy but instead simply withhold empathy from their victims. Essentially, the problem is that they deny, and refuse to recognize, the harm that befalls victims of sexual abuse. Given the desire of sexual offenders to continue offending without feeling personal distress (i.e. guilt or shame), it is not surprising that they distort their perceptions of victim reactions to be consistent with their desire to believe that they are doing no harm, or that the victim deserves to be sexually assaulted. Consistent with this view, Marshall and Moulden (2001) found that victim-specific empathy deficits in rapists were related to distorted beliefs about women. Similarly, Marshall, Hamilton, and Fernandez (2001b) found that child molesters were not only primarily deficient in empathy towards their own victim, but also manifested far greater signs of cognitive distortions that were significantly correlated with victim empathy deficits. Challenging these distortions about victim harm is meant to remove the barriers to empathy by allowing the offender to recognize the harm he has caused. Many programmes incorporate an educational component when addressing empathy. For example, Hildebrand and Pithers (1989) described providing offenders with written and video descriptions of victims' accounts of their sexual abuse. Role-plays are incorporated to facilitate the offender's ability to experience vicariously the abuse from the victim's perspective (Mann, Daniels and Marshall 2002). Offenders also write hypothetical letters both from the victim to themselves and in the form of a reply from the offender to the victim (Fernandez and Serran 2002). These letters are meant to express the victim's distress and the offender's acceptance of this and his responsibility for the offence. This component has been evaluated (Marshall *et al.* 1997a; Marshall, O'Sullivan and Fernandez 1996a) the results revealing a significant increase in empathy for the offender's own victim.

Social functioning

Difficulties with intimacy and loneliness appear to characterize sexual offenders (Ward, Hudson and McCormack 1997). Marshall (1989, 1993, 1994a; Marshall, Hudson and Hodkinson 1993) has suggested that insecure attachments with parents provide sexual offenders with an inadequate template for future relationships. Such insecure attachments are based on early experiences of abuse, neglect or rejection by parents, which not only creates a fear of intimacy, but also deprives these men of opportunities to learn the skills and confidence necessary for healthy intimate relationships. Sexual offenders frequently identify intimacy with sex, and given that peer-aged relationships may be threatening, they turn to sexual relations with children or non-consenting adults. Marshall *et al.* (1996b) described procedures for enhancing intimacy and reducing loneliness among sexual offenders. First, offenders identify the origins of intimacy difficulties and learn how their own behaviour contributes to their lack of intimacy. Next, the benefits of increased intimacy are reviewed, including methods of enhancing sexual relations with peer-aged partners. Pathways to the goals of increased intimacy, such as sharing enjoyable activities and communicating openly with their partners, are also part of this treatment component. Related topics such as jealousy and loneliness are addressed, and techniques to manage and alter these emotional states are introduced and explored. Marshall *et al.* (1996b) evaluated this component and found that their clients' sense of intimacy was enhanced and their loneliness reduced. Given the constraints of prison in terms of access to loved ones, the opportunity to implement intimacy skills is limited, so these significant improvements are somewhat surprising. An important feature of Canadian prisons is, however, that all offenders (including sexual offenders) are permitted to have conjugal visits with their partners on a reasonably regular basis. These visits provide opportunities to practise their newly acquired intimacy skills.

One important aspect involved is the implementation of intimacy skills (e.g. self-confidence or feelings of self-worth). Crowell, Fraley and Shaver (1999), for example, reviewed evidence showing that securely attached people (i.e. those with effective intimacy skills) had significantly higher self-esteem than those classified as insecurely attached. The same has been found to be true among children with secure and insecure attachments to their parents (Thompson 1999). We have found that intimacy, loneliness and self-esteem are significantly correlated in sexual offenders prior to treatment (Marshall *et al.* 1997b), and that treatment-induced changes in self-esteem predict changes in intimacy and loneliness (Marshall *et al.* 1997a). Since treatmentinduced changes in self-esteem are also correlated with changes in other treatment targets, such as empathy (Marshall *et al.* 1997a) and deviant sexual arousal (Marshall 1997), it is a significant treatment target. Creating an effective therapeutic climate within treatment is an essential feature that facilitates the enhancement of self-esteem as well maximizing the benefits for all other treatment targets. Treating clients empathically and warmly (both of which include respectfulness and support) has been shown to provide the conditions necessary for sexual offenders to gain the most benefits from treatment (Marshall *et al.*, 2002), including increasing their self-esteem. In addition, clients are helped to identify their strengths, of which they are to systematically remind themselves repeatedly each day, and they are encouraged to attend to their appearance and self-presentation and to pursue educational and occupational upgrading (Marshall, Anderson and Champagne 1997c). Finally, offenders are requested to increase the range and variety of their social activities because this has been shown to increase self-confidence (Khanna and Marshall 1978). Combining these elements has been demonstrated to enhance the self-esteem of sexual offenders (Marshall *et al.* 1997a).

Relapse prevention (self-management)

Relapse prevention (Marlatt 1982; see also Ward, Purvis and Devilly, this volume) was first employed in the treatment of substance misusers to maintain treatment gains. Although the relapse prevention model was demonstrated to be effective with addicts, there have been challenges to the way in which it has been employed with sexual offenders (Laws, Hudson and Ward 2000). Marques (1982) was the first to provide an outline of how this approach might be applied to sexual offenders. A detailed description of the approach was then published (Pithers *et al.* 1983), which resulted in an immediate adoption of the approach by the majority of North American treatment programmes (Knopp, Freeman-Longo and Stevenson 1992).

The relapse prevention approach described by Pithers (1990) and his colleagues is that most widely used in sexual offender treatment. It assumes that re-offences or relapses do not occur 'out of the blue' but are the product of a variety of events and situations that develop over time. The model also proposes that all sexual offenders will at some point slip or lapse from their state of complete abstinence. Some will recover and return to their abstinence, whereas others may continue along the path to a re-offence. In relapse prevention, the aim is to examine past offending in order to identify the points along the way that increased and contributed to the risk of the individual's (re)offending. Once these events, situations and feelings have been recognized, the offender generates ways to either avoid or cope with the increased risk.

In a recent evaluation of the relapse prevention model, Ward and Hudson (1996) identified two main criticisms: (1) adaptation from the original model used with addicts resulted in changes that are conceptually confusing; and (2) aspects of the model are not supported by the limited evidence available. Marques *et al.* (1989) found that, after treatment, clients improved their knowledge of relapse prevention concepts and the factors that placed them at risk, and they identified strategies for coping with risk factors. Unfortunately, the data available on the long-term effectiveness of Marques' programme are disappointing. Moreover, Beckett *et al.* (1994) measured several community programmes in England and found quite disappointing results. In the most successful of these programmes, only 57 per cent of participants demonstrated improved relapse prevention knowledge after treatment, while no changes were observed in three of the programmes. Mann (1996) suggested that the negative findings may have been a function of the time-limited nature of the programmes. She then compared three extensive prison-based programmes: a therapeutic community with no cognitive behavioural or relapse prevention component; a cognitive behavioural programme with no RP component; and a cognitive behavioural programme with an extensive RP component. The results supported the usefulness of cognitive-behavioural treatment, the benefits being clearly attributable to the inclusion of the RP component.

Although RP approaches appear to have potential benefits, recent attempts to improve their effectiveness have focused on the avoidance aspects of the approach. In RP programmes, clients are required to identify risk factors and then develop strategies for avoiding those factors. As Mann (2000) points out, the general psychological literature indicates that avoidance goals are very difficult to maintain, whereas approach goals are more readily achieved. For example, the only way to avoid feelings of loneliness is to develop positive relationships. Thus, the goals for offenders in this case will be to acquire the skills to develop enjoyable and satisfying relationships rather than having a goal of avoiding loneliness. Approach goals are those which identify ways of meeting the basic needs of autonomy, competence and relatedness (see Ward, 2002, for a discussion of these goals) that result in a fulfilling life. Ward's contention is that a person living such a fulfilling life will have no reason to offend. In fact, focusing on positive goals rather than avoidance strategies is simply a change in emphasis as the goal of treatment with sexual offenders has for many years been the development of ways of meeting their needs prosocially, with the assumption being that success in these endeavours will remove the motivation to offend.

In addition, Ward and Hudson (Hudson and Ward 2000; Ward and Hudson 2000) have outlined multiple pathways to offending among sexual offenders, whereas the original RP model described only one pathway (see also Ward, Purvis and Devilly, this volume). In response to these criticisms and reformulations of RP, we have changed both our emphasis and our descriptors. What was previously called the 'offence chain/cycle' we have renamed 'offence pathways', and we describe what were called 'relapse prevention plans' as 'self-management plans'. The latter descriptor is not only more approach-orientated, but also conveys to clients that the future management of their problems is their responsibility. Our clients' self-management plans express goals that are attainable, are adapted specifically to their capacities and circumstances and will lead to life satisfaction and fulfilment.

Renaming the offence cycle serves to indicate that offences rarely follow a formulaic pattern. They typically occur when an opportunity occurs coincident with both internal and external disinhibiting processes and those processes and opportunities may be different on different occasions of offending. Thus, at least two or more offence pathways (or sets of internal and external circumstances) should be identified. It is, however, not necessary to identify every possible factor that may have played a part in every offence, since the goal of treatment is to instil a generic disposition that is responsive to all potential future circumstances. This more positive approach to what was previously called RP is meant to instill hope and optimism in our offenders, and there is evidence that hope is a primary factor in maintaining treatment gains (Moulden and Marshall 2002).

Deviant sexual arousal

Deviant sexual preferences have long been a central target of sexual offender treatment programmes. Although more recent evidence suggests that only a limited number of sexual offenders display sexual arousal to deviant themes at assessment (Marshall and Fernandez 2003) it nevertheless remains true that some do, and these responses must be changed if treatment is to be effective. Essentially, two approaches have been employed to achieve the goal of reducing or eliminating deviant sexual preferences or sexual responsiveness to deviant themes: behavioural interventions and pharmacological treatment.

Behavioural procedures involve strategies to enhance attraction to normative themes (masturbatory reconditioning) and reduce the sexual valence of deviant behaviours (aversive conditioning or satiation therapy). Masturbatory reconditioning techniques involve having the offender masturbate to ejaculation while rehearsing normative sexual behaviours (i.e. consenting sex with an adult). These procedures rely on the offender carrying out the tasks in his natural environment. The evidence to date on the effectiveness of these procedures is not convincing (Laws and Marshall 1991) despite their widespread popularity. Electrical aversive conditioning has largely been abandoned, presumably for ethical and therapy-relationship reasons, although evidence suggests that these procedures are effective (Quinsey and Earls 1990). Covert sensitization (a covert variant of aversive conditioning) is a popular approach to reducing deviant interests, but again the supportive evidence is limited. For a detailed description of this procedure, see Marshall *et al.* (1999, pp.120–122). In fact, only satiation therapy appears to have satisfactory data supporting its use (Laws and Marshall 1991). In this procedure, the client masturbates to orgasm and then immediately post-orgasm explicitly rehearses every variation of his deviant fantasies that he can think of for at least ten minutes. Immediately after orgasm, men enter what is called the 'refractory state' in which they are unresponsive to sexual stimulation. Associating the rehearsal of deviant fantasies with this refractory state dramatically diminishes the attractiveness of these deviant stimuli (Johnston, Hudson and Marshall 1992; Marshall 1979).

Psychopharmacological approaches involve the administration of either an agent (anti-androgen or hormonal agent) that reduces the testosterone level or one that dampens the intensity of urges (e.g. a selective serotonin re-uptake inhibitor). Prentky (1997) suggests that use of anti-androgen interventions are most effective with offenders who engage in highly repetitive behaviour, are driven by uncontrollable sexual urges or experience extremely intrusive sexual fantasies. This suggests that sex-drive reducing medication is warranted only when:

- the offender's sexual history reveals a high rate of deviant activity that is persistently evident over an extended period of time

- phallometric assessments indicate strong deviant sexual arousal or very high sexual arousal to all stimuli

- the offender self-reports excessive masturbation or persistent, intrusive deviant fantasies

- he displays an excessive use of pornography

- the offender engages in institutional sexualized behaviour toward staff or other inmates

- hormonal assays reveal a high level of testosterone.

Bradford (1997) has reviewed the evidence on the value of these medical interventions, and it seems clear that they can be useful. It is, however, best to view these procedures as an adjunct to comprehensive cognitive-behavioural programmes since the offenders must eventually learn to manage their behaviours without the drugs.

Programmes for special populations

Treatment for the majority of sexual offenders is challenging, but clients with particular characteristics require specialized approaches. Although it is impossible to cover each of these populations in detail, specific programmes for particular unique populations are described (Marshall *et al.* 1998).

Appropriate treatment for developmentally delayed offenders has been outlined by Haaven and his colleagues (Coleman and Haaven 1998, 2001; Haaven, Little and Petre-Miller 1990). In Haaven's programme, which has been adapted quite broadly, concepts are simplified and visual images are used to convey these concepts. For example, posters are used to detail the client's concept of himself as he was before entering treatment (i.e. the 'Old Me') and as he aims to become (i.e. the 'New Me'). Small steps toward treatment goals are repeated and rewarded until they are entrenched before moving to the next step. Indeed, repetition and rewards are crucial, as is a slow move toward greater self-reliance.

Offenders who score high on psychopathy also present special problems. These clients can appear to be effectively participating in treatment, but this sometimes disguises the fact that they have simply learned what to say but have not integrated treatment concepts. Psychopathic offenders present challenges to treatment providers whether or not they are sexual offenders (McMurran 2001). Specialized programmes have been developed (Hughes *et al.* 1997), although not yet for sexual offenders. Juvenile sexual offenders also present special difficulties. There are now numerous reports in the literature detailing appropriate approaches with these young offenders (Graham, Richardson and Bhate 1998; Worling 1998). Recent evaluations of these programmes indicate that they effectively reduce subsequent recidivism (Worling and Curwen 1998).

Treatment effectiveness

Dispute continues regarding the effectiveness of treatment for sexual offenders, much of the criticism being aimed at the methodological adequacy of studies purportedly demonstrating effectiveness. McConaghy (1999) and Quinsey *et al.* (1993) claim there are no studies that adequately demonstrate benefits to treatment, but others disagree. The criticisms of McConaghy and Quinsey *et al.* are predicated on the assumption that the only acceptable design for adequately answering the question 'Is treatment effective?' is that of randomly assigning sexual offender volunteers to treatment or no treatment. These offenders (both treated and untreated) would then be released into the community and followed for several years to determine the effects of treatment. Other than possible ethical objectives to this random design (see Marshall and Pithers 1994), it is unlikely that prison administrators, for example, would allow sexual offenders who wanted treatment to be denied entry to a programme. However, a satisfying evaluation of treatment needs to approximate as closely as possible to this ideal design.

The committee administering the Association for the Treatment of Sexual Abusers collaborative outcome study determined that the entry standard for studies would require them to have at least a reasonably well-matched comparison group of untreated offenders released from the same setting as the treated group. Using this standard, the ATSA group identified 42 studies reporting treatment outcome involving over 9000 subjects. A clear benefit from treatment was observed. Of the treated subjects, 9.9 per cent re-offended over the extended follow-up period, whereas 17.3 per cent of the untreated group re-offended – a clear, significant effect. Treatment for sexual offenders clearly can be effective, but problems persist because treatment, just as clearly, does not prevent all participants from re-offending. The problem for future research is to identify what features of offenders, or characteristics of treatment, facilitate or impede treatment effectiveness.

Implications

Treating sexual offenders is a complex issue, and there is no magic cure. To be effective, treatment providers must consider a myriad of issues. First and foremost, it is essential to reduce the risk of recidivism and protect the public. In order to do this, it is necessary to help offenders to learn skills and attitudes that help them control their behaviour and develop a healthy lifestyle. Creating appropriate treatment environments, maximizing thera-peutic processes that facilitate treatment engagement and being flexible are necessary for creating optimal opportunities for change. Interventions do not occur in a vacuum: offenders should have the opportunity to use their newfound skills on a daily basis and be challenged and reinforced. Final treatment reports should be useful for management and decisionmaking by focusing on issues related to static and dynamic risk factors, the factors related to the offence pathways and the offenders' self- management plan, as well as by making practical recommendations that highlight both areas of strength and areas that need further development.

Interventions cannot be assessed unless treatment providers are willing to conduct research to determine whether treatment is having an impact. Evaluating whether or not the various components of treatment achieve their goals (e.g. whether addressing cognitive distortions actually produces more accurate perceptions of others) is also essential and should precede outcome evaluation. Further research is required before firm conclusions can be made about what works in different contexts.

In this chapter, we have attempted to outline some important issues related to effective intervention. The treatment of sexual offenders is a relatively new area, and opportunities exist to refine treatment programmes better to meet the needs of the diverse clients we are serving. The dedication and commitment that treatment providers and researchers bring to their work will go a long way towards improving existing programmes and reducing the risk of sexual abuse for women and children in the community.

References

Abel, G.G., Becker, J.V. and Cunningham-Rathner, J. (1984) 'Complications, Consent, and Cognitions in Sex Between Children and Adults.' *International Journal of Law and Psychiatry 7*, 89–103.

Abel, G.G., Levis, D. and Clancy, J. (1970) 'Aversion Therapy Applied to Taped Sequences of Deviant Behaviour in Exhibitionism and Other Sexual Deviations: A Preliminary Report.' *Journal of Behavior Therapy and Experimental Psychiatry 1*, 58–66.

Abel, G.G., Rouleau, J.L. and Cunningham-Rathner, J. (1986) 'Sexually Aggressive Behavior.' In W. Curran, A.L. McGarry and S.A. Shah (eds) *Forensic Psychiatry and Psychology: Perspectives and Standards for Interdisciplinary Practice.* Philadelphia: Davis.

Allen, D.W. (1980) 'A Psychoanalytic View.' In D.J. Cox and R.J. Daitzman (eds) *Exhibitionism: Description, Assessment and Treatment.* New York: Garland STPM Press.

Andrews, D.A. and Bonta, J. (1998) *The Psychology of Criminal Conduct,* 2nd edn. Cincinnati, OH: Anderson Press.

Andrews, D.A., Zinger, I., Hoge, R.D., Bonta, J., Gendreau, P. and Cullen, F.T. (1990) 'Does Correctional Treatment Work? A Clinically-relevant and Psychologically-informed Meta-analysis.' *Criminology 28*, 369–404.

Barbaree, H.E. (1991) 'Denial and Minimization Among Sex Offenders: Assessment and Treatment Outcome.' *Forum on Corrections Research 3*, 30–33.

Becker, J.V. and Kaplan, M.S. (1993) 'Cognitive Behavioural Treatment of the Juvenile Sex Offender.' In H.E. Barbaree, W.L. Marshall and S.M. Hudson (eds) *The Juvenile Sex Offender*. New York: Guilford Press.

Beckett, R., Beech, A., Fisher, D. and Fordham, A.S. (1994) *Community-based Treatment of Sex Offenders: An Evaluation of Seven Treatment Programmes*. Home Office Occasional Paper. London: Home Office.

Bond, I.K. and Evans, D.R. (1967) 'Avoidance Therapy: Its Use in Two Cases of Underwear Fetishism.' *Canadian Medical Association Journal 96*, 1160–1162.

Bradford, J. (1997) 'Medical Intervention in Sexual Deviance.' In D.R. Laws and W.D. O'Donahue (eds) *Sexual Deviance: Theory, Assessment, and Treatment*. New York: Guilford Press.

Brake, S.C. and Shannon, D. (1997) 'Using Pretreatment to Increase Admission in Sex Offenders.' In B.K. Schwartz and H.R. Cellini (eds) *The Sex Offender: New Insights, Treatment Innovations and Legal Developments*. Kingston, NJ: Civic Research Institute.

Bumby, K.M. (1996) 'Assessing the Cognitive Distortions of Child Molesters and Rapists: Development and Validation of the MOLEST and RAPE Scales.' *Sexual Abuse: A Journal of Research and Treatment 8*, 37–54.

Burton, D. and Smith-Darden, J. (2001) *North American Survey of Sexual Abuser Treatment and Models: Summary Data 2000*. Brandon, VT: Safer Society Press.

Cautela, J.R. (1967) 'Covert Sensitization.' *Psychological Reports 20*, 459–468.

Coleman, E. and Haaven, J. (1998) 'Adult Intellectually Disabled Sexual Offenders: Program Considerations.' In W.L. Marshall, Y.M. Fernandez, S.M. Hudson and T. Ward (eds) *Sourcebook of Treatment Programs for Sexual Offenders*. New York: Plenum Press.

Coleman, E. and Haaven, J. (2001) 'Assessment and Treatment of Intellectually Disabled Sexual Abusers.' In M.S. Carich and S.E. Mussack (eds) *Handbook for Sexual Abuser Assessment and Treatment*. Brandon, VT: Safer Society Press.

Conn, J.H. (1949) 'Brief Psychotherapy of the Sex Offender: A Report of a Liaison Service Between a Court and a Private Psychiatrist.' *Clinical Psychopathology 10*, 347.

Crowell, J.A., Fraley, R.C. and Shaver, P.R. (1999) 'Measurement of Individual Differences in Adolescent and Adult Attachment.' In J. Cassidy and P.R. Saver (eds) *Handbook of Attachment: Theory, Research and Clinical Applications*. New York: Guilford Press.

Fernandez, Y.M. (2002) *In their Shoes: Examining the Issue of Empathy and its Place in the Treatment of Offenders*. Oklahoma City, OK: Wood N' Barnes Publishing.

Fernandez, Y.M. and Serran, G. (2002) 'Empathy Training for Therapists and Clients.' In Y.M. Fernandez (ed) *In their Shoes: Examining the Issue of Empathy and its Place in the Treatment of Offenders*. Oklahoma City, OK: Wood N' Barnes Publishing.

Furby, L., Weinrott, M.R. and Blackshaw, L. (1989) 'Sex Offenders Recidivism: A Review.' *Psychological Bulletin 105*, 3–30.

Gendreau, P. (1996) 'The Principles of Effective Intervention with Offenders.' In A.T. Harland (ed) *Choosing Correctional Options that Work: Defining the Demand and Evaluating the Supply*. Thousand Oaks, CA: Sage.

Gendreau, P., Paparozzi, M., Little, T. and Goddard, M. (1993) 'Does "Punishing Smarter" Work? An Assessment of the New Generation of Alternative Sanctions in Probation.' *Forum on Corrections Research 5*, 31–34.

Gordon, A. and Hover, G. (1999) 'The Twin Rivers Sex Offender Treatment Program.' In W.L. Marshall, Y.M. Fernandez, S.M. Hudson and T. Ward (eds) *Sourcebook of Treatment Programs for Sexual Offenders.* New York: Plenum Press.

Graham, F., Richardson, G. and Bhate, S.R. (1998) 'Development of a Service for Sexually Abusive Adolescents in the Northeast of England.' In W.L. Marshall, Y.M. Fernandez, S.M. Hudson and T. Ward (eds) *Sourcebook of Treatment Programs For Sexual Offenders.* New York: Plenum Press.

Grossman, L.S. (1985) 'Research Directions in the Evaluation and Treatment of Sexual Offenders: An Analysis.' *Behavioural Sciences and the Law 3*, 421–435.

Haaven, J., Little, R. and Petre-Miller, D. (1990) *Treating Intellectually Disabled Sex Offenders: A Model Residential Program.* Orwell, VT: Safer Society Press.

Hanson, R.K. (2000) *Risk Assessment.* Beaverton, OR: Association for the Treatment of Sexual Abusers.

Hanson, R.K. and Harris, A.J.R. (2000) 'Where Should We Intervene? Dynamic Predictors of Sexual Offense Recidivism.' *Criminal Justice and Behavior 27*, 6–35.

Hanson, R.K., Gizzarelli, R. and Scott, H. (1994) 'The Attitudes of Incest Offenders: Sexual Entitlement and Acceptance of Sex with Children.' *Criminal Justice And Behavior 21*, 187–202.

Hanson, R.K., Gordon, A., Harris, A.J.R. *et al.* (2002) 'First Report of the Collaborative Outcome Data Project on the Effectiveness of Psychological Treatment for Sex Offenders.' *Sexual Abuse: A Journal of Research and Treatment 14*, 2, 169–194.

Hayashino, D.S., Wurtele, S.K. and Klebe, K.J. (1995) 'Child Molesters: An Examination of Cognitive Factors.' *Journal of Interpersonal Violence 10*, 106–116.

Hildebrand, D. and Pithers, W.D. (1989) 'Enhancing Offender Empathy for Sexual-abuse Victims.' In D.R. Laws (ed) *Relapse Prevention with Sex Offenders.* New York: Guilford Press.

Hudson, S.M. and Ward, T. (2000) 'Relapse Prevention: Assessment and Treatment Implications.' In D.R. Laws, S.M. Hudson and T. Ward (eds) *Remaking Relapse Prevention with Sex Offenders: A Sourcebook.* Thousand Oaks, CA: Sage.

Hughes, G., Hogue, T., Hollin, C. and Champion, H. (1997) 'First-stage Evaluation of a Treatment Programme for Personality Disordered Offenders.' *Journal of Forensic Psychiatry 8*, 515–527.

Johnston, P., Hudson, S.M. and Marshall, W.L. (1992) 'The Effects of Masturbatory Reconditioning with Nonfamilial Child Molesters.' *Behaviour Research and Therapy 30*, 559–561.

Khanna, A. and Marshall, W.L. (1978) 'A Comparison of Cognitive and Behavioural Approaches for the Treatment of Low Self-esteem.' Paper presented at the 12th Annual Convention of the Association for the Advancement of Behavior Therapy, Chicago, IL, November.

Knopp, F.H., Freeman-Longo, R. and Stevenson, W.F. (1992) *Nationwide Survey Of Juvenile and Adult Sex-offender Treatment Programs and Models.* Brandon, VT: Safer Society Press.

Koss, M.P. and Harvey, M.R. (1991) *The Rape Victim: Clinical and Community Interventions,* 2nd edn. Newbury Park, CA: Sage.

Laws, D.R. (1989) *Relapse Prevention with Sex Offenders.* New York: Guilford Press.

Laws, D.R. and Marshall, W.L. (1991) 'Masturbatory Reconditioning: An Evaluative Review.' *Advances in Behaviour Research and Therapy 13,* 13–25.

Laws, D.R., Hudson, S.M. and Ward, T. (2000) *Remaking Relapse Prevention With Sex Offenders: A Sourcebook.* Thousand Oaks, CA: Sage.

McConaghy, N. (1999) 'Methodological Issues Concerning Evaluation of Treatment for Sexual Offenders. Randomization, Treatment Dropouts, Untreated Controls, and Within-treatment Studies.' *Sexual Abuse: A Journal of Research and Treatment 11,* 183–193.

McGuire, J. (2002) 'Criminal Sanctions Versus Psychologically-based Interventions with Offenders: A Comparative Empirical Analysis.' *Psychology, Crime and Law 8,* 183–208.

McIvor, G., Rowlings, C., Skinner, K. and Campbell, V. (1997) *The STOP Programme: The Development and Implementation of Prison-based Groupwork with Sex Offenders.* Occasional Paper No. 2/1977. Edinburgh: Scottish Prison Service.

McMurran, M. (2001) 'Offenders with Personality Disorders.' In C.R. Hollin (ed) *Handbook of Offender Assessment and Treatment.* Chichester: Wiley.

Maletzky, B.M. (1991) *Treating the Sexual Offender.* Newbury Park, CA: Sage.

Mann, R. (1996) 'Measuring the Effectiveness of Relapse Prevention Intervention with Sex Offenders.' Paper presented at the 15th Annual Research and Treatment Conference of the Association for the Treatment of Sexual Abusers, Chicago, IL, November.

Mann, R. (2000) 'Managing Resistance and Rebellion in Relapse Prevention Intervention.' In D.R. Laws, S.M. Hudson and T. Ward (eds) *Remaking Relapse Prevention with Sex Offenders.* Thousand Oaks, CA: Sage.

Mann, R., Daniels, M. and Marshall, W.L. (2002) 'The Use of Role-plays in Developing Empathy.' In Y.M. Fernandez (ed) *In their Shoes: Examining the Issue of Empathy and its Place in the Treatment of Offenders.* Oklahoma City, OK: Wood N' Barnes Publishing.

Marlatt, G.A. (1982) 'Relapse Prevention: A Self-control Program for the Treatment of Addictive Behaviors.' In R.B. Stuart (ed) *Adherence, Compliance, and Generalization in Behavioral Medicine.* New York: Brunner/Mazel.

Marolla, J. and Scully, D. (1986) 'Attitudes Towards Women, Violence, and Rape: A Comparison of Convicted Rapists and Other Felons.' *Deviant Behavior 7,* 337–355.

Marques, J.K. (1982) 'Relapse Prevention: A Self-control Model for the Treatment of Sex Offenders.' Paper presented at the 7th Annual Forensic Mental Health Conference, Asilomar, CA, USA, March.

Marques, J.K. (1988) 'How to Answer the Question "Does Sexual Offender Treatment Work".' *Journal of Interpersonal Violence 14,* 437–451.

Marques, J.K., Day, D.M., Nelson, C. and Miner, M.H. (1989) 'The Sex Offender Treatment and Evaluation Project: California's Relapse Prevention Program.' In D.R. Laws (ed) *Relapse Prevention with Sex Offenders*. New York: Guilford Press.

Marquis, J.N. (1970) 'Orgasmic Reconditioning: Changing Sexual Object Choice Through Controlling Masturbation Fantasies.' *Journal of Behavior Therapy and Experimental Psychiatry 1*, 263–271.

Marshall, W.L. (1979) 'Satiation Therapy: A Procedure for Reducing Deviant Sexual Arousal.' *Journal of Applied Behavioral Analysis 12*, 10–22.

Marshall, W.L. (1989) 'Invited Essay: Intimacy, Loneliness, and Sexual Offenders.' Behavior Research and Therapy 27, 491–503.

Marshall, W.L. (1992) 'The Social Value of Treatment for Sexual Offenders.' *Canadian Journal of Huiman Sexuality 1*, 109–114.

Marshall, W.L. (1993) 'The Role of Attachment, Intimacy, and Loneliness in the Etiology and Maintenance of Sexual Offending.' *Sexual and Marital Therapy 8*, 109–121.

Marshall, W.L. (1994a) 'Pauvreté des liens d'attachement et déficiences dans les rapports intimes chez les agresseurs sexuels.' *Criminologie XXVII*, 55–69.

Marshall, W.L. (1994b) 'Treatment Effects on Denial and Minimization in Incarcerated Sex Offenders.' *Behavior Research and Therapy 32*, 559–564.

Marshall, W.L. (1997) 'The Relationship Between Self-esteem and Deviant Sexual Arousal in Nonfamilial Child Molesters.' *Behavior Modification 21*, 86–96.

Marshall, W.L., Anderson, D.A. and Champagne, F. (1997c) 'Self-esteem and its Relationship to Sexual Offending.' *Psychology, Crime, and Law 3*, 161–186.

Marshall, W.L., Anderson, D.A. and Fernandez, Y. M. (1999). *Cognitive-behavioural Treatment of Sexual Offenders*. Toronto: Wiley.

Marshall, W.L., Bryce, P., Hudson, S.M., Ward, T. and Moth, B. (1996b) 'The Enhancement of Intimacy and the Reduction of Loneliness Among Child Molesters.' *Journal of Family Violence 11*, 219–235.

Marshall, W.L., Champagne, F., Brown, C. and Miller, S. (1997b) 'Empathy, Intimacy, Loneliness, and Self-esteem in Nonfamilial Child Molesters.' *Sexual Abuse: A Journal of Research and Treatment 9*, 321–333.

Marshall, W.L., Champagne, F., Sturgeon, C. and Bryce, P. (1997a) 'Increasing the Self-esteem of Child Molesters.' *Sexual Abuse: A Journal of Research and Treatment 9*, 321–333.

Marshall, W.L. and Fernandez, Y.M. (2000) 'Phallometric Testing with Sexual Offenders: Limits to its Value.' *Clinical Psychology Review 20*, 807–828.

Marshall, W.L. and Fernandez, Y.M. (2003). *Phallometric Testing with Sexual Offenders. Theory, Research and Practice*. Brandon VT: Safer Society Press.

Marshall, W.L., Fernandez, Y.M., Hudson, S.M. and Ward, T. (eds) (1998) *Sourcebook of Treatment Programs for Sexual Offenders*. New York: Plenum Press.

Marshall, W.L., Hamilton, K. and Fernandez, Y.M. (2001b) 'Empathy Deficits and Cognitive Distortions in Child Molesters.' *Sexual Abuse: A Journal of Research and Treatment 13*, 123–131.

Marshall, W.L., Hudson, S.M. and Hodkinson, S. (1993) 'The Importance of Attachment Bonds in the Development of Juvenile Sex Offenders.' In H.E. Barbaree, W.L. Marshall and S.M. Hudson (eds) *The Juvenile Sex Offender.* New York: Guilford Press.

Marshall, W.L. and McGuire, J. (2003) *Effect Sizes in the Treatment of Sexual Offenders. International Journal of Offender Treatment and Comparative Criminology 46,* 653–663.

Marshall, W.L. and Moulden, H. (2001) 'Hostility Toward Women and Victim Empathy in Rapists.' *Sexual Abuse: A Journal of Research and Treatment 13,* 249–255.

Marshall, W.L., O'Sullivan, C. and Fernandez, Y.M. (1996) 'The Enhancement of Victim Empathy Among Incarcerated Child Molesters.' *Legal and Criminological Psychology 1,* 95–102.

Marshall, W.L. and Pithers, W.D. (1994) 'A Reconsideration of Treatment Outcome with Sex Offenders.' *Criminal Justice and Behavior 21,* 10–27.

Marshall, W.L., Serran, G., Moulden, H. *et al.* (2002). 'Therapist Features in Sexual Offender Treatment: Their Reliable Identification and Influence on Behavior Change.' *Clinical Psychology and Psychotherapy 9,* 395–405.

Marshall, W.L., Thornton, D., Marshall, L.E., Fernandez, Y.M. and Mann, R.E. (2001) 'Treatment of Sexual Offenders Who Are in Categorical Denial: A Pilot Project.' *Sexual Abuse: A Journal of Research and Treatment 13,* 205–216.

Mathis, J.L. (1980) 'Group Therapy.' In D.J. Cox and R.J. Daitzman (eds) *Exhibitionism: Description, Assessment, and Treatment.* New York: Garland STPM Press.

Moulden, H.M. and Marshall, W.L. (2002) *Hope in the Treatment of Sexual Offenders: A Potential Application of Hope Theory.* Submitted for publication.

Murphy, W.D. (1990) 'Assessment and Modification of Cognitive Distortions in Sex Offenders.' In W.L. Marshall, D.R. Laws and H.E. Barbaree (eds) *Handbook of Sexual Assault: Issues, Theories, and Treatment of the Offender.* New York: Plenum Press.

Murphy, W.D. and Carich, M.S. (2001) 'Cognitive Distortions and Restructuring in Sexual Abuser Treatment.' In M.S. Carich and S.E. Mussack (eds) *Handbook for Sexual Abuser Assessment and Treatment.* Brandon, VT: Safer Society Press.

Pithers, W.D. (1990) 'Relapse Prevention with Sexual Aggressors: A Method for Maintaining Therapeutic Change and Enhancing External Supervision.' In W.L. Marshall, D.R. Laws and H.E. Barbaree (eds) *Handbook of Sexual Assault: Issues, Theories, and Treatment of the Offender.* New York: Plenum Press.

Pithers, W.D., Marques, J.K., Gibat, C.C. and Marlatt, G.A. (1983) 'Relapse Prevention with Sexual Aggressors: A Self-control Model of Treatment and Maintenance of Change.' In J.G. Greer and I.R. Stuart (eds) *The Sexual Aggressor: Current Perspectives of Treatment.* New York: Van Nostrand Reinhold.

Prentky, R.A. (1997) 'Arousal Reduction in Sexual Offenders: A Review of Antiandrogen Interventions.' *Sexual Abuse: A Journal of Research and Treatment 9,* 4, 335–347.

Prentky, R.A. and Burgess, A.W. (1990) 'Rehabilitation of Child Molesters: A Cost–Benefit Analysis.' *American Journal of Orthopsychiatry 60,* 80–117.

Quinsey, V.L. and Earls, C.M. (1990) 'The Modification of Sexual Preferences.' In W.L. Marshall, D.R. Laws and H.E. Barbaree (eds) *Handbook of Sexual Assault: Issues, Theories, and Treatment of the Offender.* New York: Plenum Press.

Quinsey, V.L., Harris, G., Rice, M.E. and Lalumiere, M.L. (1993) 'Assessing Treatment Efficacy in Outcome Studies of Sex Offenders.' *Journal of Interpersonal Violence 8*, 512–523.

Schlank, A.M. and Shaw, T. (1996) 'Treating Sex Offenders Who Deny their Guilt: A Pilot Study.' *Sexual Abuse: A Journal of Research and Treatment 8*, 17–23.

Serran, G.A., Fernandez, Y.M., Marshall, W.L. and Mann, R. (2003) 'Process Issues in Treatment: Applications to Sexual Offender Programs.' *Professional Psychology: Research and Practice 34*, 368–374.

Stermac, L.E. and Segal, Z.V. (1989) 'Adult Contact with Children: An Examination of Cognitive Factors.' *Behavior Therapy 20*, 573–584.

Thompson, R.A. (1999) 'Early Attachment and Later Development.' In J. Cassidy and P.R. Shaver (eds) *Handbook of Attachment: Theory, Research and Clinical Applications.* New York: Guilford Press.

Ward, T. (2000) 'Sexual Offenders' Cognitive Distortions as Implicit Theories.' *Aggression and Violent Behavior: A Review Journal 5*, 491–507.

Ward, T. (2002).'Good Lives and the Rehabilitation of Offenders: Promises and Problems.' *Aggression and Violent Behavior 7*, 513–528.

Ward, T. and Hudson, S. M. (1996) 'Relapse Prevention: A Critical Analysis.' *Sexual Abuse: A Journal of Research and Treatment 8*, 177–200.

Ward, T. and Hudson, S.M. (2000) 'Sexual Offenders' Implicit Planning: A Conceptual Model.' *Sexual Abuse: A Journal of Research and Treatment 12*, 189–202.

Ward, T., Hudson, S.M. and McCormack, J. (1997) 'Attachment Style, Intimacy Deficits, and Sexual Offending.' In B.K. Schwartz and H.R. Cellini (eds) *The Sex Offender: New Insights, Treatment Innovations, and Legal Developments*, volume II. Kingston, NJ: Civic Research Institute.

Worling, J.R. (1998) 'Adolescent Sexual Offender Treatment at the SAFE-T Program.' In W.L. Marshall, Y.M. Fernandez, S.M. Hudson and T. Ward (eds) *Sourcebook of Treatment Programs for Sexual Offenders.* New York: Plenum Press.

Worling, J. and Curwen, T. (1998) *The Adolescent Sexual Offender Project: A 10-year Follow-up Study.* Report on the SAFE-T Program, Thistletown Regional Centre for Children and Adolescents, Toronto. Toronto: Ontario Ministry of Community and Social Services.

CHAPTER 7

Treatment of Sex Offenders in the UK in Prison and Probation Settings

Anthony R. Beech and Dawn D. Fisher

Introduction

The treatment of sexual offenders has undergone a series of changes since the early work focusing on the use of psychoanalytic techniques in the first half of the twentieth century. With the rising interest in behaviour therapy in the 1960s, sexual offenders began to be treated with behaviour modification to suppress deviant arousal, and social skills training to increase appropriate interpersonal behaviour. For the next decade or so, treatment was limited to these two approaches, and aversive conditioning using electric shock or aversive odours was commonplace (Beech and Mann 2002).

With the advent of cognitive approaches in the 1970s, attention turned to the thought processes of sexual offenders and the role of so-called 'cognitive distortions', i.e. pro-offending attitudes and beliefs used by sexual offenders to justify their offending and minimize any guilt they might feel. Work on challenging these thoughts began to be incorporated into treatment programmes, along with a focus on developing empathy for the victims of abuse. The inculcation of empathy was seen as vital in tackling any victim-blaming attitudes or denial of the harm caused by abuse (Abel, Blanchard and Becker 1978).

By the mid-980s, the concept of relapse prevention, first developed in the addictions field by Marlatt and Gordon (1985), was adapted for application to sexual offenders (Marques 1982; Pithers *et al.* 1983). The relapse prevention approach signified a combining of cognitive and behaviour therapy with its emphasis on the use of cognitive processes to influence behaviour and the need for behavioural rehearsal in learning appropriate coping strategies.

Since the mid-1980s, most treatment programmes for sexual offenders have incorporated such approaches into an integrated package, aiming to change sexual arousal, enhance social and empathy skills, restructure offence-supportive attitudes and enhance self-management through the use of relapse prevention techniques (Fisher and Beech 1999).

The rehabilitation of sexual offenders in the UK through treatment has become a big industry over the past ten years, in both prison and community settings. We now describe the current situation regarding treatment provision in prison and community settings.

Treatment ethos

The method of treatment used by both the Prison and the Probation Service in the UK is best described as cognitive-behavioural therapy (CBT). This approach has developed through the combination of both cognitive and behavioural approaches to therapy. (For an overview of the CBT approach see Marshall, Anderson and Fernandez 1999.) To give a brief synopsis, the behavioural component addresses the overt and covert behaviour of an individual and the principles of learning theory. This was originally confined to the use of procedures to alter behaviour, i.e. rewarding desired behaviours and punishing unwanted ones, but has since broadened out to include modelling (demonstrating a desired behaviour) and skills training (teaching specific skills through behavioural rehearsal). The cognitive component of the CBT approach addresses the thoughts or cognitions that individuals experience, which are known to affect mood state and hence have an influence upon subsequent behaviour. Cognitive therapy therefore aims to encourage an individual to think differently about events, thus giving rise to different affect and behaviour. The vital components of cognitive therapy involve the use of self-instruction and self-monitoring. Strong emphasis is given to getting offenders to understand that how one thinks affects how one feels and behaves directly. By combining these two approaches, CBT provides a comprehensive approach to treating sex offenders that now has research evidence to support its efficacy (Alexander 1999; Friendship, Mann and Beech 2003; Hanson *et al.* 2002). CBT has been shown in the 'What Works' literature (McGuire 1995) to be the most effective method of treating offenders.

Group, rather than individual, work is the usual method of delivering CBT to sexual offenders in the UK. The group work approach is seen as being suitable for all types of sexual offender. Beech and Fordham (1997) outlined the benefits of being in a group and group work as the following:

- Groups provide an environment that can offer both support and challenge to the individual.

- Group work provides the opportunity for discussion with peers.

- Group work provides opportunities for increasing self-esteem and empathic responding.

- Groups also offer a forum for support and the sharing of problems, which may be a completely new experience for many child sex abusers, who are generally isolated individuals, often with interpersonal deficits and feelings of inadequacy.

Having the experience of being valued, being able to help others, practising social skills and getting to know others in detail can greatly improve an individual's self-esteem and interpersonal functioning. Given that feelings of inadequacy and lack of appropriate relationships may be an important vulnerability factor for many child sex abusers (Thornton, Beech and Marshall in press), improvement in these areas is an important element in reducing re-offending.

Treatment for sexual offenders in prison

A strategy for the treatment of sexual offenders in prison began in 1991 with the implementation of the Sex Offender Treatment Programme (SOTP). This initiative was devised to be a framework for the integrated assessment and treatment of sex offenders (Mann 1999; Mann and Thornton 1998).

SOTP is currently running in 26 prisons in England and Wales, with around 1000 men completing treatment every year. This makes it the biggest treatment programme in the world at the present time. SOTP aims to treat all types of sex offender, whether they have committed offences against adults or children. In terms of the number of men going through treatment, current estimates would suggest that:

- 80 per cent of the men entering treatment have offended against children

- 15 per cent are men who have offended against adults

- 5 per cent are men who have killed their victim, with the suspicion or knowledge that there was a sexual component to the killing (information obtained from the Prison Service's Lifer Section and Offender Behaviour Programmes Unit).

Treatment provision for serious[1] sexual offenders in English and Welsh Prison Service typically consists of the following components (see Mann 1999).

Assessment

Here the offender is assessed for his suitability to undertake a group work programme. Exclusions are made, are made at this point, on the basis of the following:

- He is in total denial of the offence.

- He is suffering from psychotic illness or was at the time of the offence.

- He has a high score (26 or above) on the Hare Psychopathy Checklist (Hare 1991), suggesting that he has psychopathic characteristics, which

---

1   We use the term 'serious' here to mean the type of sexual offence that invariably receives a custodial sentence, rather than the type of sexual offence that is seen as less serious by the courts and hence is more likely to receive a community sentence. Such offences here typically include indecent exposure, the making of indecent telephone calls and downloading child pornography from the Internet.

would in turn suggest that he would not benefit from the group work programme currently provided for sexual offenders.

As part of the assessment, offenders will complete a battery of psychometric tests and will also be assessed for their level of need using the Structured Risk Assessment protocol (Thornton 2002) in addition to the assessment of actuarial risk, using Risk Matrix-2000 (Thornton *et al.* in press).

The CORE Programme

If a sexual offender is assessed as being suitable to take part in treatment and does not have learning difficulties,[2] he will first undertake the CORE Programme. The goals of this programme (Mann 1999) are:

- to reduce denial and minimization

- to enhance an understanding of the victims' experiences

- to develop strategies to avoid re-offending.

When the CORE Programme was introduced in 1991, this was the sum total of treatment a sex offender would receive, which comprised 35–40 two-hour sessions. This programme was then revised and expanded, and by late 1994 the 'revised' programme was rolled out generally, providing around 160 treatment contact hours. This revised programme has been recently superseded by the CORE 2000 programme. CORE 2000, although essentially covering the same areas as the revised programme, now places more emphasis on treatment as a collaborative effort. Here, the primary purposes of the programme are to increase the offender's motivation to avoid re-offending and to develop the self-management skills necessary to achieve this. Cognitive restructuring, modelling and positive reinforcement are seen as central to such treatment. While motivation is developed through undermining the excuses and rationalizations (cognitive distortions) that offenders use to justify their offending, empathy with their

---

2   If an offender is assessed as having learning difficulties, he will go
      through an adapted programme specifically designed for those with an
      IQ of 70–80. This has an emphasis on the use of non-verbal material
      and a reduced empathy component.

victims is increased by creating an emotional and intellectual awareness of the victim's experience of the offence and by examining the consequences of offending on their own lives.

The EXTENDED Programme

If an offender is assessed as having many treatment needs, he will also undertake a second stage of treatment, termed the EXTENDED Programme. The goals of this programme (Mann 1999) are to:

- identify and challenge patterns of dysfunctional thinking
- improve the management of emotions
- improve relationship and intimacy skills
- address deviant fantasy and sexual arousal
- understand the links of all of the above to sexual offending.

This programme has again been recently revised and emphasizes the importance of learning to manage negative emotions, particularly through the use of positive and calming cognitions rather than behavioural coping strategies, which may not always be available to the offender. The EXTENDED Programme now runs for around 68 two-hour sessions and focuses on the schemas (the underlying core beliefs held by the offender) and interpersonal skills deficits found in many offenders. Offenders will be offered additional individual work on managing deviant arousal where this is deemed appropriate by treatment managers in the various establishments where this programme is run. There are plans to develop a specific programme targeting arousal.

The ROLLING Programme

This programme is aimed at offenders with fewer treatment needs than those attending CORE 2000. It covers a number of offence-specific tasks, which offenders have to complete before leaving the programme. Tasks include such things as completing an offence account, writing a victim apology letter, and identifying and challenging distorted thinking. Tasks are set according to assessed needs, and the offender can remain in the programme for as long as required to complete the tasks satisfactorily. Being a rolling programme, this means that offenders can join and leave the group at any time, which makes it a very flexible programme to run.

Treatment for sexual offenders in the community

In terms of treatment provision in the community, three 'pathfinder programmes' have been accredited by the Joint Prison and Probation Services Accreditation Panel for England and Wales. The three programmes are the West Midlands Programme, the Thames Valley Programme (TV-SOGP) and the Northumbria Programme. The Joint Accreditation Panel is made up of a group of experts from both UK and North America whose task is to accredit treatment programmes that they consider to be of a suitable standard. Programmes are judged on a range of criteria that meet the 'What Works' principles. The 42 areas of the National Probation Service in England and Wales are in the process of implementing one of these 'geographically near' programmes. In terms of numbers entering probation-based treatment, this initiative predicted that it would have 2000 men in treatment or who have completed treatment by the end of 2004 (David Middleton, UK National Probation Directorate 2002).

One of the differences between the accredited programmes offered within the prison and probation services is that the probation programmes have to cater for a wide range of offenders (exhibitionists, rapists and child abusers) with only one programme, whereas the prison service is able to offer a range of programmes to suit the needs of different offenders, as outlined above. Within the probation service, limited resources mean that only one programme can be run, so the programme has to offer a number of modules that offenders attend according to their needs. There is also the need for flexibility so that offenders can repeat modules as necessary.

As an example of community treatment, TV-SOGP (see HM Prison Service 2003) has four programme blocks that offenders attend according to their assessed needs. The first block is the foundation block, which is an intensive two-week schedule. This is aimed at reducing denial and increasing motivation and taking responsibility for the offending behaviour, identifying and challenging distorted thinking, understanding the links between thoughts, feelings and behaviour, and thus recognizing the role played by deviant sexual thoughts. It also introduces the ideas of relapse prevention, problem-solving and simple strategies to control deviant sexual thoughts. The programme then moves to weekly or twice-weekly sessions for the remainder of the blocks. The next block is victim empathy, which aims to help the offender to understand the perspective of the victim, the effects of sexual abuse, the behaviour of the victim and the far-reaching consequences of abuse on all those affected. The third block is life skills, which essentially covers problem-solving, coping strategies and interpersonal relationships. The aim here is to improve an offender's ability to relate to and have more realistic expectations of others. The final block is relapse prevention, which aims to assist offenders in developing realistic relapse plans and the skills and strategies required to put them into practice.

An offender assessed as having many problems would undertake the entire programme, whereas those with fewer problems, i.e. only offence-specific needs, would not attend life skills. Offenders who have successfully completed a programme in prison may attend only relapse prevention, using it as a form of maintenance in the community. Offenders can repeat blocks as necessary or omit them according to need.

A model of treatment change

Programmes for sexual offenders have generally been developed to address the factors shown by research to be either contributory or characteristic factors in child abuse, so have been shown to work well with this group (Beech, Fisher and Beckett 1999). Given, however, that not all sexual offenders are child abusers, it is not expected that such programmes will be ideal for all sexual offenders needing treatment. It is therefore unclear how well the treatment may map on to the treatment needs of Internet offenders, exhibitionists, rapists and sexual murderers. In Figure 7.1, we have constructed a model of treatment that is typically given to all sexual offenders both in prison and in the community. We should clearly note, however, that this model has been primarily worked out for the treatment of men who have offended against children. This model is the basis of the TV-SOGP.

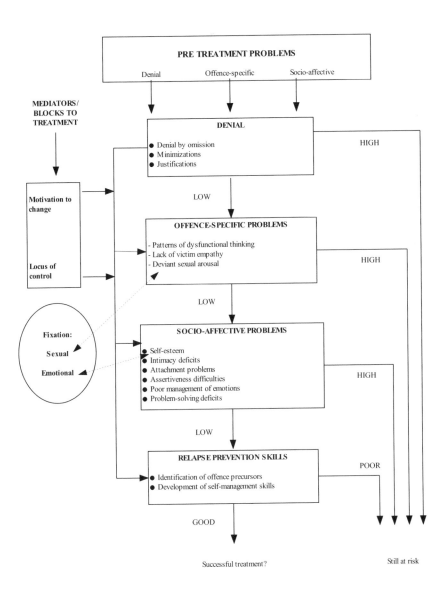

Figure 7.1 Model of treatment for child sexual abusers
Adapted from Fisher and Beech (2002)

The model is divided into four main sections: denial and minimization, offence-specific problems, social adequacy problems and relapse prevention. A further group of factors called mediators to treatment effects are also included. It should be noted that a clear model of treatment specifically for rapists and for sexual murderers has not yet been specifically delineated. In addition, some aspects of the schematic model of treatment in the prison programme – denial, victim empathy and relapse prevention – are dealt with in the CORE programme. Other elements are dealt with in the EXTENDED programme, for example relationship and intimacy skills, deviant fantasy and arousal, and patterns of dysfunctional thinking.

Denial and minimization

Sex offenders are well known for their high levels of denial and minimization (Beech and Fisher 2002; Maletzky 1991). Here, denial is used in the broadest sense to include the total denial of having committed a sexual offence through to denying specific aspects of the offence, i.e. admitting one piece of behaviour but not another. Minimization refers to the lessening of the offence in some way, e.g. its frequency, duration or severity.

Although it is acknowledged that level of denial is not a predictor of recidivism (Hanson and Bussière 1998), and reducing the level of denial does not equate with changes in other areas such as attitude towards the offence(s) and victim(s) (Beckett *et al.* 1994), it is nonetheless the first area that needs to be addressed in treatment as it is difficult to work on any offence-related problem if the offender is denying that such an offence(s) even took place (Fisher and Beech 2002).

In addition, although denial is not in itself a criminogenic need, it would seem to be vital when working with sex offenders to work on this, for the following reasons:

- Lessening denial allows the individual to talk openly about himself, and his thoughts, attitudes, feelings and behaviours. This means that he can identify the factors that contributed to his offending and the areas in which he needs further work.

- Admitting his role in the offending enables the individual to take responsibility for his behaviour (having an internal locus of control). He is then in a position to look at the choices and decisions he made and see that he could do things differently in the future. Fisher, Beech and Browne (1998) found that internal locus of control prior to treatment was a predictor of treatment success.

Once the individual has acknowledged that he has committed an offence, he is more receptive to considering the factors that may have contributed to the development of the offence behaviour, so work can then begin on the 'offence-specific' problems.

Offence-specific problems

The next section of the model concerns those factors directly relevant to sexual offending. These include the individual's beliefs and attitudes towards sex, offending behaviour and also their pattern of sexual arousal.

PATTERNS OF DYSFUNCTIONAL THINKING

It has been well documented that sex offenders typically hold beliefs about their offending that allow them to justify and rationalize their behaviour (Abel, Becker and Cunningham-Rathner 1984; Murphy 1990). Work on raising awareness of these thinking errors (cognitive distortions) and enabling individuals to recognize and challenge their own distorted thinking forms an important part of treatment in both probation- and prison-based treatment for sexual offenders in the UK. In probation programmes, this is seen as part of the core work carried out with child abusers. Similarly, in the prison programme, this work is carried out in the initial core programme (Mann 1999) of group treatment.

In CORE 2000 and the probation programmes, cognitive therapy techniques are employed in order to get offenders to identify and challenge their distorted thinking. In the prison service, further work is carried out on patterns of dysfunctional thinking in the EXTENDED Programme (Mann 1999), which in part attempts to identify the underlying causes. It has been suggested that such thinking errors/cognitive distortions arise from a core set of dysfunctional schema held by the offender (Ward *et al.* 1997). Such core schemas may, according to Ward and Keenan (1999), include seeing children as sexual beings and seeing sexual contact between adults and children as not being harmful to children. Using cognitive therapy tech-

niques, these schemas are examined and deconstructed, and group participants practise managing schema-related thinking using such techniques
such as 'disputing' and 'cognitive restructuring', practised in role-play
exercises (Mann and Beech 2002).

LACK OF VICTIM EMPATHY

A major target in cognitive-behavioural programmes for sex offenders, in
terms of changing the level of pro-offending attitudes/dysfunctional thinking, is the development of empathy for the offender's victim(s). Enhancing
victim empathy is seen as a core treatment objective of most sex offender
programmes in both the probation and prison programmes. A number of
studies have described sex offenders' lack of empathy for their own victims
rather than a general empathy deficit (Fernandez *et al.* 1999; Fisher 1998;
Scully 1988). Working on the inculcation of specific victim empathy, it is
suggested by these and other authors, makes it less likely that the offender
will commit further offences as victim empathy should act as a block to
further offending.

In terms of feedback from child abusers who have been through
treatment, these men have reported that the victim empathy component of
the UK prison programme, which includes role-play, has the most profound
effect in really getting them to understand the harm that they have caused
their victims (Beech *et al.* 1999).

DEVIANT SEXUAL AROUSAL

The other area contained within the offence-specific section concerns sexual
arousal and attitudes towards sex. The experience of being sexually aroused
to fantasies of coercive sex or of children is an issue that needs to be
addressed when treating some rapists and preferential child sexual abusers.
It should be noted that not all offenders have primary arousal to deviant
fantasies. Many will have appropriate fantasies and are offending because
appropriate sexual outlets are unavailable to them. This typically occurs
where distorted thinking is employed to justify their behaviour. Sexual
attitudes and beliefs therefore need to be explored in treatment.

Individuals who are aroused only by deviant activity and have no interest in appropriate sexual activity will remain strongly motivated to offend. It may be necessary to refer these individuals for individual work using fantasy modification techniques, despite there being poor evidence for their efficacy (Laws and Marshall 1991). In some instances, it may also be necessary to refer the individual to a psychiatrist for anti-libidinal medication. Here, offenders would still be expected to continue with the programme while on such medication. An extensive use of individual work is used in some prisons with clients defined as having deviant sexual interests through the use of techniques such as masturbatory reconditioning, covert sensitization and ammonia aversion. Ammonia aversion is typically employed to pair the fantasy that arouses an individual with an unpleasant sensation. Here, objective monitoring of deviant arousal may be undertaken using the penile plethsythmograph, a machine that monitors penile arousal to audio and/or visual stimuli related to the deviant sexual interests that the offender is suspected of holding or known to hold. This instrument is not, however, currently employed in the probation service and is in use in only a few prisons in the UK at the present time.

Socio-affective problems

This field of treatment covers a wide range of areas that relate to the efficacy of an individual's social functioning. There is a growing body of evidence highlighting various deficits in child abusers, such as problems in self-esteem, relationship and intimacy deficits, assertiveness difficulties and poor emotional regulation, which can be grouped together under this heading as they refer to how well individuals relate to others and feel about themselves. How child abusers feel about themselves is also related to how well they cope generally in life. The range of factors addressed in the treatment of socio-affective problems includes the following.

SELF-ESTEEM

Sex offenders are generally regarded as having low self-esteem, which, it is believed, may contribute to their offending and hinder progress in therapy. Finkelhor (1984) and Groth (1979) have suggested that low self-esteem and sex offending are related, whereas Marshall *et al.* (1997) have found that the enhancement of self-esteem facilitated the attainment of a number of specific treatment goals and was associated with reductions in deviant arousal. Fisher, Beech and Browne (1999) reported significantly lower levels of self-esteem in child abusers compared with non-offenders.

Because self-esteem appears to be linked with how the individual relates to others and copes with life, it is likely that improvements in these areas will lead to a corresponding increase in self-esteem, and that low self-esteem may conversely increase the likelihood of an offender committing further sexual offences. Mann and Beech (2002) report that the general literature on self-esteem suggests that those who have low self-esteem are more likely to see themselves as not being in control of their lives (external locus of control) and may therefore refuse to take responsibility for their own actions, thus making it less likely that they will exhibit self-regulatory behaviour. Some evidence of the link between self-esteem and offending has been reported by Thornton *et al.* (in press). These authors have found that 'treated men', i.e. those who had been through prison or community sex offender treatment programmes, who were subsequently reconvicted for a further sexual offence(s), had significantly lower levels of self-esteem compared with those who had not been convicted of further sexual offences.

INTIMACY DEFICITS

Marshall (1989) has proposed that deficits in intimacy cause sex offenders to seek sexual satisfaction with either children or non-consenting adults. He further argues (Mulloy and Marshall 1999) that sex offenders identify all types of intimacy with sex and thus think that sexual behaviour of any kind will meet their intimacy needs. Evidence certainly suggests that child sex offenders report higher levels of emotional loneliness/fear of intimacy/isolation than non-offenders (Bumby and Hansen 1997; Fisher *et al.* 1999; Garlick, Marshall and Thornton 1996). This pattern is most pronounced in preferential, fixated offenders who, while reporting a high level of emotional isolation, also report high levels of emotional identification/fixation with children (Fisher *et al.* 1999).

Lack of intimacy can, it could also be argued, lead to an increase in deviant fantasies, which for a number of child abusers (especially the preferential/fixated type) are an important precursor to sexual offending (Swaffer *et al.* 2000). Proulx, McKibben and Lusignan (1996) report evidence of a relationship between emotional loneliness and deviant fantasy in child abusers and rapists. Proulx *et al.'s* findings highlight the importance of working on this area with child sexual abusers, particularly those offenders who perceive that children can meet their emotional needs better than age-appropriate adults.

ATTACHMENT PROBLEMS

Marshall's work on intimacy has highlighted the influence of childhood events on later sexual offending, particularly a history of poor emotional relationships with parents/primary carers. There is evidence that many sex offenders do indeed have a history of poor parental attachment. Smallbone and Dadds (1998), for example, found that a poor relationship with the mother was a predictor of general antisocial behaviour, and poor paternal attachments predicted sexual coercion in adulthood. Awad, Saunders and Levene (1984) reported the parents of adolescent sex offenders as being either rejecting, abusive or emotionally detached. Grossman and Grossman (1990) suggest that insecure parent–child bonding results in a child who is unfriendly, dependent, moody and low in self-esteem, and who has social competency problems. Such attachment difficulties lead to offenders having difficulty forming relationships with age-appropriate adults. Work on attachment difficulties is not specifically undertaken in the current programmes, but the sequelae of such difficulties are addressed in the life skills modules of probation programmes and the EXTENDED Programme. The management of emotions and the improvement in relationship and intimacy skills is addressed in these programmes.

ASSERTIVENESS DIFFICULTIES

Research evidence that child abusers are lacking in assertion skills is somewhat mixed. Although some studies report child abusers to be underassertive (Abel *et al.* 1984; Pithers *et al.* 1987), others have failed to find differences in assertiveness between sex offenders and non-offenders or non-sexual offenders (Overholser and Beck 1986). More recent evidence (Fisher *et al.* 1999) suggests that it is again only fixated/preferential child abusers who are under-assertive, regressed/situational offenders being indistinguishable from non-offenders in terms of reported assertiveness problems. For fixated/preferential offenders, it is therefore important to work on their assertiveness level in life skills work. Basic assertiveness skills are addressed in the life skills modules of the probation programmes and the EXTENDED programme, with sessions on appropriate conflict resolution and expressing feelings, but it is recognized that those offenders with extensive deficits will need to be referred to specific programmes.

MANAGEMENT OF NEGATIVE EMOTIONAL STATES

Many sex offenders do not cope effectively with negative mood states (e.g. anger, boredom, humiliation, resentment, anxiety and depression) and use sexual thoughts and behaviours to cope (Cortoni, Heil and Marshall 1996). Evidence also suggests that such emotional disturbance can be a precursor to deviant fantasy (Proulx *et al.* 1996) and negative mood state (Pithers *et al.* 1987; Ward and Hudson 1998). It is therefore important that treatment includes work on teaching more effective coping strategies to deal with emotional states. The most recent version of the prison EXTENDED Programme, for example, emphasizes the importance of learning to manage negative emotions, particularly through the use of positive and calming cognitions, whereas the TV-SOGP teaches problem-focused coping and positive self-talk.

Although many offenders report negative mood states as the precursors of their offending, it should be noted that this is most likely to apply to those whom Ward and Hudson would describe as having an avoidant pathway to offending. Those with an approach pathway may offend when in a positive emotional state.

PROBLEM-SOLVING DEFICITS

Problem-solving concerns the ability to identify problems effectively, generate possible solutions, choose the most effective solution and put it into practice. Effective problem-solving is beneficial to all aspects of an individual's life, including his ability to relate well to others and deal with the inevitable interpersonal problems that arise in all types of relationship. Problem-solving can therefore be beneficial to sex offenders who have interpersonal difficulties.

Barbaree, Marshall and Connor (1988) examined the problem-solving abilities of sex offenders and reported that although they could identify as many potential solutions to problems as non-offenders, they typically chose an inadequate solution. Barbaree *et al.* report that sex offenders generally have poor general problem-solving skills and have developed inadequate generic coping styles, rather than simply being deficient in specific skills. In addition to poor coping strategies, a disorganized irresponsible lifestyle and poor impulse control have also been found to be a characteristic of some sex offenders, one that is predictive of re-offending (Thornton 2002).

To tackle these problems, Barbaree *et al.* suggest that treatment should include training in problem-solving and the development of a problem-focused coping style. Robinson (1995) also reported that cognitive skills training (which includes problem-solving) had a significant impact on sex offenders, reducing recidivism by 57 per cent in programme-completers. He concluded that, of all offenders, 'sex offenders appeared to derive the greatest benefits from the programme'.

Socio-affective problems therefore appear to be an important element of treatment for many sex offenders as it can be argued that, despite working successfully on denial and offence-specific problems, an individual may remain at risk of offending if he also remains socially inadequate and unable to form appropriate relationships.

Relapse prevention

The last treatment section of the model is labelled relapse prevention. Here, we should note that, in the current provision of treatment for sexual offenders in UK prisons, RP work typically follows work on pro-offending attitudes in the CORE 2000 programme, whereas work on socio-affective problems is addressed (for those who are considered in need of it) in the EXTENDED programme. Within the probation programmes, RP work is the last module of work undertaken in the programme and can be repeated as a booster or maintenance programme as needed.

This area of work concerns getting the offender to identify particular types of precursor (thoughts, moods or situations) to his offending. Once these 'warning signs' have been identified, the aim of therapy is to empower the offender to develop appropriate self-management skills to prevent relapse (Beech and Fisher 2002; Laws 1999; Pithers *et al.* 1983). Offenders thus develop both an awareness of all their risk factors and appropriate strategies to cope safely with these factors.

Programmes in the UK have until recently stressed the importance to offenders of not putting themselves in risky situations, hence emphasizing the use of avoidance techniques at the expense of highlighting the positives of not re-offending. The latest version of the prison CORE 2000 programme, however, highlights to offenders the idea that there are positives about not re-offending and new 'appealing life goals', i.e. 'Old Me/New Me'.

Mediators of treatment effectiveness

This section not so much describes therapy as investigates the characteristics of the offender that have to be taken into consideration because of their influence on treatment efficacy. Here, we describe three factors that could be regarded as mediators of treatment effectiveness: motivation to change, locus of control and level of emotional fixation.

Motivation to change

This is the key factor in the success of treatment. Unless an individual is motivated to use what he has learned in therapy, he will not apply his newly acquired skills and knowledge to changing his lifestyle, and therefore his likelihood of recidivism will not be reduced. It is thus vital that treatment encourages motivation to change.

It is likely that most offenders enter treatment with an ambivalent attitude towards changing their offending behaviour. Many will have enjoyed the offence but not the negative consequences for themselves. Others may be reluctant to change because they have little else in their lives.

Some may be unmotivated because they do not believe that they have the ability to change and may be very fearful of what change will involve. By demonstrating that change is possible, by showing that there are alternatives to offending, and by offenders understanding that an abuse-free life will ultimately be more rewarding than continuing to offend, it is possible to develop a motivation to change in offenders. The delivery style of group facilitators will be a key element in this, and they will need to be supportive, encouraging, praising and respectful. Beech and Fordham (1997) report that an important component of group-based treatment is the instillation of hope in group members, i.e. indicating to abusers that there is the possibility of change to leading an 'offence-free life'. As indicated in Figure 7.1 above, motivation to change will affect all of the areas targeted in treatment (denial, offence-specific problems, socio-affective difficulties and relapse prevention skills).

Locus of control

This concerns the extent to which an individual regards himself as having little influence over his life and therefore regards things that happen as being due to others. Such individuals are not likely to benefit from treatment unless they can be encouraged to take responsibility for their behaviour and become more internally controlled (Fisher *et al.* 1998). This would seem to link strongly to denial in that unless the individual is able to admit the offence behaviour and detail the processes that led to the offence, he is not in a position to take responsibility for his actions.

Offenders can be encouraged to take responsibility and develop a more internal locus of control in a number of ways. Functional analysis of the offence (using decision chains: Ward *et al.* 1995) can be used to identify the thoughts that preceded the behaviour and the decisions made that led to the offence. Distorted thinking that has been used to excuse or blame others can be highlighted and the offender helped to challenge such thinking; relapse prevention provides the offender with a number of strategies he can use to avoid offending in the future. In addition, use of frameworks of offending, such as the Finkelhor Four Stage Model (Finkelhor 1984), can provide a very helpful illustration to many offenders of the process of offending to which they can relate. This helps them to acknowledge that offending did not 'just happen' but was an active process in which they made the decision to act as they did, whether this process was over a long time period or happened very quickly. Locus of control will perhaps also affect all of the areas targeted in treatment, empirical evidence suggesting that locus of control is strongly related to level of denial and a positive treatment outcome in therapy in terms of reductions on measurements of offence-related attitudes (Fisher *et al.* 1998).

Level of fixation

Fixation can mean that a child sexual abuser is primarily focused both sexually and emotionally on children. We have already discussed how treatment to address deviant sexual interest/sexual fixation is attempted. We have also shown that there are some emotionally fixated child sexual abusers who are unable to relate to adults, because they are either fearful of them or have no interest in them, who at the same time perceive that their emotional needs can be met only through relationships with children. Empirical support for this has been reported by Beech and Fisher (2002), who found a significant relationship in highly fixated child abusers between adult intimacy problems and level of emotional fixation with children. Hence, fixation (both sexual and emotional) can, we suggest, act as a significant barrier to treatment. Thus, even though other offence-specific problems (i.e. patterns of dysfunctional thinking/victim empathy deficits) can be addressed and work on socio-affective problems and RP skills can be inculcated, they will be of limited value if this core fixation cannot be successfully addressed. This problem tends to be present in the highest-risk predatory child sexual abusers, and it may be that such individuals are not responsive to the treatment methods currently available.

Issues in working with sexual offenders

In this section, we address some issues of programme design and management that are not solely related to the content or process of sexual offender treatment. Because there has been so little written about some of these areas, there is often little empirical work to draw on. Below, we describe some of the issues involved in working with sexual offenders.

Engaging offenders in treatment

Sexual offenders are in some ways quite different from general psychotherapy clients. Sexual offenders often enter treatment because they are mandated to do so, rather than through free choice. Furthermore, whereas general psychotherapy clients are usually motivated to change because of being distressed by their psychological state, sexual offenders often enjoy their offending and are not motivated to change. In addition, the stigma and vilification experienced by sexual offenders from the rest of society is unparalleled, so that in treatment they may be extremely sensitive to indications of labelling, hostility or lack of empathy on the part of therapists. If treatment providers fail to take these dynamics into account, the value of treatment may be lessened.

Therapist qualities and training

As Beech and Mann (2002) note, little has been written about the qualities that should be looked for in an effective sexual offender therapist. Marshall *et al.*'s (2003) review of therapist characteristics contains a list of desirable qualities such as warmth, empathic ability, emotional expressiveness and confidence. Mann (2001) further lists four essential qualities for an effective therapist, based on experience of training and supervising sex offender treatment providers. These are a positive attitude towards the offenders themselves, a self-evaluating approach, an inquiring mind and a warm interpersonal style.

Even less has been written about how therapists should be trained. In North America, most therapists working with sexual offenders are trained within psychology or social work traditions and undertake general study and training followed by a treatment internship. In the UK, sexual offender therapists tend to be psychologists, probation officers or prison officers. Both the prison and the probation services provide intensive residential training for staff working on specific treatment programmes. This is because training can assist in ensuring that all therapists adhere to the same style and work towards the same goals.

Maintaining the treatment integrity of programme delivery

Treatment integrity is about ensuring that therapists adhere to the goals of the programme and carry out therapy in an appropriate manner. Treatment integrity can be threatened by programme drift and programme non-compliance. Programme drift (Hollin, 1995; Johnson, 1981) is the term for what happens when therapists drift away from the aims of the programme. Programme non-compliance (Hollin, 1995) occurs when the practitioners start changing the programme, omitting some bits and adding new material, as they see fit.

Both prison and community programmes incorporate supervision and monitoring into the programme schedules in order to guard against such programme drift. Supervision also allows therapists to improve in confidence and competence and to resolve uncertainties, resulting in a more sophisticated delivery of the programme. Monitoring involves a supervisor or consultant attending a treatment session or watching a tape of a session. Monitoring typically focuses on adherence to the treatment manual, therapist style and use of therapeutic techniques (modelling, positive reinforcement and cognitive restructuring) (Beech and Mann 2002). As a result of monitoring, feedback can be provided to therapists, recognizing skill levels and, if necessary, suggesting that therapists can improve in some areas.

Policy implication of work with sexual offenders

With regard to the policy implications of work with sex offenders, the key issues focus on the availability of treatment and the suitability of the treatment offered to different types of sex offenders.

The responsivity principle is a big issue in the 'What Works' literature (McGuire 1995). This principle of effective practice states that treatment programmes should be geared to offenders' abilities and learning styles. As previously noted, most current accredited work has been set up to treat male adult sexual offenders in prison and the community. In terms of the treatment of adolescents, the prison programme is carried out in three sites, but there is no accredited provision for adolescents at the present time in the community. Similarly, there is currently no accredited programme for female sexual offenders, although again some work is being carried out with this population at one prison site. The treatment needs of these populations are therefore an important issue.

The responsivity principle also means, arguably, that distinct programmes should be designed for offenders with learning difficulties, offenders from different cultural backgrounds and personality-disordered offenders. At the current time, the Prison Service has a programme geared towards offenders with borderline learning difficulties, but the Probation Service does not. There is a current joint prison and health initiative geared towards developing programmes for those working with personality-disordered offenders. Some work has been carried out looking at the needs of sexual offenders from different ethnic backgrounds (Webster *et al.* in press) but no specific programmes have been set up for such offenders at the time of writing. Research would, however, suggest that men from different ethnic backgrounds do as well as UK white males in terms of treatment change (Webster *et al.* in press).

It is also apparent from this review that the majority of treatment offered is by the prison and probation services. There are, however, many sex offenders who do not come under these jurisdictions, such as those dealt with by social services and the health services. The health services offer some treatment for sex offenders via the forensic services, i.e. Special Hospitals, secure units and forensic community services. Social services frequently have to refer to private practitioners and organizations for assessment and treatment where it is offered. Owing to funding limitations, it is often the case that there will be no opportunity for treatment following assessment.

As noted above, it may be that, at the present time, the highest-risk (predatory) child sexual abusers may not be responsive to the treatment methods currently available. Hence the identification of these individuals is of the highest priority in order that the effective community risk management of such individuals can be put into place. This may involve police surveillance or residence in a supervised setting, although it should be noted there are currently no such facilities available as the only residential treatment facility for child abusers (the Lucy Faithfull Foundation's Wolvercote Unit) has recently closed. It is important for effective risk management that all those involved with the offender have close liaison and good communication as an offender will often be involved with a variety of agencies, each of which may have important information to share. It is also important to have information regarding the progress made in treatment as not all offenders who complete a treatment programme will have responded sufficiently to reduce their risk, and this needs to be known by those charged with supervising the individual.

References

Abel, G.G., Becker, J.V. and Cunningham-Rathner, J. (1984) 'Complications, Consent and Cognitions in Sex Between Children and Adults.' *International Journal of Law and Psychiatry 7*, 89–103.

Abel, G.G., Blanchard, G.T. and Becker, J. (1978) 'An Integrated Treatment Program for Rapists.' In R. Rada (ed) *Clinical Aspects of the Rapist.* New York: Grune & Stratton.

Alexander, M.A. (1999) 'Sexual Offender Treatment Efficacy Revisited.' *Sexual Abuse: A Journal of Research and Treatment 11*, 101–116.

Awad, G., Saunders, E. and Levene, J. (1984) 'A Clinical Study of Male Adolescent Sex Offenders.' *International Journal of Offender Therapy and Comparative Criminology 28*, 105–115.

Barbaree, H.E., Marshall, W.L. and Connor, J. (1988) 'The Social Problem-solving of Child Molesters.' Unpublished manuscript. Queen's University, Kingston, Ontario, Canada.

Beckett, R.C., Beech, A.R., Fisher, D. and Fordham, A.S. (1994) *Community-based Treatment for Sex Offenders: An Evaluation of Seven Treatment Programmes.* London: HMSO.

Beech, A.R. and Fisher, D.D. (2002) 'The Rehabilitation of Child Sex Offenders.' *Australian Psychologist 37*, 206–214.

Beech, A.R. and Fordham, A. (1997) 'Therapeutic Climate of Sexual Offender Treatment Programmes.' *Sexual Abuse: A Journal of Research and Therapy 9*, 219–237.

Beech, A.R. and Mann, R.E. (2002) 'Recent Developments in the Treatment of Sexual Offenders.' In J. McGuire (ed) *Offender Rehabilitation: Effective Programmes and Policies to Reduce Reoffending.* Chichester: Wiley.

Beech, A.R., Fisher, D. and Beckett, R.C. (1999) *STEP 3: An Evaluation of the Prison Sex Offender Treatment Programme.* London: HMSO.

Bumby, K.M. and Hansen, D.J. (1997) 'Intimacy Deficits, Fear of Intimacy and Loneliness Among Sexual Offenders.' *Criminal Justice and Behaviour 24*, 315–331.

Cortoni, F., Heil, P. and Marshall, W.L. (1996) 'Sex as a Coping Mechanism and its Relationship to Loneliness and Intimacy Deficits in Sexual Offending.' Paper presented at the 15th Annual Research and Treatment Conference of the Association for the Treatment of Sexual Offenders, Chicago, October.

Fernandez, Y.M., Marshall, W.L., Lightbody, S. and O' Sullivan, C. (1999) 'The Child Molester Empathy Measure.' *Sexual Abuse: A Journal of Research and Treatment 11,* 17–31.

Finkelhor, D. (1984) *Child Sexual Abuse: New Theory and Research.* London: Macmillan.

Fisher, D. (1998) 'Assessing Victim Empathy.' Unpublished Ph.D. Thesis: University of Birmingham, UK.

Fisher, D.D. and Beech, A.R. (1999) 'Current Practice in Britain with Sexual Offenders.' *Journal of Interpersonal Violence 14,* 233–249.

Fisher, D.D. and Beech (2002) 'Treating the Adult Sex Offender.' In K.D. Browne, H. Hanks, P. Stratton and C. Hamilton (eds) *The Prediction and Prevention of Child Abuse: A Handbook.* Chichester: Wiley.

Fisher, D., Beech, A.R. and Browne, K. (1998) 'Locus of Control and its Relationship to Treatment Change and Abuse History in Child Sexual Abusers.' *Legal and Criminological Psychology 3,* 1–12.

Fisher, D., Beech, A.R. and Browne, K.D. (1999) 'Comparison of Sex Offenders to Non-sex Offenders on Selected Psychological Measures.' *International Journal of Offender Therapy and Comparative Criminology 43,* 473–491.

Friendship, C., Mann, R.E. and Beech, A.R. (2003) 'Evaluation of a National Prison-based Treatment Program for Sexual Offenders in England and Wales.' *Journal of Interpersonal Violence 18,* 744–759.

Garlick, Y., Marshall, W.L. and Thornton, D. (1996) 'Intimacy Deficits and Attribution of Blame Among Sexual Offenders.' *Legal and Criminological Psychology 1,* 251–258.

Grossman, K.E. and Grossman, K. (1990) 'The Wider Concept of Attachment in Cross-cultural Research.' *Human Development 33,* 31–47.

Groth, A.N. (1979). *Men who Rape: The Psychology of the Offender.* New York: Plenum Press.

Hanson, R.K. and Bussière, M.T. (1998) 'Predicting Relapse: A Meta-analysis of Sexual Offender Recidivisim Studies.' *Journal of Consulting and Clinical Psychology 66,* 348–362.

Hanson, R.K., Gordon, A., Harris, A.J.R. *et al.* (2002) 'First Report of the Collaborative Outcome Data Project on the Effectiveness of Psychological Treatment for Sex Offenders.' *Sexual Abuse: A Journal of Research and Treatment 14,* 169–194.

Hare, R.D. (1991) *Manual for the Revised Psychopathy Checklist.* Toronto: Multi-Health Systems.

Her Majesty's Prison Service (2003) *The Treatment and Risk Management of Sexual Offenders in Custody and the Community.*

Hollin, C. (1995) 'The Meaning and Implications of "Programme Integrity".' In J. McGuire (ed) *What Works: Reducing Reoffending.* Chichester: Wiley.

Johnson, V.S. (1981) 'Staff Drift: A Problem in Treatment Integrity.' *Criminal Justice and Behavior 8,* 223–232.

Laws, D.R. (1999) 'Relapse Prevention: The State of the Art.' *Journal of Interpersonal Violence 14,* 285–302.

Laws, D.R. and Marshall, W.L. (1991) 'Masturbatory Reconditioning with Sexual Deviates: An Evaluative Review.' *Advances in Behaviour Research and Therapy 13*, 13–25.

McGuire, J. (1995) *What Works: Reducing Reoffending.* Chichester: Wiley.

Maletzky, B.M. (1991) *Treating the Sexual Offender.* Newbury Park, CA: Sage.

Mann, R.E. (1999) 'The Sex Offender Treatment Programme HM Prison Service England & Wales.' In S. Hofling, D. Drewes and I. Epple-Waigel (eds) *Auftrag Prävention: Offensive gegen sexuellen Kindesmißbrauch.* Munich: Atwerb-Verlag KG.

Mann, R.E. (2001) 'Implementing and Managing Sex Offender Treatment Programmes.' Paper presented at the Conference of the International Association for Forensic Mental Health, Vancouver, BC, Canada, April.

Mann, R. and Beech, A.R. (2002) 'Cognitive Distortions, Schemas and Implicit Theories.' In T. Ward, D.R. Laws and S.M. Hudson (eds) *Theoretical Issues and Controversies in Sexual Deviance.* London: Sage.

Mann, R.E. and Thornton, D. (1998) 'The Evolution of a Multisite Sexual Offender Treatment Program.' In W.L. Marshall, Y.M. Fernanadez, S.M. Hudson and T. Ward (eds) *Sourcebook of Treatment Programs for Sexual Offenders.* New York: Plenum Press.

Marlatt, G.A. and Gordon, J.R. (1985) *Relapse Prevention: Maintenance Strategies in the Treatment of Addictive Behaviours.* New York: Guilford Press.

Marques, J.K. (1982) 'Relapse Prevention: A Self-control Model for the Treatment of Sex offenders.' Paper presented at the 7th Annual Forensic Mental Health Conference, Asilomar, CA, USA, March.

Marshall, W.L. (1989) 'Intimacy, Loneliness and Sexual Offenders.' *Behavior Research and Therapy 27*, 491–503.

Marshall, W.L., Anderson, D. and Fernandez, Y. (1999) *Cognitive-behavioural Treatment of Sexual Offenders.* Chichester: Wiley.

Marshall, W.L., Champagne, F., Sturgeon, C. and Bryce, P. (1997) 'Increasing the Self-esteem of Child Molesters.' *Sexual Abuse: A Journal of Research and Treatment 9*, 321–333.

Marshall, W.L., Fernandez, Y., Serran, G.A., Mulloy, R. and Thornton, D. (2003) 'Process Issues in the Treatment of Sexual Offenders: A review of the relevant literature.' *Aggression and Violent Behaviour 8*, 205–234.

Middleton, D. (2002) *The Treatment and Risk Management of Sexual Offenders in Custody and in the Community.* Published by the National Probation Directorate. London: Home Office, ref. NPD/037/2002. Online: www.probation.homeoffice.gov.uk/files/pdf/The%20Treatment%20and%20Risk%20Management%20of%20Sexual%20Offenders%20in%20Cus.pdf

Mulloy, R. and Marshall, W.L. (1999) 'Social Functioning.' In W.L. Marshall, D. Anderson and Y. Fernandez (eds) *Cognitive-behavioural Treatment of Sexual Offenders.* Chichester: Wiley.

Murphy, W. (1990) 'Assessment and Modification of Cognitive Distortions in Sex Offenders.' In W.L. Marshall, D.R. Laws and H.E. Barbaree (eds) *Handbook of Sexual Assault: Issues, Theories and Treatment of the Offender.* New York: Plenum Press.

Overholser, C. and Beck, S. (1986) 'Multimethod Assessment of Rapists, Child Molesters, and Three Control Groups on Behavioural and Psychological Measures.' *Journal of Consulting and Clinical Psychology 54*, 682–687.

Pithers, W.D., Buell, M.M., Kashima, K.M., Cumming, G.F. and Beal, L.S. (1987) 'Precursors to Relapse of Sexual Offenders.' Paper presented at the 7th Annual Conference of the Association for the Behavioural Treatment of Sexual Abusers, Newport, OR, USA, October.

Pithers, W.D., Marques, J.K., Gibat, C.C. and Marlatt, G.A. (1983) 'Relapse Prevention: A Self-control Model of Treatment and Maintenance of Change for Sexual Aggressives.' In J. Greer and I.R. Stuart (eds) *The Sexual Aggressor: Current Perspective on Treatment.* New York: Van Nostrand Reinhold.

Proulx, J., McKibben, A. and Lusignan, R. (1996) 'Relationship Between Affective Components and Sexual Behaviours in Sexual Aggressors.' *Sexual Abuse: A Journal of Research and Treatment 8*, 279–289.

Robinson, D. (1995) *The Impact of Cognitive Skills Training on Post-release Recidivism Among Canadian Federal Offenders.* Ottawa, Ontario, Canada: Correctional Service of Canada, Research Division.

Scully, D. (1988) 'Convicted Rapists' Perceptions of Self and Victim: Role Taking and Emotions.' *Gender and Society 2*, 200–213.

Smallbone, S.W. and Dadds, M.R. (1998) 'Childhood Attachment and Adult Attachment in Incarcerated Adult Male Sex Offenders.' *Journal of Interpersonal Violence 13*, 555–573.

Swaffer, T., Hollin, C., Beech, A., Beckett, R.C. and Fisher, D. (2000) 'An Exploration of Child Sexual Abusers' Sexual Fantasies Before and After Treatment.' *Sexual Abuse: A Journal of Research and Treatment 12*, 61–68.

Thornton, D. (2002) 'Constructing and Testing a Framework for Dynamic Risk Assessment.' *Sexual Abuse: A Journal of Research and Treatment 14*, 137–151.

Thornton, D. Beech, A. and Marshall, W.L. (in press). 'Pre-treatment Self-esteem and Post-treatment Sexual Recidivism.' *International Journal of Offender Therapy and Comparative Criminology.*

Ward, T. and Hudson, S.M. (1998) 'A Model of the Relapse Process in Sexual Offenders.' *Journal of Interpersonal Violence 13*, 700–725.

Ward, T., Hudson, S.M., Johnston, L. and Marshall, W.L. (1997) 'Cognitive Distortions in Sex Offenders: An Integrative Review.' *Clinical Psychology Review 17*, 479–507.

Ward, T. and Keenan, T. (1999) 'Child Molesters' Implicit Theories.' *Journal of Interpersonal Violence 14*, 8, 821–838.

Ward, T., Louden, K., Hudson, S. and Marshall, W.L. (1995) 'A Descriptive Model of the Offence Chain in Child Molesters.' *Journal of Interpersonal Violence 10*, 453–473.

Webster, S.D., Aktar, S., Bowers, L., Mann, R.E. and Marshall, W.L. (in press) 'The Impact of the Prison Service Sex Offender Treatment Programme on Minority Ethnic Offenders: A Preliminary Study.' *Crime, Psychology and Law.*

CHAPTER 8

Managing Children and Young People who are Sexually Aggressive

Andrew Kendrick

Introduction

There has been a recent government focus on policy and legislation to combat sexual offending and the abuse of children. The issue of children and young people who are sexually aggressive has also been attracting increasing attention, both in the professional arena and in the broader public consciousness. However, research knowledge and the development of services for young people who are sexually aggressive lag behind those for adult sex abusers. Although we know that a significant proportion of sexual abuse is perpetrated by children and adolescents, there are still significant gaps in our knowledge. The development of services for children and young people who are sexually aggressive is also very patchy, and although there has been significant progress in the range of services available, this has tended to be local developments, and there has been a lack of a strategic overview.

It is vital to address the development of services for children and young people who are sexually aggressive because the evidence shows that many adult sex offenders begin their sexually abusive behaviour in adolescence (Abel, Mittelman and Becker 1985; Ryan 1997a). It is also argued that the identification of sexually aggressive behaviour, and intervention at an early stage, is important as children and young people are more tractable and their behaviour is easier to change (Expert Panel on Sex Offending 2001; O'Callaghan and Print 1994). Work with children and young people who are sexually aggressive needs to be set squarely in the context of child protection and the prevention of further abusive behaviour.

In this chapter, I will look at the current situation in the UK with regard to research knowledge and the development of policy and practice for this group of children and young people. I will draw on official statistics and research that shed some light on the scale of this problem and will identify current central Government policy initiatives focusing on children and young people who are sexually aggressive. The developments in practice across a range of settings and contexts will be described and the evidence on the effectiveness of interventions discussed.

A range of terms has been used in the research and practice literature for this group of children and young people (e.g. sexually abusive young people, adolescent sexual abusers, adolescent sex offenders, juvenile sexual offenders, children and young people who sexually abuse others). The Cosgrove report (Expert Panel on Sex Offending 2001) identified the confusion created by the use of different terms in different agencies and recommended that the term 'sexually aggressive young people' should be used. I have therefore used this term, except when discussing other people's work, when I have used the term the authors themselves have used.

Problems of definition also surround what is normal sexual development and what is inappropriate sexual behaviour at different stages of development (Masson 1995; Vizard, Monck and Misch 1995). There has been a long-standing assumption about the way in which sexually aggressive behaviour develops into adulthood. Indeed, the National Children's Home Report stated that:

> the young abuser is likely to grow into a pattern of sex offending rather than out of it, and there is a need for early intervention to prevent long-term addictive, abusive behaviour patterns developing. (1992, p.v)

This is being increasingly questioned, however, and evidence suggests that most sexually aggressive children and young people will not go on to offend in adulthood, particularly if they receive appropriate supervision and specialist provision (Association for the Treatment of Sexual Abusers 2000; Beckett 1999).

The scale of the problem

There appears to be a growing consensus that between roughly a quarter and a third of sexual abuse is perpetrated by children and adolescents (Expert Panel on Sex Offending 2001; Grubin 1998; Masson and Erooga 1999; Masson and Morrison 1999; Monck and New 1996; National Children's Home 1992; Ryan 1997a; see also Masson, this volume).

The situation from crime figures in Scotland is less clear than in England and Wales because sexual offences by children and young people can be dealt with by the Children's Hearings system or the court system. Children up to the age of 16 years will be dealt with by the Children's Hearings system, except in the case of serious offences, such as sexual offences, which may be dealt with by the court system. Between the ages of 16 and 18, young people will be dealt with by the court system unless they are already subject to a supervision requirement from the Children's Hearing system, in which case they may be referred back to a Children's Hearing (Kendrick and Mair 2002; Murray and Hallett 2000). In the year 2001, there were 5987 crimes of indecency recorded by the police in Scotland, but these figures are not broken down by age. Prison statistics show that 20 of the 243 (8.2%) direct sentenced receptions to penal establishments in 2001 for crimes of indecency involved young offenders (i.e. young men aged 16–20 years old) (Scottish Executive 2002a). Although published statistics for referrals to the Children's Hearings system do not give a breakdown of the type of offence, the report *A Commitment to Protect* stated that 'the Children's Hearing System dealt with nearly three hundred referrals related to allegations of sexual offences committed by children. These offences included indecent assault, lewd and libidinous practices, incest and rape' (Social Work Services Inspectorate 1997, p.43). This compares with some 25,000 referrals on offence grounds per year. In addition, 750 young people aged under 18 years were convicted of offences of indecency in the ten-year period to 1995 (SWSI 1997).

A small number of studies in the UK provides some evidence of the extent of sexually aggressive behaviour by children and young people. James and Neil (1996) surveyed GP practices, paediatricians, child psychiatrists, residential and field social workers, probation officers and police Family Protection Units in Oxfordshire in order to identify the prevalence of juvenile sexual offending over a 12-month period. Thirty-four sexually abusive youths were identified, giving a prevalence rate of 1.5 per 1000 males aged between 12 and 17 years.

It is, however, important to remember that crime statistics and studies of child sexual abuse as reported to official agencies can only show the extent of reported offences, much sexual aggression by children and young people not being recognized as such, not being dealt with as abusive or criminal behaviour, and not being reported to the police or other agencies (Masson and Morrison 1999; Ryan 1997a; Ryan *et al* 1987; Vizard *et al.* 1995).

Developments in policy: Towards a national strategy

There have been important recent developments in relation to the policy for children and young people who are sexually aggressive, linked to broader policy debates about services and legislation for adult sex offenders. *A Commitment to Protect* concluded that 'young people's sexual offending must be more effectively addressed at an early stage if their progression to more serious offending in adulthood is to be prevented' (SWSI 1997, p.49) and called for the establishment of an 'Expert Panel on Sex Offending' to assist strategic collaboration and provide a national oversight of all work with sex offenders in Scotland.

The SWSI also carried out an inspection of the management of sex offender cases in the community in eight local authorities in Scotland (SWSI 2000). This included 46 cases of children and young people who had committed sexual offences or displayed sexually aggressive behaviour and who might have presented a risk to children or other vulnerable members of the community. This inspection found that the supervision and management of the cases of children and young people who were sexually aggressive had yet to reach the general standard of adult cases. Although some authorities were beginning to establish a local agenda for action, poor information about the extent of sexually aggressive behaviour by children hindered effective work with this group. In some authorities, there was a lack of cross-over of knowledge from criminal justice social work to children's services, which would have benefited from skills, knowledge and expertise in managing sexually aggressive behaviour. Fisher and Beech also contrast recent developments for adolescents with those for adults: 'the availability of assessment and treatment is...largely dependent on local developments, and these do not constitute a coherent service that requires a framework of resources and policies' (1999, p.247).

Most of the Scottish authorities inspected (six out of eight) had no local strategy or guidelines for staff in children's services working with sexually aggressive young people. Although cases were identified that were well managed and demonstrated a high standard of social work practice, none of the authorities was able consistently to demonstrate a satisfactory management of risk from sexual aggression by young people (SWSI 2000). Masson (1995) found that although there was an increase in the development of policy and procedures in Area Child Protection Committee (ACPC) areas in England and Wales in the early 1990s, this involved fewer than one-fifth of ACPCs, and there were significant regional differences.

Following the recommendation of *A Commitment to Protect* (SWSI 1997), the Expert Panel on Sex Offending, chaired by Lady Cosgrove, was established in 1998 with the aim of developing a cohesive framework for dealing with sex offending in Scotland (Expert Panel on Sex Offending 2001). It developed a strategic approach that focused on four themes for protecting children and young people:

1.   developing personal safety programmes to protect children and young people from all forms of abuse

2.   the early identification of and intervention with young people demonstrating sexually aggressive behaviour through the promotion of safe and healthy relationships

3.   reviewing existing legislation and measures that protect children and young people from sex offenders outside the home

4.   developing proposals to involve local people positively in community safety.

The Cosgrove report, building on previous work, highlighted the different and distinct needs of children and young people who are sexually aggressive and observed that although they may be more amenable than adult offenders to learning new attitudes, behaviours and skills, personal change programmes need to be consistent with their stage of development (Expert Panel on Sex Offending 2001; see also O'Callaghan and Print 1994). The report confirmed that whereas some good collaborative and flexible practice in the assessment and treatment of children and young people was taking place, it tended to be on an ad hoc basis, and there was little skilled specialist provision for children and young people who are sexually aggressive.

The Expert Panel called for the Scottish Executive to review current provision in relation to assessment and intervention programmes and provision for children and young people who have committed a sexual offence or who are displaying sexually aggressive behaviour. It also recommended that the Scottish Executive should develop a national strategy for a specialist assessment and intervention service for children and young people who offend or display sexually aggressive behaviour. This service should include access to a robust and comprehensive risk and needs assessment, and to offence-specific personal change programmes to be available both in the community and in secure and non-secure residential settings. Finally, all children and young people identified as being at risk of sexual offending or who are displaying sexually aggressive behaviour should have access to an appropriate personal change programme (Expert Panel on Sex Offending 2001).

The Scottish Executive has accepted these recommendations, and the Education Department and the SWSI will be responsible for developing this part of the strategy on sex offending in Scotland (Scottish Executive 2002b).

Characteristics of children and young people who are sexually aggressive

Although a number of factors have been associated with sexually aggressive behaviour, children and young people who are sexually aggressive are a heterogeneous group (Lovell 2002; see also Masson, this volume). While assumptions have been made about the causal factors leading to sexual aggression, e.g. the link between being a victim of sexual abuse and becoming sexually aggressive, we shall see that the situation is much more complex and multilayered than this.

Females who are sexually aggressive

Most children and young people who are sexually aggressive are male. In the UK, however, the issue of women who sexually abuse children has only recently come to the fore as an important area of work (Saradjian and Hanks 1996; see also Kemshall, this volume). As with sexually aggressive males, early identification and intervention are important. Saradjian and Hanks' study of 50 women who had sexually abused children found that, by adolescence, all but three 'had already been engaged in sexual behaviours inappropriate to their age and developmental stage' (1996, p.66). Blues, Moffat and Telford (1999) concluded that, in relation to factors contributing to abusing behaviour and treatment, there are more similarities than differences between boys and girls who sexually abuse: 'The biggest difference would seem to be in how both society and professionals view and respond to them' (Blues *et al.* 1999, p.182; see also Lane, with Lobanov-Rostovsky 1997).

Social isolation and social skills deficits

Research has identified that sexually aggressive children and young people are socially isolated, with deficits in social skills, problems with anger management and high level of social anxiety (Epps 1999a; Masson and Erooga 1999; O'Callaghan and Print 1994), although Vizard *et al.* caution that 'this is yet another area in which sweeping statements have crept into the literature...but for which the empirical evidence is poor or difficult to interpret' (1995, p.737). O'Callaghan and Print found:

> adolescent sexual abusers exhibiting relatively high degrees of withdrawal and social anxiety compared to those involved in non-sex offences. Approximately twice as many sexual abusers as non-sex offenders reported that they had been bullied in school and many felt that they had few friends or social contacts. (1994, p.153)

Education and learning disability

Research has shown that children and young people who are sexually aggressive often exhibit problem behaviour in education (truancy, exclusion and the need for special educational resources) or have learning difficulties or disability (Dolan *et al.* 1996; Masson and Erooga 1999; O'Callaghan 1998; Vizard *et al.* 1995). O'Callaghan and Print, however, in a comparison of the characteristics of 50 adolescent male sex offenders with those of 28 adolescents convicted for non-sexual offences, found that 'whilst half the sexual abusers perceived themselves as having learning difficulties, as compared to 19 per cent of non-sex offenders, their general intelligence level was very similar to the non-sex offender group' (1994, p.153; see also Lightfoot and Evans 2000).

Experience of trauma and victimization

Way states that 'many questions remain about the relationship between prior victimisation histories and sexually assaultive behaviour' (2002, p.26). Although adolescent sexual offenders report a higher prevalence of child-hood sexual abuse victimization than males in the general population, studies have reported widely different rates of victimization (4–75 per cent) (Way 2002). Comparisons between sexually aggressive young people and non-sexual offenders have sometimes, and sometimes not, found a high proportion of sexual abuse victimization among the sexually aggressive group (O'Callaghan and Print 1994). In recent UK research, however, Salter *et al.* (2003) conducted a longitudinal study of 224 male victims of sexual abuse and identified 26 who had subsequently become sexual abusers. They concluded that their results:

> show that the risk of childhood victims of sexual abuse becoming abusers themselves is lower than previously thought, despite the fact that cases referred to the specialist clinic were almost certainly more severe and complex than community cases. (Salter *et al.* 2003, p.474)

Studies of the experience of trauma and victimization have tended to focus on sexual abuse. Some studies, however, indicate that sexually aggressive young people have higher rates of physical abuse and neglect than non-sexual offenders (Way 2002; see also Becker 1998; Vizard *et al.* 1995). As Way has observed (see also Becker 1998; Mulholland and McIntee 1999):

> A strict correspondence of childhood sexual abuse and later sexual offending behaviour has been widely disputed and summarily discarded...Yet, when we

expand the definition of childhood maltreatment beyond sexual abuse, re-searchers and practitioners report that these adolescents recount high rates of childhood maltreatment beyond sexual abuse...Physical abuse, neglect and family violence. (2002, p.49)

Family dysfunction

Ryan writes that some of the 'common characteristics of the families of sexually abusive youths are emotional impoverishment, lack of appropriate affect, dangerous secrets, distorted attachments, and a history of disruptions in care and function' (1997b, p.139). Vizard *et al.* (1995), however, stress that the data on family dysfunction are difficult to interpret. Skuse *et al.* (1998) studied 25 adolescent boys who had been sexually abused, 11 of whom had sexually abused other children. Three factors were associated with an increased risk of being in the sexually abusive group: experiencing intrafamilial violence, witnessing intrafamilial violence and discontinuity of care: 'at this stage...it may be more appropriate to view a climate of violence as conferring an increased risk, whether or not the boy is a direct victim of the physical abuse' (Skuse *et al.* 1998, p.178; see also Bentovim 2002). Salter *et al.* also concluded that their results:

> reinforce the importance of intrafamilial violence as a potential mediator between being a victim and perpetrator of sexual abuse...Parallels between our findings and others include the relevance of parental emotional rejection, the effect of experiencing and witnessing physical violence, and lack of material care, or neglect. (2003, p.474)

The range of provision for sexually aggressive children and young people

We have seen that, compared with services for adult abusers, services for sexually aggressive children and young people are less well developed. Against this, it has been strongly argued that there is a need for a 'continuum of care' and provision for this group (Bengis 1997; National Children's Home 1992). Morrison states that 'in an environment where pressures on resources intensify daily, the requirement is to go beyond promoting the need to work with abusers, to finding reliable ways of determining the low,

medium and high risks groups and what level of intervention is required'
(2001, p.32). He argues for a four-tier continuum of services:

> *level 1* – educational and supportive service to family where there has been
> early presentation of sexually problematic behaviour in the context of a rea-
> sonably positive functioning family
>
> *level 2* – psycho-educational group to strengthen parental skills and commit-
> ment where there have been further sexual behaviour problems
>
> *level 3* – community-based treatment programme for young person and
> parents
>
> *level 4* – specialist community/residential programmes for the most complex
> and high-risk group where there are multiple problems and serious abusive
> behaviours.
>
> (Morrison 2001, pp.34–35).

Worling and Curwen suggest that there is a good deal of consensus
regarding the specialized treatment of sexually aggressive children and
young people. Treatment goals include:

> increasing offender accountability; assisting offenders to understand and in-
> terrupt the thoughts, feelings, and behaviors that maintain sexual offending;
> reducing deviant sexual arousal, if present; developing healthy attitudes
> towards sex and relationships; and reducing the offenders' personal trauma, if
> present.
>
> (2000, p.966).

Cognitive-behavioural interventions focus on changing patterns of deviant
arousal, correcting distorted thinking and increasing social competence
(Beckett 1994; Ryan and Lane 1997), whereas relapse prevention work
identifies diversionary strategies and coping skills to stop the reoccurrence
of sexually aggressive behaviour (O'Callaghan and Print 1994; Pithers *et al.*
1988; Richardson and Graham 1997).

Longo, however, is concerned that 'there is no literature that defines the
"best practice" in treating children with sexual behaviour problems' (2002,
p.218). He argues that the influence of work with adult sex abusers has led
to: the misuse of technology; not taking into account the developmental

stage of children and young people; using inappropriate language and materials; and the inappropriate use of highly confrontational approaches. There is an increasing demand that a more holistic approach be taken with children and young people, rather than there being an exclusive focus on their sexually aggressive behaviour:

> Holistic treatment means treating the whole person not just a particular problem...When we see the whole person as a person with many facets, many of which are damaged parts, then we are better able to understand the nature of what we must treat and the complexities of doing so.
>
> (Longo 2002, p.229; see also Morrison 2001)

Farmer and Pollock have argued that 'the context in which therapeutic help was offered seemed to be of considerable importance' (1998, p.182).

Assessment and decision-making

Assessment is crucial to the process of decision-making regarding risk, monitoring and the provision of services. *Managing the Risk* (SWSI 2000), however, found that even where assessments had taken place, local authorities rarely used these to inform plans to reduce risk. Fewer than half the cases that included an assessment of the risk of further sexual aggression recorded clear arrangements for the young person's supervision in circumstances of risk. Epps (1999b) stresses that the protection of other children is central to the assessment of risk. Will (1999) describes three main purposes of assessment: assessing risk, developing a formulation on which an initial treatment plan can be based, and assessing the young person's motivation to accept treatment designed to reduce the likelihood of repeating the sexually abusive behaviour. He outlines three stages to the assessment process. Stage One is a general overall assessment of the young person and his family or carers, which involves obtaining a developmental history of the young person and a family history and assessment. Stage Two is a detailed assessment of the young person's abusive behaviour, including its antecedents and consequences. Will suggests that important information to be gained includes: establishing a common language for sexual organs and functions; sources of the young person's sexual knowledge, sexual experience and behaviour; and any history of sexually abusive behaviour. The final stage of the assessment process is developing a formulation for intervention and risk management (Will 1999; see also Calder, Hanks and Epps 1997; Graham, Richardson and Bhate 1997; Vizard 2002).

Community-based services

Community-based programmes for sex offenders are a recent development. The SWSI in Scotland carried out a survey of specialist services for sex offenders in the community. Fifteen local authorities provided information on 20 programmes, and the first programmes were established in 1991. All but one of the programmes indicated that they would work with young people aged 16–18 years, but 12 stated that they would not accept children and young people under 16 years of age. Only a small number specialized in work with children and young people who were sexually aggressive (SWSI 1997). An increasing number of community-based services are being described in the literature. One of the first in the UK describes itself as having developed:

> an eclectic methodology based largely on humanistic, client-centre and cognitive restructuring therapies...In addition to group therapy, most programme participants will be involved in individual therapy sessions and in many cases families and/or carers will be involved in therapeutic work.
>
> (O'Callaghan and Print 1994, p.157).

Although other projects may have developed a slightly different focus, there is much similarity in approach (Baker 2002; Buist and Fuller 1997; Leheup and Myers 1999; Monck and New 1996).

Foster and residential care

There is a number of serious issues concerning work with sexually aggressive children and young people in residential and foster care. There has been a great deal of concern about the danger of children and young people being abused by other young people in these settings (Brogi and Bagley 1998; Green and Masson 2002; Kendrick 1997; Lindsay 1999a, 1999b). We have seen that sexually aggressive children and young people have frequently experienced discontinuity of care, which can involve placement in residential care, foster care or special education settings. Some children and young people will be living in these settings before their sexually aggressive behaviour is known and will abuse other children and young people in these locations (Kendrick and Mair 2002; SWSI 2000).

In addition, children and young people will frequently be placed in residential or foster care following the discovery of their sexually aggressive behaviour. There is, however, a shortage of appropriate resources and placements for this group of children and young people. Bankes, Daniels and Quartly (1999) report instances of young people's sexually aggressive behaviour being minimized or ignored in order to achieve placement. Children and young people who are sexually aggressive may be placed with children who have been victims of abuse and are vulnerable to further exploitation. In *Managing the Risk* (SWSI 2000), 24 of the 46 young people were looked after away from home, most in residential settings. It is essential that if a young person is known to have a history of sexual aggression, decisions about placement must be based on careful assessment of the risks, agreed protection plans and appropriate levels of supervision (Epps 1999b; SWSI 2000). Such placements have important implications for placement policies, staffing level and the training and supervision of staff. There are also significant issues in relation to building design and structure, peer group characteristics, behaviour management and control, communication and decision-making, and confidentiality (Centre for Residential Child Care 1995; Epps 1997a, 1997b; Skinner 1992).

Farmer and Pollock (1998), in their study of sexually abused and abusing children in substitute care, found that little work focused on the abusing behaviour. It is only relatively recently that a range of specialist foster and residential provision for sexually aggressive children and young people has been developed (Bankes *et al.* 1999; Clarke 2002; Epps 1997a; Kendrick and Mair 2002). Epps states that one of the 'advantages of working in a residential context is that it allows for greater control over the environmental and situational variables that contribute to sexually abusive behaviour' (1997a, p.45). The issue of through-care and integration back into the community is, however, also a particular problem with sexually aggressive adolescents placed away from home (Greer 1997; Hird 1997).

Group work

Group work has emerged as a central method of working with sexually aggressive young people (Print and O'Callaghan 1999). As O'Callahan and Print observe:

> Groupwork provides the adolescent with a safe environment in which to explore his sexual behaviour, thoughts and feelings. Social skills and im-proved self-esteem are often developed through group empathy, support and role-modelling, and peer pressure is very effective in breaking down denial and minimisation. (1994, p.165)

Baker also sees the advantages of group work with teenagers but cautions against group work with pre-pubertal children as this 'exposes them to the risk of contamination with information about a range of novel sexual acts that may arouse their interest and increase their risk' (2002, p.334). O'Boyle, Lenehan and McGarvey (1999) describe a six-step programme that addresses: developing group identity, trust and calm; developing individual commitment to the group process; developing intellectual and emotional understanding of the impact of abuse; enabling young people to talk through their offence cycles; developing young people's knowledge of sex and sexuality; raising awareness of young people's own sexual desires and risk situations; and developing skills to manage such risks (see also Thomason 2000).

Family work

Working with the families of children and young people who are sexually aggressive is also crucial (Burnham *et al.* 1999). Morrison (2001) considers that engagement with families continues to be too low a priority but must be an integral part of any developmentally based programme. O'Callaghan and Print also stress that for a weekly treatment programme to be effective:

> it is essential that the work is supported and maintained by others in the young person's day-to-day network. Parents and carers must play a crucial role in this task, and their inclusion and involvement in the programme is therefore important. (1994, p.176)

Hackett (2001) usefully provides a guide for the parents of young people who have sexually abused that, as well as addressing the many questions parents will ask of themselves, looks at this aspect of the work from the parents' perspective.

Relapse prevention

> The overall goals of RP [relapse prevention] are to increase the clients' awareness and range of choices concerning their behavior, to develop specific coping skills and self-control capacities, and to develop a general sense of mastery or control over their lives. (Pithers *et al.* 1988, p.146)

Relapse prevention approaches have become central to the work of programmes with sexually aggressive young people. They require that the young person accepts responsibility for his action, is able to recognize and monitor the thoughts, emotions and behaviour that lead up to a sexually aggressive act, is able to recognize high-risk situations, and is able to use learned coping skills and strategies effectively (Pithers *et al.* 1988; Richardson and Graham 1997; Ryan and Lane 1997).

The aim of relapse prevention is that the young person can transfer the knowledge and skills learned through treatment into the community setting. Pithers *et al.* (1988) and Maletzky (1991) stress that learned coping skills need to be 'overlearned' so that they become automatic. O'Boyle *et al.* (1999) give the example of a young man in residential care identifying a potential risk situation when he was visiting home and out seeing friends. He escaped from the situation by going home and telling his mother and then returning to the children's home and explaining his early return, and he was able to explain the risks of the situation (see also Ennis, Williams and Kendrick 1995).

Relapse prevention also stresses the importance of external supervision and monitoring involving both the professional network and the young person's family (Thomas 1997), as well as the need for the more general development of interpersonal skills, anger and stress management skills, and problem-solving skills (Pithers *et al.* 1988).

Research on effectiveness

A major issue in relation to the development of interventions with children and young people who sexually abuse others concerns their long term effectiveness. Although there is a rapidly expanding literature on the effectiveness of programmes working with adult offenders, the literature on interventions with children and young people is much less well developed. Vizard *et al.* (1995), reviewing the literature, noted 'the small amount of information on post-treatment outcome' (p.749) and urged for the establishment of long-term prospective studies.

One of the most rigorous recent evaluative studies was carried out by Worling and colleagues in Canada (Worling and Curwen 2000). This study examined the success of specialized adolescent sexual offender treatment by comparing recidivism rates between treated offenders and a comparison group. The Sexual Abuse, Family Education and Treatment (SWFE-T) programme is a specialized, community-based programme that provides sexual-abuse specific assessment, treatment, consultation and long-term support to the child victims of incest and their families, children with sexual behaviour problems and their families, and adolescent sexual offenders and their families.

Recidivism data were collected for all 148 adolescent sexual offenders assessed in the programme between 1987 and 1995. Of these, 58 adolescents were included in the treatment group, these including young people who had completed the programme or dropped out following at least one year of treatment. The comparison group of 90 adolescents included those who had been assessed by the programme but were receiving treatment elsewhere, had refused treatment or had dropped out of the programme before a year of treatment. The mean follow-up period was over six years from initial contact, and recidivism data were based on criminal charges. Worling and Curwen reported that 'significant differences were found between the Treatment and Comparison groups with respect to all categories of reoffending' (2000, p.971). The sexual assault recidivism rate for the treatment group was 5 per cent, and that of the comparison group was 18 per cent. The authors conclude that the results:

support the efficacy of specialized community-based treatment at the SAFE-T Program for reducing the risk of adolescent sexual recidivism…participation in specialized treatment was [also] associated with a 41% reduction in violent nonsexual recidivism and a 59% reduction in non-violent reoffending. (Worling and Curwen 2000, p.976)

Conclusion

The development of work with children and young people who are sexually aggressive has been gathering pace over recent years but is still far from ideal. Specialist services for this group continue to be patchy, and knowledge in mainstream services is underdeveloped. Given that the central outcome of successful work with sexually aggressive children and young people is child protection, it is crucial that the framework for a national strategy is taken forward with some urgency. Working with children and young people who are sexually aggressive is stressful and personally demanding. It is important that workers are supported through supervision, training and development. The picture of a child or young person who is sexually aggressive moving inexorably towards more serious sexual offences in adulthood seems to have faded and blurred. Focused work with this group of young people can help in breaking the cycle of their sexually aggressive behaviour, supporting them towards a positive future and protecting other children.

References

Abel, G.G., Mittelman, M.S. and Becker, J.B. (1985) 'Sex Offenders: Results of Assessment and Recommendations for Treatment.' In H. Ben-Aaron, S. Hacker and C. Webster (eds) *Clinical Criminology: Current Concepts.* Toronto: M&M Graphics.

Association for the Treatment of Sexual Abusers (2000) *The Effective Legal Management of Juvenile Sexual Offenders.* On line: www.atsa.com/ppjuvenile.html

Baker, T. (2002) 'The Community Management of Young People Who Sexually Abuse.' In M.C. Calder (ed) *Young People who Sexually Abuse: Building the Evidence Base for your Practice.* Lyme Regis: Russell House Publishing.

Bankes, N., Daniels, K. and Quartly, C. (1999) 'Placement Provision and Placement Decisions: Resources and Processes.' In M. Erooga and H. Masson (eds) *Children and Young People who Sexually Abuse Others: Challenges and Responses.* London: Routledge.

Becker, J. (1998) 'What We Know About the Characteristics and Treatment of Adolescents who Have Committed Sexual Offenses.' *Child Maltreatment 3,* 317–329.

Beckett, R. (1994) 'Cognitive-behavioural Treatment of Sex Offenders.' In T. Morrison, M. Erooga and R. Beckett (eds) *Sexual Offending Against Children: Assessment and Treatment of Male Abusers.* London: Routledge.

Beckett, R. (1999) 'Evaluation of Adolescent Sexual Abusers.' In M. Erooga and H. Masson (eds) *Children and Young People who Sexually Abuse Others.* London: Routledge.

Bengis, S. (1997) 'Comprehensive Service Delivery with a Continuum of Care.' In G. Ryan and S. Lane (eds) *Juvenile Sexual Offending: Causes, Consequences, and Correction.* San Francisco: Jossey-Bass.

Bentovim, A. (2002) 'Research on the Development of Sexually Abusive Behaviour in Sexually Abused Males: The Implications for Clinical Practice.' In M.C. Calder (ed) *Young People who Sexually Abuse: Building the Evidence Base for your Practice.* Lyme Regis: Russell House Publishing.

Blues, A., Moffat, C. and Telford, P. (1999) 'Work with Adolescent Females who Sexually Abuse: Similarities and Differences.' In M. Erooga and H. Masson (eds) *Children and Young People who Sexually Abuse Others: Challenges and Responses.* London: Routledge.

Brogi, L. and Bagley, C. (1998) 'Abusing Victims: Detention of Child Sexual Abuse Victims in Secure Accommodation.' *Child Abuse Review 7*, 315–329.

Buist, M. and Fuller, R. (1997) *A Chance to Change: An Intervention with Young People who Have Sexually Abused Others.* Edinburgh: Stationery Office.

Burnham, J., Moss, J., Debelle, J. and Jamieson, R. (1999) 'Working with Families of Young Sexual Abusers: Assessment and Intervention Issues.' In M. Erooga and H. Masson (eds) *Children and Young People who Sexually Abuse Others: Challenges and Responses.* London: Routledge.

Calder, M.C., Hanks, H. and Epps, K.J. (1997) *Juveniles and Children who Sexually Abuse: A Guide to Risk Assessment.* Lyme Regis: Russell House Publishing.

Centre for Residential Child Care (1995) *Guidance for Residential Workers Caring for Young People who Have Been Sexually Abused and Those who Abuse Others.* Glasgow: Centre for Residential Child Care.

Clarke, P. (2002) 'Therapeutic Communities: A Model for Effective Intervention with Teenagers Known to have Perpetrated Sexual Abuse.' In M.C. Calder (ed) *Young People who Sexually Abuse: Building the Evidence Base for your Practice.* Lyme Regis: Russell House Publishing.

Dolan, M., Holloway, J., Bailey, S. and Kroll, L. (1996) 'The Psychosocial Characteristics of Juvenile Sexual Offenders Referred to an Adolescent Forensic Service in the UK.' *Medicine, Science and the Law 36*, 4, 343–352.

Ennis, J., Williams, B., and Kendrick, A. (1995) 'Working with Perpetrators of Child Sexual Abuse: Issues for Social Work Practice.' *Child Care in Practice 2*, 1, 60–70.

Epps, K. (1997a) 'Managing Risk.' In M. Hoghughi, S. Bhate and F. Graham (eds) *Working with Sexually Abusive Adolescents.* London: Sage.

Epps, K.J. (1997b) 'Pointers for Carers.' In M. Calder, with H. Hanks and K. Epps *Juveniles and Children who Sexually Abuse: A Guide to Risk Assessment.* Lyme Regis: Russell House Publishing.

Epps, K.J. (1999a) 'Causal Explanations: Filling the Theoretical Reservoir.' In M.C. Calder (ed) *Working with Young People who Sexually Abuse: New Pieces of the Jigsaw Puzzle.* Lyme Regis: Russell House Publishing.

Epps, K.J. (1999b) 'Looking After Young Sexual Abusers: Child Protection, Risk Management and Risk Reduction.' In M. Erooga and H. Masson (eds) *Children and Young People who Sexually Abuse Others: Challenges and Responses.* London: Routledge.

Expert Panel on Sex Offending (2001) *Reducing the Risk: Improving The Response to Sex Offending.* Edinburgh: Scottish Executive.

Farmer, E. and Pollock, S. (1998) *Sexually Abused and Abusing Children in Substitute Care.* Chichester: Wiley.

Fisher, D. and Beech, A.R. (1999) 'Current Practice in Britain with Sexual Offenders.' *Journal of Interpersonal Violence 14,* 3, 240–256.

Graham, F., Richardson, G. and Bhate, S. (1997) 'Assessment.' In M. Hoghughi, S. Bhate and F. Graham (eds) *Working with Sexually Abusive Adolescents.* London: Sage.

Green, L. and Masson, H. (2002) 'Adolescents Who Sexually Abuse and Residential Accommodation: Issues of Risk and Vulnerability.' *British Journal of Social Work 32,* 149–168.

Greer, W.C. (1997) 'Aftercare: Community Integration Following Institutional Treatment.' In G. Ryan and S. Lane (eds) *Juvenile Sexual Offending: Causes, Consequences and Correction,* 2nd edn. San Francisco: Jossey-Bass.

Grubin, D. (1998) *Sex Offending Against Children: Understanding the Risk.* London: Home Office.

Hackett, S. (2001) *Facing the Future: A Guide for Parents of Young People who Have Sexually Abused.* Lyme Regis: Russell House Publishing.

Hird, J. (1997) 'Working in Context.' In M. Hoghughi, S. Bhate and F. Graham (eds) *Working with Sexually Abusive Adolescents.* London: Sage.

James, A.C. and Neil, P. (1996) 'Juvenile Sexual Offending: One-year Period Prevalence Study Within Oxfordshire.' *Child Abuse and Neglect 20,* 6, 477–485.

Kendrick, A. (1997) 'Safeguarding Children Living away from Home from Abuse: A Literature Review.' In R. Kent *Children's Sasfeguards Review.* Edinburgh: Stationery Office.

Kendrick, A. and Mair, R. (2002) 'Developing Focused Care: A Residential Unit for Sexually Aggressive Young Men.' In M.C. Calder (ed) *Young People Who Sexually Abuse: Building the Evidence Base for your Practice.* Lyme Regis: Russell House Publishing.

Lane, S., with Lobanov-Rostovsky, C. (1997) 'Special Populations: Children, Females, the Developmentally Disabled, and Violent Youth.' In G. Ryan and S. Lane (eds) *Juvenile Sexual Offending: Causes, Consequences, and Correction.* San Francisco: Jossey-Bass.

Leheup, R. and Myers, S. (1999) 'A Description of a Community-based Project to Work with Young People who Sexually Abuse.' In M.C. Calder (ed) *Working with Young People who Sexually Abuse: New Pieces of the Jigsaw Puzzle.* Lyme Regis: Russell House Publishing.

Lightfoot, S. and Evans, I.M. (2000) 'Risk Factors for a New Zealand Sample of Sexually Abusive Children and Adolescents.' *Child Abuse and Neglect 24,* 9, 1185–1198.

Lindsay, M. (1999a) 'The Neglected Priority: Sexual Abuse in the Context of Residential Child Care.' *Child Abuse Review 8*, 405–418.

Lindsay, M. (1999b) 'Dilemmas and Potential Work with Sexually Abusive Young People in Residential Settings.' In M.C. Calder (ed) *Working with Young People who Sexually Abuse: New Pieces of the Jigsaw Puzzle*. Lyme Regis: Russell House Publishing.

Longo, R. (2002) 'A Holistic Approach to Treating Young People Who Sexually Abuse.' In M.C. Calder (ed) *Young People who Sexually Abuse: Building the Evidence Base for your Practice*. Lyme Regis: Russell House Publishing.

Lovell, E. (2002) *Children and Young People who Display Sexually Harmful Behaviour*. Accessed 15 April 2003. Online: www.nspcc.org.uk/inform/Info_Briefing/HarmfulBehaviour.asp

Maletzky, B.M. (1991) *Treating the Sexual Offender*. Newbury Park, CA: Sage.

Masson, H. (1995) Researching Policy and Practice in Relation to Children and Young People who Sexually Abuse.' *Research, Policy and Planning 15*, 3, 8–16.

Masson, H. and Erooga, M. (1999) 'Children and Young People who Sexually Abuse Others: Incidence, Characteristics and Causation.' In M. Erooga and H. Masson (eds) *Children and Young People who Sexually Abuse Others: Challenges and Responses*. London: Routledge.

Masson, H. and Morrison, T. (1999) 'Young Sexual Abusers: Conceptual Frameworks, Issues and Imperatives.' *Children and Society 13*, 203–215.

Monck, E. and New, M. (1996) *Report of a Study of Sexually Abused Children and Adolescents, and of Young Perpetrators of Sexual Abuse who Were Treated in Voluntary Agency Community Facilities*. London: HMSO.

Morrison, T. (2001) 'Surveying the Terrain: Current Issues in the Prevention and Management of Sexually Abusive Behaviour by Males.' *Journal of Sexual Aggression 7*, 1, 19–39.

Mulholland, S.J. and McIntee, J. (1999) 'The Significance of Trauma in Problematic Sexual Behaviour.' In M.C. Calder (ed) *Working with Young People who Sexually Abuse: New Pieces of the Jigsaw Puzzle*. Lyme Regis: Russell House Publishing.

Murray, C. and Hallett, C. (2000) 'Young People who Sexually Abuse: The Scottish Context.' *Journal of Social Welfare and Family Law 22*, 3, 245–260.

National Children's Home (1992) *The Report of the Committee of Inquiry into Children and Young People who Sexually Abuse Other Children*. London: NCH.

O'Boyle, K., Lenehan, K. and McGarvey, L. (1999) 'Developing Groupwork with Young People who Sexually Abuse.' In M.C. Calder (ed) *Working with Young People who Sexually Abuse: New Pieces of the Jigsaw Puzzle*. Lyme Regis: Russell House Publishing.

O'Callaghan, D. (1998) 'Practice Issues in Working with Young Abusers who Have Learning Disabilities.' *Child Abuse Review 7*, 435–448.

O'Callaghan, D. and Print, B. (1994) 'Adolescent Sexual Abusers: Research, Assessment and Treatment.' In T. Morrison, M. Erooga and R. Beckett (eds) *Sexual Offending Against Children: Assessment and Treatment of Male Abusers*. London: Routledge.

Pithers, W.D., Kashima, K.M., Cumming, G.F. and Beal, L.S. (1988) 'Relapse Prevention: A Method of Enhancing Maintenance of Change in Sex Offenders.' In A. Salter *Treating Child Sex Offenders and Victims*. Newbury Park, CA: Sage.

Print, B. and O'Callaghan, D. (1999) 'Working in Groups with Young Men who Have Sexually Abused Others.' In M. Erooga and H. Masson (eds) *Children And Young People who Sexually Abuse Others.* London: Routledge.

Richardson, G. and Graham, F. (1997) 'Relapse Prevention.' In M. Hoghughi, S.R. Bhate and F. Graham (eds) *Working with Sexually Abusive Adolescents.* London: Sage.

Ryan, G. (1997a) 'Incidence and Prevalence of Sexual Offences Committed by Juveniles.' In G. Ryan and S. Lane (eds) *Juvenile Sexual Offending: Causes, Consequences and Correction,* 2nd edn. San Francisco: Jossey-Bass.

Ryan, G. (1997b) 'The Families of Sexually Abusive Youth.' In G. Ryan and S. Lane (eds) *Juvenile Sexual Offending: Causes, Consequences and Correction,* 2nd edn. San Francisco: Jossey-Bass.

Ryan, G. and Lane, S. (1997) 'Integrating Theory and Method.' In G. Ryan and S. Lane (eds) *Juvenile Sexual Offending: Causes, Consequences and Correction,* 2nd edn. San Francisco: Jossey-Bass.

Ryan, G., Lane, S., Davis, J. and Isaac, C. (1987) 'Juvenile Sex Offenders: Development and Correction.' *Child Abuse and Neglect 11,* 385–395.

Salter, D., McMillan, D., Richards, M., Talbot, T., Hodges, J. and Bentovim, A (2003) 'Development of Sexually Abusive Behaviour in Sexually Victimised Males: A Longitudinal Study.' *Lancet 361,* 471–476.

Saradjian, J. and Hanks, H. (1996) *Women who Sexually Abuse Children: From Research to Clinical Practice.* Chichester: Wiley.

Scottish Executive (2002a) *Prison Statistics Scotland, 2001.* Edinburgh: Scottish Executive.

Scottish Executive (2002b) *Analysis of External Consultation on, and The Scottish Executive's Response to, 'Reducing the Risk: Improving the Response to Sex Offending', the Report of the Expert Panel on Sex Offending.* Edinburgh: Scottish Executive.

Skinner, A. (1992) *Another Kind of Home: A Review of Residential Child Care.* Edinburgh: Scottish Office.

Skuse, D., Bentovim, A., Hodges, J. *et al.* (1998) 'Risk Factors for Development of Sexually Abusive Behaviour in Sexually Victimised Adolescent Boys: Cross Sectional Study.' *British Medical Journal 317,* 175–179.

SWSI (Social Work Services Inspectorate) (1997) *A Commitment to Protect – Supervising Sex Offenders: Proposals for more Effective Practice.* Edinburgh: Stationery Office.

SWSI (Social Work Services Inspectorate) (2000) *Managing the Risk: An Inspection of the Management of Sex Offender Cases in the Community.* Edinburgh: Scottish Executive.

Thomas, J. (1997) 'The Family in Treatment.' In G. Ryan and S. Lane (eds) *Juvenile Sexual Offending: Causes, Consequences, and Correction,* 2nd edn. San Francisco: Jossey-Bass.

Thomason, P. (2000) *Focused Work with Sexually Abusive Adolescents.* Brighton: Pavilion.

Vizard, E. (2002) 'The Assessment of Young Sexual Abusers.' In M.C. Calder (ed) *Young People who Sexually Abuse: The Evidence Base for your Practice.* Lyme Regis: Russell House Publishing.

Vizard, E., Monck, E. and Misch, P. (1995) 'Child and Adolescent Sex Abuse Perpetrators: A Review of the Research Literature.' *Journal of Child Psychology and Psychiatry 36,* 5, 731–756.

Way, I. (2002) 'Childhood Maltreatment Histories of Male Adolescents with Sexual Offending Behaviours: A Review of the Literature.' In M.C. Calder (ed) *Young People who Sexually Abuse: Building the Evidence Base for your Practice.* Lyme Regis: Russell House Publishing.

Will, D. (1999) 'Assessment Issues.' In M. Erooga and H. Masson (eds) *Children and Young People who Sexually Abuse Others.* London: Routledge.

Worling, J.R. and Curwen, T. (2000) 'Adolescent Sexual Offender Recidivism: Success of Specialized Treatment and Implications for Risk Prediction.' *Child Abuse and Neglect* 24, 7, 965–982.

CHAPTER 9

Relapse Prevention: Theory and Practice

Tony Ward, Mayumi Purvis and Grant Devilly

Introduction

Over the past 20 years, the utilization of relapse prevention strategies has become a crucial component of therapy for reccurring and somewhat intractable disorders. Following the reduction of the presenting clinical problem(s), it has become common to shift the focus of therapy from the process of creating change to that of maintaining treatment gains or preventing relapse. Thus, the presence of a relapse prevention component is considered pivotal to the continued success of achieving abstinence from ongoing psychological problems, e.g. substance misuse or pathological gambling. A relapse prevention module should ideally be embedded within a treatment programme and also function as an overarching or umbrella concept capable of unifying the entire therapeutic programme (Laws 2003).

Relatedly, a number of clinicians and researchers have argued in recent years that the treatment of sexual offenders ought to be based on an understanding of the process of relapse (e.g. Pithers 1990). It has been suggested that there are clear patterns evident in the behaviour of sexual offenders that translate into distinct clusters of cognitive, affective and behavioural offence variables (Ward *et al.* 1995). Models of the relapse process set out to provide a rich description of the cognitive, behavioural, motivational and contextual factors associated with a sexual offence (Ward and Hudson 2000). Theory at this level typically includes an explicit temporal factor and focuses on proximal causes or the 'how' of sexual offending. In addition, the high recidivism rates of sexual offenders have led many theorists and researchers to view sexual deviance as analogous to addiction (Laws 1989). In light of these observations, treatment strategies such as relapse prevention have been taken from the addiction area and applied to sexual offenders (Ward and Hudson 1996).

A brief historical summary of relapse prevention

The ancestry of relapse prevention lies in the vast array of literature on substance abuse (Laws 2003; Ward and Hudson 2000). Marlatt (1982, 1985) developed the original relapse prevention model for the treatment and management of addictive behaviours, in particular alcoholism. Before briefly outlining the model, we should draw attention to one of Marlatt's most notable theoretical contributions: the construct of the relapse process. Rather than viewing relapse as a condition in which a person moves directly from a state of abstinence to a state of relapse, Marlatt assumed that relapse occurred in discrete steps over time (Ward and Hudson 1996). This led to the critical distinction within the RP model between a *lapse* (a single event involving the recurrence of a prohibited behaviour) and a *relapse* (a return to an addictive pattern). Whether a lapse leads to a relapse depends on several individual and situational factors (Blackburn 2000).

In Marlatt's cognitive-behavioural model, a high-risk situation occurs when a person is placed in a position in which their commitment to abstinence is threatened, essentially because of a lack of effective coping skills. There are three different ways in which high-risk situations can be created. The first occurs when a person is unexpectedly placed in a situation that he or she has difficulty managing (e.g. being offered a cigarette by a superior at work: Ward and Hudson 1996). A second pathway represents a direct route from lifestyle imbalances to high-risk situations. Here, the person experiences difficulty in coping with stressors and, as a result of feeling overwhelmed, relies on old methods of coping (i.e. the addictive behaviour). The high-risk situation here is likely to be an internal one, typically a negative affective state. The third major, and covert, pathway involves apparently irrelevant decisions[1] , i.e. seemingly trivial decisions that appear reasonable and unrelated to addiction but that collectively help set up high-risk situations. The individual may not be fully aware of the motives behind these decisions (i.e. to indulge in a prohibited behaviour) as apparently irrelevant decisions function to avoid self-criticism and social disapproval, and provide an excuse for lapsing.

Once in a high-risk situation, prior experiences with the drug in question may cause individuals to anticipate a number of pleasurable and positive effects, and to discount any negative consequences (the problem of immediate gratification, or PIG). The presence of a PIG can facilitate the chances of a lapse occurring. Failure to deal adaptively with the high-risk situation leads to decreased self-efficacy, lapse and the abstinence violation effect (AVE), essentially a recognition that the commitment to abstinence has been violated (Blackburn 2000; Laws 2003). Depending on how the AVE is managed, a relapse may or may not occur. According to Marlatt, the AVE consists of two major components: an attribution concerning the cause of the lapse and an affective reaction to this attribution (Marlatt and Gordon 1985). For example, if a lapse is thought to be caused by external, unstable and specific factors (e.g. 'I had to have the cigarette so as not to offend my boss'), the effect should be minimal and the possibility of relapse unlikely (Ward and Hudson 1996). If, however, a lapse is attributed to internal and unavoidable factors (e.g. 'I am weak'), a negative emotional reaction will probably be felt and the chance of relapse increased (Laws 2003). The greater the intensity of the AVE, the more likely it is that an individual will relapse, i.e. return to his or her previous level of addictive behaviour. From this perspective, one of the functions of addictive behaviour is to cope with emotional stressors; basically, it represents a maladaptive coping strategy.

---

1   'Apparently irrelevant decisions' have been also been referred to in the literature as 'seemingly irrelevant choices' and 'seemingly unimportant decisions'.

Pithers' relapse prevention model

The sex offender variation of RP, based on Marlatt's (1985) model, was originally developed by Pithers *et al.* (1983) and has remained relatively unchanged since its inception (Laws 2003).

Pithers (1990) outlined a RP programme for child molesters and rapists based on the idea of a cognitive-behavioural chain, a construct similar to that of the relapse process. Cognitive-behavioural chains refer to the idea that sexual offences are not isolated events; they are rather the final event in a lengthy sequence of thoughts and actions (Barbaree and Seto 1997; Nelson and Jackson 1989). Pithers *et al.* (1983) were the first to outline the sexual offence chain in relapse prevention terms and postulated that it consisted of four stages. First, there is a lifestyle, personality or situational event, which forms the background to the offence behaviour. Second, the offender becomes dysphoric (i.e. experiences a negative mood state) as a result of the stressors and consequently enters a high-risk situation. Third, the offender 'lapses' (e.g. fantasises about having sex with a child), and in the final stage he or she relapses (e.g. assaults the child).

In adapting Marlatt's RP model to sex offenders, Pithers and his colleagues made a number of conceptual changes. In particular, Marlatt's definition of lapse and relapse were altered to accommodate the nature of the sexual offending domain. For Marlatt, a lapse was defined as an initial reccurrence of the prohibited behaviour (e.g. a puff of a cigarette or a sip of alcohol). It is, however, clearly unacceptable with sex offenders to define a lapse in these terms, i.e. as the first instance of a sexually abusive behaviour and the victimization of a woman or child. To remedy this problem, Pithers redefined a lapse as the intentional involvement in risky behaviour (e.g. deviant sexual fantasizing, volunteering to baby-sit) and a relapse as the initial occurrence of any sexual offence (as opposed to frequent engagement in the prohibited behaviour, as specified by Marlatt).

In the Pithers model, the relapse process is described as an affective/cognitive/behavioural chain resulting in the recurrence of sexually deviant behaviour (Pithers *et al.* 1983). In his description and visual representation of the relapse process, Pithers identifies only one pathway to high-risk situations, the covert route, in which apparently irrelevant decisions lead directly to a situation in which the offender's control over his sexually abusive behaviour is threatened (see Pithers *et al.* 1988). Pithers states that a high-risk situation is typically characterized by a negative emotional state, interpersonal conflict or external conditions (e.g. baby-sitting) (Ward and Hudson 1996).

According to Pithers' model of the relapse process, the offender is initially in an abstinent state with high self-efficacy beliefs regarding the avoidance of sexual offending. However, with the advent of apparently irrelevant decisions, a high-risk situation emerges that, if not coped with effectively, results in a lapse. For example, the apparently irrelevant decision to accept a neighbour's request to baby-sit their child may result in a high-risk situation. Failure to cope effectively with this situation could potentially lead to a lapse (e.g. sexual fantasies about children).

Following the lapse, the offender experiences the AVE. According to Pithers' definition of the AVE, there is conflict between a sex offender's self-image as reformed and the recent experience of a lapse (Ward and Hudson 1996). How this dissonance effect is resolved determines whether or not a lapse becomes a relapse. If the AVE is attributed to treatment failure (i.e. the person views himself as an unreformed sexual offender, or treatment has failed), a relapse will be expected and viewed as inevitable. In addition, Pithers argues that a key component of the AVE in sex offenders is the problem of immediate gratification, in which an offender focuses on positive consequences of sexual assault and ignores the negative. This process serves to augment the intensity of the AVE and make it even more likely that relapse will occur (Ward and Hudson 1996). Note that, for Pithers, the PIG occurs as part of the AVE and facilitates the transition from a lapse to a relapse, whereas for Marlatt it mediates the transition from a high-risk situation to a lapse.

Problems with Pithers' relapse prevention model

Marlatt's and Pithers' models have both been extensively critiqued in detail elsewhere (see Ward and Hudson 1996) and we will focus on only the main problems here.

Because Pithers' model relies so heavily on the original RP theory developed by Marlatt, it is vulnerable to many of this theory's problems. We will briefly summarise these problems before considering criticisms specific to Pithers' own version of the relapse process in sexual offenders.

General criticisms

A first point is that Pithers, like Marlatt, postulates the existence of a number of mechanisms associated with the relapse process that either appear to conflict with each other or are not clearly connected. Second, Pithers does not convincingly address the interactions between the major constructs such as high-risk situations, lapses, apparently irrelevant decisions and so on. Contrary to what Pithers' model suggests, an offender frequently experiences a number of lapses before ultimately relapsing as there are usually a number of feedback loops or interactions between the various components that eventually may lead to relapse (Hall 1989; Kirkley and Fisher 1988; Saunders and Allsop 1987). An individual might, for example, move back and forth from lifestyle stresses to high-risk situations several times before finally relapsing. Third, Pithers also runs the risk of evoking unconscious decision-making (by the way of apparently irrelevant decisions) without accounting for the mechanisms involved. Finally, Pithers over-emphasizes the role of skill deficits in relapse compared with decision-making (Rohsenow *et al.* 1991).

Specific problems are as follows.

Negative affect as a high-risk situation

Pithers identifies negative affect as an example of a high-risk situation but neglects to clarify how this is so. Ward and Hudson (1996) have argued that negative emotional states are related to high-risk situations in two ways. First, such states might constitute high-risk situations on their own and lead to relapse if the offender fails to cope effectively with them. Second, such states could lead to high-risk situations via apparently irrelevant decisions, in which negative affect is a risk factor possibly associated with lifestyle imbalance. Pithers does not acknowledge this and therefore overlooks the possibility that apparently irrelevant decisions may be involved only in the establishment of certain high-risk situations.

Another problem is the connection between apparently irrelevant decisions and negative affective states. In Pithers' model, covert planning (apparently irrelevant decisions) is the only pathway to high-risk situations. This inflexibility means that the model can account only for external high-risk situations (being with a potential victim) and not internal high-risk situations (e.g. negative affect) as a negative emotional state is non-volitional. That is, it is not really plausible to argue that a person can intentionally plan to be in a negative emotional state in order to provide a reason to lapse. Following on from this, we suggest that a distinction needs to be made between external high-risk situations and those situations that refer to internal, non-volitional states such as negative affect (Ward and Hudson 1996). The fact that it does not cover all the possible pathways involved in re-offending is perhaps the most serious weakness in Pithers' model.

The abstinence violation effect

Pithers' reliance on Marlatt's earlier (and less satisfactory) conceptualization of the abstinence violation effect is a significant weakness of his model (Ward and Hudson 1996). Instead of comprising the AVE, it is possible that cognitive dissonance and the formulation of attributions can occur and function quite independently. That is, each set of processes can lead to relapse on their own and do not need to function as integrated components of the same process.

A further problem is that, in the Pithers model, the AVE and the PIG function together to mediate the transition from a lapse to relapse. This is, however, conceptually confusing and theoretically questionable. The two mechanisms act in opposition to each other: the AVE is associated with negative affect (guilt, feelings of failure, decreased self-efficacy beliefs, etc.), whereas the PIG comprises positive emotions and appetitive process, e.g. sexual arousal and positive views regarding abusive sex (Ward and Hudson 1996). The decision to link the PIG and the AVE together in this way contrasts sharply with the Marlatt model, in which the PIG occurs prior to the AVE and functions primarily to lead the offender from a high-risk situation to a lapse. In our view, Pithers makes this error because of his prior decision to redefine lapse as risky behaviour reflecting the intention to commit a sexual offence. The problem is that the offender is at this point in a sexually aroused state and is unlikely to experience an AVE. In fact, consistent with this observation, Ward, Hudson and Marshall (1994) have found that child molesters tend to experience the AVE following a relapse rather than a lapse.

Lapse and relapse distinctions

Although Pithers makes the necessary distinction between a lapse and relapse, he neglects to draw a further distinction between the first instance of a sexual offence and a return to pre-treatment levels of offending or increased severity of offending. There is an important difference between committing one offence and committing many or, as may be more common, increasing the severity of offending during a single assault (Ward and Hudson 1996). It would perhaps be useful to create a further distinction based on the severity or frequency of offending. For example, a single instance of sexually aggressive behaviour could be labelled Relapse One, and multiple offences or increased severity could be labelled Relapse Two (Marshall, Hudson and Ward 1992; Ward and Hudson 1996). It is a sensible and ethically appropriate strategy to continue to apply relapse prevention principles following the first sexual offence, although it is important in therapy to teach offenders to regard relapse as something to avoid (Ward and Hudson 1996).

Offender type

Pithers' RP approach has been found to be limited in its general scope regarding its applicability to different offenders. In particular, sexual offenders who view adult–child sexual contact as legitimate and favourable are not easily accommodated within the model. Owing to the positive regard these men have for sexual contact with children, they tend to experience a higher level of positive emotions throughout the offence cycle and take a more active pathway rather than the covert route described by Pithers (Ward *et al.* 1995). In addition, impulsive opportunism has been found by researchers to be a common precursor to sexual offending, particularly for rapists (Knight and Prentky 1990; Marshall and Serran 2000). However, as these offenders may still be motivated to desist from sexually offending, it is likely that they will exhibit a relapse process that is representative of their characteristics but inconsistent with Pithers' conception of the relapse process (Ward and Hudson 1996).

In closing, it should be highlighted that the adoption of the sex offender RP model from the substance abuse domain is problematic as the extent to which sexual offending can be viewed as an addiction is, at best, controversial (Cooper *et al.* 1999). In fact, research exists which indicates that the offence process of sexual offenders is not consistent with an addiction perspective (e.g. see Hudson, Ward and McCormack 1999).

A self-regulation model of the relapse process

Unlike the RP models described above which are merely theory based, the self- regulation model of relapse prevention (Ward and Hudson 2000) has its foundations in both theoretical and empirical work. Using the written descriptions of offending obtained from 26 child molesters, Ward *et al.* (1995) developed a descriptive model of sexual offending (i.e. the offence chain). This model was later tested and validated by Hudson *et al.* (1999), who furthered the understanding of offence pathways. By incorporating 86 offence descriptions into the descriptive model of child sexual offending, Hudson *et al.* (1999) identified eight distinct offence pathways of child molesters, the majority of offenders falling into one of three (major) pathways.

The three major pathways consisted of a positive-affect pathway, a negative-affect pathway and a mixed pathway. The positive-affect pathway is characterized by a positive mood in the beginning, followed by direct and explicit offence planning. The offender perceives his relationship with the victim to be mutual in nature and therefore evaluates his sexually abusive behaviour positively. There is consequently a commitment to continue offending in the future. These child sex offenders may refer to their relationship with their victim as 'We were partners' or 'We were in love.' Conversely, the negative-affect pathway features negative emotions throughout the entire offence process, with implicit planning featuring as the precursor to the sexual offence. Child sex offenders who follow this pathway may suggest, 'I never thought of anything happening between her and me – it just happened.' Alternatively, the mixed pathway begins with a negative affect and is followed by explicit distal planning. Later, proximal planning leads the offender to feel positive ('I enjoyed it – felt loved') or negative ('I used my position of power to do to her what I wanted') affect. Post-offence evaluations are negative (fear of being caught or feelings of disgust and regret), and subsequently the offender does not intend to offend again. Polaschek *et al.* (2001) developed a similar model for rapists and again found several common offence pathways for rape offenders. The most recent development in this research programme has, however, been that of the self-regulation model (Ward and Hudson 2000), which is a reformulation of the offence pathways research using self-regulation theory. It represents a theoretically coherent and empirically grounded model that is currently the focus of a number of research programmes (e.g. Bickley and Beech 2002).

The self-regulation model of relapse prevention for sex offenders

Self-regulation pertains to the use of internal and external process that enables individuals to engage in goal-directed behaviour; this can refer to either the achievement or the avoidance of desired goals (Baumeister and Heatherton 1996; Karoly 1993). Cochran and Tesser (1996) make the distinction between acquisitional (approach) and inhibitory (avoidance) goals. Acquisitional goals concern the establishment of a skill or situation and involve approach behaviour, whereas inhibitory goals relate to the decrease or complete suppression of a behaviour or situation and necessitate avoidance behaviour.

The self-regulation model of the relapse process builds upon ongoing research into the offence process and theoretical and empirical research on self-regulation (Ward and Hudson 2000). The model constitutes nine phases and four pathways organized around the nature of sexual offence goals (approach versus avoidant) and the types of strategy used to achieve those goals. Ward and Hudson (1998, 2000) describe the phases of the model as follows:

PHASE 1: LIFE EVENT

An individual is attempting to remain offence-free when some kind of life event occurs (e.g. relationship stress or a problem at work). The individual appraises this event according to existing beliefs and attitudes, his goals at that moment and the context in which it is occurring. This then activates certain patterns of thoughts, emotions and intentions. The loss of a job may, for example, conjure up feelings of inadequacy and a desire to retaliate against the world.

PHASE 2: DESIRE FOR DEVIANT SEX OR ACTIVITY

The life event and ensuant appraisal results in the emergence of a desire for offensive sex and the presence of emotions associated with these desires. This may lead to the activation of an offence script (cognitive representations from the individual's long-term memory that contain information that guides offending behaviour) and covert rehearsal of the offence, which in turn lowers the individual's inhibitions against indulging in deviant fantasies. As offence scripts can be activated and executed without conscious intention, the individual may initially have minimal awareness of the overall goal. The accompanying affective states may be happiness, sexual arousal, anxiety and anger.

PHASE 3: OFFENCE-RELATED GOALS ESTABLISHED

At this point, the offender considers the acceptability of his maladaptive desire and decides what, if anything, he should do about it. As the desire for deviant sex is established, the resultant offence-related goal is also identified. Here, there are two possible goals: avoidance and approach goals. Avoidance goals are associated with the desire to remain offence-free and are essentially negative in nature as the goal is not to achieve a particular state of affairs. The individual is therefore likely to experience a negative affective state as he will be fearful and anxious about the possibility of offending. In contrast, approach goals reflect the motivation to sexually offend. Individuals may experience either a positive or a negative affective state depending on their aims. If, for example, the aim is to be sexually gratified, the affect is likely to be positive, but if the aim is to punish or humiliate someone, the affect is likely to be extremely negative.

PHASE 4: STRATEGY SELECTED

Although not necessarily an explicit decision, the selection of strategies designed to achieve the goal occurs at this stage. Strategies can be selected automatically based on the activated offence script. There are four possible pathways: avoidant-passive, avoidant-active, approach-automatic and approach-explicit. Two pathways are associated with avoidance goals, and two are associated with approach goals.

The *avoidant-passive* pathway contains both the desire not to offend and also the inability to prevent the offence from happening. As far as self-regulation goes, this is an under-regulation or disinhibition pathway as negative affective states either function as disinhibitors or lead to behaviours that result in a loss of control. These individuals find it difficult to control their offending owing to their lack of effective coping skills and ongoing problems with impulsivity; they also typically use covert planning.

In the *avoidant-active* pathway, individuals actively attempt to control deviant thoughts and fantasies but employ strategies that are ineffective or counterproductive. This is consequently a misregulation pathway as the strategies used to avoid offending paradoxically increase the likelihood of an offence occurring. An offender may, for example, use alcohol to suppress the desire to offend, but in reality the use of alcohol decreases his inhibitions, which simply increases his chance of committing a sexually abusive act.

The *approach-automatic* pathway is also an under-regulation or disinhibition pathway. The individual has over-learned offence scripts that navigate the individual's behaviour towards sexually abusive behaviour, and consequently the associated strategies are unlikely to be under intentional control. Individuals may experience either a positive or a negative affective state.

Finally, the *approach-explicit* pathway constitutes conscious, explicit planning and involves finely tuned strategies aimed at sexual offending. This pathway represents an intact self-regulation pathway as the individuals concerned possess good self-regulation skills. The problem lies instead in the nature of the underlying goals, which essentially support and encourage sexual abuse. The affective state experienced by the individual could again be either positive or negative depending on the goal. For example, if the goal is to establish an 'intimate relationship' with a child, the offender may experience strong positive affective states. In contrast, if the aim is to intimidate or punish someone (e.g. a woman), strong negative states such as anger are likely to be present.

It is expected that, for the two pathways associated with avoidance goals (i.e. not to offend), negative affective states will predominate following the offence because of individuals' perception that they have 'failed'. Alternatively, those pathways associated with approach goals (i.e. to offend) will be likely to yield positive affective states following an offence because of the offender's perceived success.

PHASE 5: HIGH-RISK SITUATION

At this point, contact or the opportunity for contact with a potential victim occurs as a result of the previous explicit or implicit planning or counterproductive strategies. The individual appraises the situation according to his goals. For those individuals whose strategies are to avoid offending, the high-risk situation signifies failure, and negative affective states are almost certainly experienced. For those individuals taking an approach strategy, a positive affective state will probably be experienced because, for them, the high-risk situation signifies success. Although it is possible for some offenders to be placed unexpectedly in a high-risk situation leading them to relapse at this phase, the type of goal held will still have some influence over how they interpret and respond to the high-risk situation.

PHASE 6: LAPSE

The lapse is the immediate precursor to the sexual offence, in which the offender's intention is to engage in an offence. At this point, it is suggested that individuals following the avoidance pathways will temporarily switch from an avoidance goal to an approach goal. The avoidant-passive offender will give up his attempts at self-control, whereas the avoidant-active offender will decide that he is unable to control his deviant sexual urges.

Approach-automatic offenders are likely to be fully controlled by situational stimuli and therefore offend impulsively, whereas the approach-explicit offender will demonstrate a careful planning and management of the situation. Consequently, because of the increase in sexual arousal and/or the anticipation of pleasure, all offenders are hypothesized to experience a positive affective state.

PHASE 7: SEXUAL OFFENCE

In a recent study, Ward *et al.* (1995) identified three distinct models of the victim–offender relationship during the offence process. These models directly influence the amount of violence employed by the offender and the severity of the sexual offence itself. The first model is characterized by a self-focus in which the offender's own needs (usually relief from heightened sexual arousal) are paramount. In the second model, there is a victim focus, the offender regarding the victim's needs as more important and sexual contact being viewed as occurring in the context of a 'caring relationship'. Offenders holding this set of beliefs are unlikely to behave in an overtly aggressive manner and often set out to please the victim; typically, they (falsely) see themselves as nurturers. In the third model, there is a mutual focus whereby the offender believes that both he and the victim desire sexual contact and are involved in a 'loving, reciprocal' relationship. It is not clear in the self-regulation model whether particular pathways are associated with certain victim–offender relationship models. It is, however, possible that individuals following avoidant pathways are likely to be self-focused, presumably because they are intent on fulfilling their own needs and succumbing to their desires. Those individuals following approach pathways may have varying foci depending on their goals. A goal to humiliate and punish the victim will, for example, suggest a self-focus, whereas a goal to please the victim may lead the offender to focus on the victim's needs.

PHASE 8: POST-OFFENCE EVALUATIONS

Following the offence, an evaluation of events is likely to occur. Avoidant pathway offenders are expected to evaluate themselves negatively in accordance with the abstinence violation effect, experiencing feelings of guilt, shame and failure. Conversely, it is anticipated that approach pathway offenders will experience positive emotional states because they have achieved their goals.

PHASE 9: ATTITUDE TOWARDS FUTURE OFFENDING

The final phase of the model concerns the impact of sexual offending on future intentions and expectations. Persons with avoidant goals may decide either: (a) to recommit to abstinence, attempt to regain control or continue misregulation; (b) to continue offending because they feel they are unable to stop; or (c) openly to choose offending as a positive option in their life and switch to an approach goal. Alternatively, approach-automatic offenders are likely to have their offence scripts reinforced, ensuring future offending, and approach-explicit offenders will learn from their experiences and develop and refine their offence strategies accordingly. The self-regulation model of the sexual offence process is an ever-evolving model as it is heavily informed by emerging data. Consequently, new pathways or even sub-pathways may be identified in the future. Empirical research with an independent group of child sexual offenders has already found support for the model's distinction between approach and avoidant goals, and the classification of child sexual offenders according to such goals (Bickley and Beech 2002). In his recent comprehensive review of relapse prevention, Laws (2003) identified the advantages of the self-regulation model as follows:

- It avoids the rigidity of the classical RP model while preserving many of its positive assessment and treatment features.

- It allows for the addition of more pathways and the incorporation of new theoretical developments. It allows for multiple levels of detail where required.

Furthermore, Laws describes the model's integration of goals and self-regulatory style as elegant and simple, without being too simplistic.

Practice implications of the self-regulation model of relapse prevention

The self-regulation model conveys a richer understanding of the specific deficits and behaviours associated with sex offenders following certain pathways and, as such, provides an effective platform for treatment. This is to be contrasted with the traditional (Pithers) RP model, which suggests that all offenders follow the same offence pathway (namely the covert route) and essentially display coping skill deficits. Indeed, some clinicians have previously viewed their task to be one of encouraging offenders to view their offences in terms of the single pathway presented in the classical RP model (Polaschek *et al.* 2001). The difficulty is that many offenders' offence processes do not fit within this framework.

From the perspective of the self-regulation model, major clinical tasks are to assess each sex offender's goal type and self-regulation style, and to identify their specific deficits. This fine-grained analysis enables treatment providers to individualize treatment plans rather than adopt a 'one-size-fits-all' approach. For example, according to the self-regulation model, the avoidant-passive offender is likely to have particular skill deficits (e.g. poor coping skills and a low awareness of his offence process), which are in need of direct modification. Therefore, for such offenders, explicitly addressing beliefs about personal agency and seeking to install skills for adequate self-management should take priority in therapeutic interventions (Hudson and Ward 2000). Attention to self-management is of particular importance for these men as the pathway they follow is one of under-regulation.

Alternatively, the avoidant-active offender follows a pathway representing misregulation (i.e. although there is a direct attempt to control deviant behaviour, counterproductive strategies are utilized, until he eventually switches to an approach goal). As the offence process is obvious to the offender, less work needs to be done on increasing his awareness of the process; instead, there needs to be a focus on identifying the links in the offending process, in particular helping him to understand that the strategies used to avoid offending can, paradoxically, result in sexually abusive behaviour (Hudson and Ward 2000; Pithers 1990).

For the approach-automatic offender, a major problem resides in his relative lack of awareness of the process of offending, in part owing to the utilization of over-learned offence scripts. A primary treatment goal would be assisting such an individual to understand his offence process, followed by teaching appropriate self-regulation strategies and an awareness of goals. In contrast, the approach-explicit offender presents a very different clinical problem, possessing effective self-regulation skills and some degree of offence-related 'expertise'. The approach-explicit pathway is fundamentally about goals rather than skills. Core schemas (self, intimacy, sexuality and a sense of being wronged and blamed) should be the primary focus of the intervention, at least in the first instance. These men may also need a reconditioning of their deviant sexual preferences. This client poses the most difficulty in treatment as his pathway is the most dissimilar from what is communicated and understood in the traditional RP model (Hudson and Ward 2000). Instead, intervention should focus on cognitive distortions and the disclosure of offence-related thoughts, feelings and motivations, the major therapeutic challenge being the changing of explicit goals (Hudson and Ward 2000).

Conclusion

An adequate model of the relapse process in sex offenders should exhibit a sound understanding of the offence process, particularly capturing the diversity of pathways and processes. Pithers' RP model has provided clinicians and researchers with a basic understanding of this process and has contributed significantly to our present-day conceptualization of sexual offending. There are, however, a number of significant conceptual and empirical problems associated with this model that limit its clinical utility. We suggest that the self-regulation model presented in this chapter avoids these problems and is able to provide clinicians with a more comprehensive framework with which to guide assessment and treatment. Furthermore, the self-regulation model provides a broader understanding of the factors associated with relapse and subsequently enables clinicians to tailor treatment to the unique needs of specific types of offender (Ward and Hudson 2000).

References

Barbaree, H.E. and Seto, M.C. (1997) 'Pedophilia: Assessment and Treatment.' In D.R. Laws and W. O'Donohue (eds) *Sexual Deviance: Theory, Assessment, and Treatment.* New York: Guilford Press.

Baumeister, R.F. and Heatherton, T.F. (1996) 'Self-regulation Failure: An Overview.' *Psychological Inquiry 7*, 1–15.

Bickley, J. and Beech, A.R. (2002) 'An Investigation of the Ward and Hudson Pathways Model of the Sexual Offence Process with Child Abusers.' *Journal of Interpersonal Violence 17*, 371–393.

Blackburn, R. (2000) *The Psychology of Criminal Conduct: Theory, Research and Practice.* Chichester: Wiley.

Cochran, W. and Tesser, A. (1996) 'The "What the Hell" Effect: Some Effects of Goal Proximity and Goal Framing on Performance.' In L.L. Martin and A. Tesser (eds) *Striving and Feeling: Interactions Among Goals, Affect, and Self-regulation.* New York: Lawrence Erlbaum.

Cooper, A., Scherer, C.R., Boies, S.C. and Gordon, B.L. (1999) 'Sexuality on the Internet: From Sexual Exploration to Pathological Expression.' *Professional Psychology: Research and Practice 30*, 154–164.

Hall, R.L. (1989) 'Relapse Rehearsal.' In D.R. Laws (ed) *Relapse Prevention with Sex Offenders.* New York: Guilford Press.

Hudson, S.M. and Ward, T. (2000) 'Relapse Prevention: Assessment and Treatment Implications.' In D.R. Laws, S.M. Hudson and T. Ward (eds) *Remaking Relapse Prevention with Sex Offenders: A Sourcebook.* Newbury Park, CA: Sage.

Hudson, S.M., Ward, T. and McCormack, J.C. (1999) 'Offence Pathways in Sexual Offenders.' *Journal of Interpersonal Violence 14*, 779–798.

Karoly, P. (1993) 'Mechanisms of Self-regulation: A Systems View.' *Annual Review of Psychology 44*, 23–52.

Kirkley, B.G. and Fisher, E.B. (1988) 'Relapse as a Model of Nonadherence to Dietary Treatment of Diabetes.' *Health Psychology 7*, 221–230.

Knight, R.A. and Prentky, R.A (1990) 'Classifying Sexual Offenders: The Development and Corroboration of Taxonomic Models.' In W.L. Marshall, D.R. Laws and H.E. Barbaree (eds) *Handbook of Sexual Assault: Issues, Theories, and Treatment of the Offender.* New York: Plenum Press.

Laws, D.R. (ed) (1989) *Relapse Prevention with Sex Offenders.* New York: Guilford Press.

Laws, D.R. (2003) 'The Rise and Fall of Relapse Prevention.' *Australian Psychologist 38*, 1, 22–30.

Marlatt, G.A. (1982) 'Relapse Prevention: A Self-control Program for the Treatment of Addictive Behaviors.' In R.B. Stuart (ed) *Adherence, Compliance, and Generalization in Behavioural Medicine.* New York: Brunner/Mazel.

Marlatt, G.A. (1985) 'Relapse Prevention: Theoretical Rationale and Overview of the Model.' In G.A. Marlatt and J.R. Gordon (eds) *Relapse Prevention.* New York: Guilford Press.

Marlatt, G.A. and Gordon, J.R. (1985) *Relapse Prevention: Maintenance Strategies in the Treatment of Addictive Behaviours.* New York: Guilford Press.

Marshall, W.L. and Serran, G.A. (2000) 'Improving the Effectiveness of Sexual Offender Treatment.' *Trauma, Violence, and Abuse 1*, 203–222.

Marshall, W.L., Hudson, S.M. and Ward, T. (1992) 'Relapse Prevention in Sexual Deviance.' In P. Wilson (ed) *Principles and Practice of Relapse Prevention.* New York: Guilford Press.

Nelson, C. and Jackson, P. (1989) 'High-risk Recognition: The Cognitive-behavioural Chain.' In D.R. Laws (ed) *Relapse Prevention with Sex Offenders.* New York: Guilford Press.

Pithers, W.D. (1990) 'Relapse Prevention with Sexual Aggressors: A Method for Maintaining Therapeutic Gain and Enhancing External Supervision.' In W.L. Marshall, D.R. Laws and H.E. Barbaree (eds) *Handbook of Sexual Assault: Issues, Theories and Treatment of the Offender.* New York: Plenum Press.

Pithers, W.D., Kashima, K.M., Cumming, G.F. and Beal, L.S. (1988) 'Relapse Prevention. A Method of Enhancing Maintenance of Change in Sex Offenders.' In A.C. Salter (ed) *Treating Child Sex Offenders and Victims: A Practical Guide.* Newbury Park, CA: Sage.

Pithers, W.D., Marques, J.K., Gibat, C.C. and Marlatt, G.A. (1983) 'Relapse Prevention: A Self-control Model of Treatment and Maintenance of Change for Sexual Aggressives.' In J. Greer and I.R. Stuart (eds) *The Sexual Aggressor: Current Perspective on Treatment.* New York: Van Nostrand Reinhold.

Polaschek, D.L.L., Hudson, S.M., Ward, T. and Siegert, R.J. (2001) 'Rapists' Offence Processes: A Preliminary Descriptive Model.' *Journal of Interpersonal Violence 16*, 523–544.

Rohsenow, D.J., Niaura, R.S., Childress, A.R., Abrams, D.B. and Monti, P.M. (1991) 'Cue Reactivity in Addictive Behaviors: Theoretical and Treatment Implications.' *International Journal of Addictions 25*, 957–993.

Saunders, W.A. and Allsop, S. (1987) 'Relapse: A Psychological Perspective.' *British Journal of Addiction 82*, 417–429.

Ward, T. and Hudson, S.M. (1996) 'Relapse Prevention: A Critical Analysis.' *Sexual Abuse: A Journal of Research and Treatment 8*, 177–200.

Ward, T. and Hudson, S.M. (1998) 'A Model of the Relapse Process in Sexual Offenders.' *Journal of Interpersonal Violence 13*, 700–725.

Ward, T. and Hudson, S.M. (2000) 'A Self-regulation Model of Relapse Prevention.' In D.R. Laws, S.M. Hudson and T. Ward (eds) *Remaking Relapse Prevention with Sex Offenders: A Sourcebook.* Newbury Park: CA: Sage.

Ward, T., Hudson, S. and Marshall, W. (1994) 'The Abstinence Violation Effect in Child Molesters.' *Behaviour Research and Therapy 35*, 431–437.

Ward, T., Louden, K., Hudson, S.M. and Marshall, W.L. (1995) 'A Descriptive Model of the Offence Chain in Child Molesters.' *Journal of Interpersonal Violence 10*, 452–472.

PART THREE

Community-based Risk Management Strategies

CHAPTER 10

Multi-Agency Public Protection Arrangements: Key Issues

Mike Maguire and Hazel Kemshall

Introduction

One of the most prominent features of crime control policy and practice over the past few years has been the huge growth of interagency partnership (see, for example, Hughes 1998). There are few areas in which this has been more pronounced than that of 'public protection', which broadly covers measures to reduce the risks posed by dangerous violent or sexual offenders. Interagency partnership has been seen as a key tool in the effective management of sexual and violent offenders in the community, providing an easier exchange of relevant information across agencies and a greater pooling of resources to provide community-based risk management interventions.

The main aims of this chapter are to outline the new partnership arrangements that have emerged in England, Wales and Scotland specifically for this purpose, and to comment on the issues they raise in respect of practicality, effectiveness and accountability. The chapter is based partly on recent material outlining these arrangements but also considers them against the background of an evaluation of multi-agency public protection panels in six police force areas carried out in 1999 (Maguire *et al.* 2001), which identified a number of major problems and challenges to be overcome if the developing system were to be effective.

The chapter also draws on research in Scotland on the use of risk assessment tools and the extent of multi-agency working across the relevant agencies (McIvor, Kemshall and Levy 2002). This study found various risk assessment tools in use across Scotland, only three of which had been validated against Scottish populations, as well as a wide variation in approach to the risk assessment of violent and sexual offenders. Multi-agency work operated in different ways at different levels and was located in various settings. Although the strengths of multi-agency working were generally recognized, difficulties in information-sharing were identified, as were significant practical difficulties in its smooth operation (McIvor *et al.* 2002).

The chapter is divided into two main sections. First, a brief overview is provided of recent history in the field, including relevant legislation in England and Wales, and in Scotland. Second, comments are made on four of the most critical aspects of public protection work: organizational structures and procedures; identification of, and exchange of information about, relevant offenders; risk assessment; and risk management.

Historical and legislative background

The longest history of formal interagency co-operation in the public protection area is to be found in relationships between the prison and probation services. In England and Wales, an important landmark was the introduction of parole in 1968, which necessitated communication and information exchange between the two agencies in respect of prisoners eligible for release on license. It was not until the late 1980s, however, that concerns about potentially dangerous offenders coming out of prison, together with the growing recognition of 'risk management' as part of the core business of the probation service (Kemshall 1998; Kemshall and Maguire 2001), persuaded probation managers in some areas to establish much closer links with prison staff, aimed at ensuring that such offenders were systematically identified in prison, and that concrete plans were made for their supervision and resettlement, well in advance of release. This included the development of formal risk assessment tools and procedures, as well as mechanisms for the prison to pass on important pieces of information about individual offenders. In Scotland, there has historically been less formal co-operation between social work departments and prisons with respect to pre-release planning and through-care (McIvor and Barry 1998), although mechanisms have been in place for a number of years for social work units in prisons to alert community-based social workers of the impending release of Schedule One offenders (i.e. those who have committed offences against children). As recently as 2002, a tripartite group comprising representatives of social work departments, the Scottish Prison Service and the Scottish Executive concluded that:

> the present system too often operates as separate elements and that the throughcare partnership should be strengthened to enable the development of a strong multi-agency approach to effective throughcare services in the future. (Scottish Executive 2002)

In England and Wales in the early 1990s, probation managers also began to liaise more closely with the police about dangerous offenders under their supervision, establishing joint protocols on information-sharing that disregarded cultural traditions against the passing on of confidential information between 'welfare' and 'enforcement' agencies. A parallel development was the arrangements for joint working and information-sharing between the police, social services and others in relation to children at risk that were set up under the Children Act 1989, especially the creation of multi-agency Area Child Protection Committees.

During the early 1990s, an increasing number of areas took this kind of thinking further by setting up formal 'public protection panels' (or bodies with similar names), which brought together various combinations of probation officers, police, prison staff, social workers, psychiatrists, housing officers and other key players in order to consider the nature and level of risk posed by individual offenders moving into an area (usually, but not always, on release from prison) and to make joint plans about how best to 'manage' that risk. Most such panels were organized by the probation service, which had primary responsibility for supervising offenders after they left prison, although others clearly had much to contribute in terms of both information and practical assistance: the police, for example, might undertake surveillance in high-risk cases, housing officers might provide suitable accommodation away from potential victims, psychiatrists might provide clearer insight into the risks, and so on.

The above activity was concerned with potential violence of all kinds, but as the decade progressed, media and public attention became increasingly focused on the risks posed specifically by sexual offenders, especially 'paedophiles' (Grubin 1998; Hebenton and Thomas 1996, 1997; Hughes, Parker and Gallagher 1996; Kitzinger 1999; Worrall 1997; see also Thomas, this volume). The government responded by passing the Sex Offenders Act 1997, under which most convicted sex offenders were required to register their address with the local police for a minimum of five years, and the police, in consultation with the probation service, were given responsibility for assessing, and where necessary 'managing', the risk that each registered offender posed (Cobley 1999, 2000; Plotnikoff and Woolfson 2000; Power 1999). These duties were generally undertaken by public protection panels (or groups with similar names) containing representatives from the police, probation and a variety of other agencies (Kemshall and Maguire 2001, 2002; Maguire *et al.* 2001). The Act also introduced the Sex Offender Order, a civil order that courts could use to place offenders under specific restrictions, such as not entering certain areas, the breach of which could lead to imprisonment (Cobley 2000).

This legislation was later strengthened and widened by the Criminal Justice and Courts Services Act 2000, under which a statutory duty is placed on *both* the police and the probation services to assess and manage the risks posed by violent, sexual and other offenders who 'may cause serious harm to the public' (s. 67). This Act also requires both the Home Office and the local 'responsible authorities' (police and probation) to produce annual reports on the public protection arrangements in place and statistics on the numbers of offenders dealt with (Home Office 2002a; Kemshall and Maguire 2003). Finally, the Sexual Offenders Bill 2003, being debated at the time of writing, proposes a further tightening of the controls on registered sex offenders, including a quicker notification of changes of address, inclusion of those convicted abroad, and the replacement of the Sex Offender Order with the stronger Sexual Offences Prevention Order.

Similar developments took place in Scotland during this period, the Cosgrove and MacLean Committees on sexual and violent offenders providing an important impetus to both policy and legislation (see Kemshall and McIvor, this volume; Expert Panel on Sex Offending 2001; Scottish

Executive 2000). In addition to the sentencing options available under the Crime and Disorder Act 1998 and the registration of Sex Offenders under the 1997 Sex Offenders Act, the MacLean Committee also proposed an Order for Lifelong Restriction (see Kemshall and McIvor, this volume), which is likely to require greater interagency co-operation in order to provide comprehensive risk assessments for use in court. The Order for Lifelong Restriction was introduced as a new sentence by the Criminal Justice (Scotland) Act 2003.

More generally, although formalized arrangements are developing in Scotland (e.g in Edinburgh: McIvor *et al.* 2002), they are not subject to the same legislative force as in England and Wales. Multi-agency risk assessment and management are viewed positively by the relevant agencies in Scotland, but it is recognized that their practical implementation still has some way to go (McIvor *et al.* 2002).

Across the UK as a whole, an important backcloth to the work being undertaken by the public sector agencies – one that has continually injected a sense of urgency into it – has been a series of outbursts of vigilante activity against 'paedophiles', combined with persistent calls for disclosure of the names and addresses of sex offenders to the local community. One of the main triggers for this was the murder in 2000 of Sarah Payne, which gave rise to a campaign, led by the *News of the World* newspaper, to 'name and shame' paedophiles and for a 'Sarah's Law' to match the American 'Megan's Law'.[1] The campaign was rekindled the following year following the conviction of the murderer Roy Whiting, but the Government, supported by most police and probation managers, continued to resist disclosure on the grounds that it would be counterproductive to public protection by driving sexual offenders 'underground' (Thomas 2001).[2] In England and Wales, the main concessions made to the demands for more community involvement

---

1   Under the US federal Megan's Law, passed in 1996, community notification is mandatory in cases in which it is adjudged 'necessary and relevant for public protection' – a judgement normally dependent upon assessed level of risk (Hebenton and Thomas 1997).

2   For a flavour of the political and practitioner debates on the issue, see 'Do we need a 'Sarah's Law'?', www.bbc.co.uk/news (13 December 2001).

have been the aforementioned requirement for the publication of annual reports and statistics, and the appointment of community representatives to local strategic management boards (Kemshall and Maguire 2003).

Multi-agency work

As noted above, a core characteristic of recent approaches to public protection and the effective management of sexual and violent offenders in the community in the UK has been the emphasis placed upon partnership working. This section discusses the main issues that have arisen in relation to the four areas in which effective partnership work appears to be most critical: organizational structures and procedures; the identification of, and exchange of information about, relevant offenders; risk assessment; and risk management. In each case, findings from the research by Maguire *et al.* (2001) are summarised, followed by a discussion of the extent to which new statutory and administrative arrangements in England and Wales appear to deal with the problems identified in that research.

Organizational structures and procedures [3]

Under the Sex Offenders Act 1997, all police force and probation areas were obliged to collaborate in assessing and managing the risk from sex offenders subject to registration, but they were given relatively little guidance on how this should be done. They also had only a short time in which to comply. As a result, they met the requirements in a number of different ways, in some cases building on pre-existing partnership arrangements, in others setting up new structures and protocols. Indeed, the most striking feature of the public protection arrangements examined in the study by Maguire *et al.* (2001) was the sheer variety of structures, practices and procedures to be found across the different areas – and in some cases even within particular police force areas. For example, the work was in some areas overseen by

---

3   This material is drawn from research undertaken in England and Wales and does not reflect the current situation in Scotland. For the latter, see McIvor *et al.* 2002.

multi-agency senior management boards, whereas in others middle managers were left to organize it themselves; in some areas, one agency was clearly the dominant partner, in others there was a much more equal partnership; some areas had single-tier panel systems, others two-tier systems; some had centralized systems, others devolved much of the responsibility; some focused mainly on sex offender register cases, others continued to pay strong attention to other types of 'potentially dangerous offender'; some had regular meetings to review a large number of cases, others called only infrequent, ad hoc meetings for high-risk cases; and some panel meetings were always attended by managers and/or specialist personnel, others by people with less 'clout' and/or less expertise.

Rather more worrying than the variety of local arrangements – some of which was the result of differences in the size and characteristics of the area covered, or the number of cases that had to be dealt with – was evidence of major variations in the quality of the work undertaken, including that of assessing risk, chairing panels, taking minutes and keeping track of cases. Such differences were especially influenced by the degree of commitment and leadership shown by senior managers and the resources they were prepared to make available to public protection work. There were also problems around the 'ownership' of the work: in some areas, one agency was regarded as having too much control (e.g. by preparing and chairing all meetings), causing partners to feel that they were not fully involved in decision-making; in others, there was a general tendency to leave tasks to others, nobody taking full responsibility for following up panel decisions.

Under the provisions of the Criminal Justice and Courts Services Act 2000, the Home Office was given greater powers to tackle the problems of uncertainty and inconsistency, and to raise the quality of public protection work across the country. In March 2001, it introduced initial guidance to police and probation areas on the 'Multi Agency Public Protection Arrangements' (MAPPA) required by the Act, clearly defining the responsibilities of each agency and setting out a blueprint for the organizational systems and practices to be followed (Home Office 2001). In terms of organizational arrangements, this included the following requirements:

1. The probation and police services should negotiate the involvement of social services, health and local authority housing in MAPPA, as well as working closely with prisons.

2. Information should be shared on all relevant offenders.

3. Those assessed as potentially posing the highest risk should be referred to a Multi-Agency Public Protection Panel (MAPPP) involving senior representatives of the relevant agencies (others being dealt with by lower-level panels or single agencies).

4. The effectiveness of the arrangements should be regularly monitored and reviewed.

5. Issues of resource allocation and multi-agency training should be considered and addressed.

More detailed guidance has since been prepared, further reducing the level of variation in practice (see Bryan and Payne 2003; Home Office 2003). The Criminal Justice Bill and the Sexual Offences Bill will also give significant impetus to these developments. The former incorporates the prison service into the 'Responsible Authorities', thus filling a significant gap in information exchange and risk management planning (Bryan and Payne 2003). A 'duty to co-operate' will also be placed on other key agencies such as health, housing, social services, education and youth offending teams.

The recent Home Office guidance aims to improve the consistency and quality of MAPPA systems and processes (Home Office 2003). The most important development has perhaps been increasing attention to the need for an active, high level, multi-agency Strategic Management Board in each area to oversee and monitor the processes, to provide a form of quality control (including arranging adequate training and inquiring into cases where things may have gone wrong), to ensure effective co-ordination between the various agencies and to communicate with local communities. If such boards operate as designed, many of the organizational problems identified by Maguire *et al.* (2001) should in time be greatly ameliorated.

Identification of, and exchange of information about, relevant offenders

Although the Sex Offenders Act 1997 defined which categories of sex offender had to be registered – and hence risk-assessed – there were many other offenders who could be dealt with by public protection panels, if they chose to consider them. These included people who were not charged specifically with sex offences but whose crimes involved a sexual element. They also included large numbers of violent offenders. Maguire *et al.* (2001) found a wide variation between areas in respect of whether and how these other kinds of cases came before panels. Areas that had developed partnership arrangements a long time before the 1997 Act tended to have a tradition of jointly 'risk-managing' serious violent offenders (especially those coming out of prison) and continued with such work after the Act, but those in which such arrangements were set up mainly in response to the Act tended to focus predominantly on the sex offender cases for which the police were given statutory responsibility, only rarely considering other kinds of potentially dangerous offender.

The Criminal Justice and Courts Services Act 2000 (s. 68), however, specified a greatly extended range of offenders to be dealt with under the new MAPPA. In addition to the categories already identified by the Sex Offenders Act, these included all sexual or violent offenders sentenced to 12 months' or more imprisonment, as well as anyone else 'likely to pose a risk of serious harm'. An idea of the impact this has had on the public protection arrangements can be gleaned from the figures given in the first annual report at a national level (Home Office 2002b). Although most panel work had in previous years concerned sex offenders, in March 2002 there were 18,513 registered sex offenders, 27,477 violent offenders and 1219 other offenders covered by the MAPPA.

Of course, not all offenders covered by the MAPPA actually come before panels. One of the most important elements of the new arrangements is guidance on effective 'gate-keeping' to the panels. The basic notion is that MAPPPs themselves (i.e. the highest-level panels, comprising senior staff from the relevant agencies) should reserve their attention and energies only for the 'critical few' – those offenders who present a very serious risk of harm, protection from whom will be enhanced by the exchange and discussion of detailed information, followed by co-ordinated action, between more than one agency. Other cases may be discussed either at lower-level or local multi-agency panels or, where multi-agency work would add little value or the risk is adjudged to be low, simply left to the agency with principal responsibility.

Making this filtering and allocation system work effectively requires robust and consistent methods of risk assessment and information exchange in advance of panel meetings in order to ensure that important cases are not missed, as well as to avoid unnecessary referrals to panels. A key advance in terms of data exchange has been the development of a national Violent and Sex Offender Register (ViSOR), which will contain details of every offender subject to the new MAPPA and will be accessible to, and updated by, all prison and probation services. ViSOR will not only facilitate the monitoring of known sexual and violent offenders in the community and upon release from prison, but also aid police investigations when serious offences have occurred (Edwards 2003). It will be piloted in Durham and the London Borough of Wandsworth in the latter part of 2003 prior to a national roll-out in 2004.

In addition, each area will appoint a 'MAPPA Registrar', responsible for maintaining and updating the system with new information, including the results of new or revised risk assessments. This provides the basis for a potentially much more efficient system of information exchange and of gate-keeping to the panels, although its effectiveness will ultimately still depend to a large extent on the quality of the preliminary risk assessments carried out by individual police and probation officers (see next section).

Risk assessment

The research by Maguire *et al.* (2001) found considerable variation in the methods and quality of risk assessment undertaken for and by MAPPPs. Where people subject to registration as sex offenders were concerned, most police forces routinely applied the Structured Anchored Clinical Judgement (SACJ) tool, later revised to become Risk Matrix 2000, in order to classify each offender provisionally as 'low', 'medium' or 'high' risk (for more details about the instrument, see Hanson and Thornton 2000; Kemshall 2001). Subsequent procedures varied, but offenders coming out as 'high' (or, in some cases, 'medium') risk were in most cases referred to a panel for further discussion, whereas little action was taken with regard to those emerging as 'low' risk beyond the basics of registration and referral to the relevant police division.

However, very few of the people required to use the SACJ regularly – for the most part, police constables or civilian staff at force headquarters – had received more than the most rudimentary training in how to use it. The instrument was generally applied in a mechanical fashion, and the predominantly junior staff were not usually encouraged to use their judgement to supplement the results it produced. Moreover, important pieces of information (e.g. prison or probation reports) were often lacking at the time the assessment was undertaken. As already noted, the result was inconsistency both in risk classification and in the appropriateness of the cases referred to panels, in some cases 'swamping' them unnecessarily, in others missing cases that should have received their attention.

Equally, where non-register cases (mainly violent offenders) were concerned, there were very large variations in risk assessment method and the thresholds of dangerousness used: some areas attempted to define and operate clear levels of 'serious harm', other areas relied upon offence categories, and still others depended on internally developed checklists in order to identify offenders who should be included in the public protection processes. Resource constraints were also a factor in some areas, staff being reluctant to 'overload' the system further with cases that were not statutorily their responsibility.

Finally, when cases were considered by panels, the initial risk assessments were quite often amended in light of new information or through the use of professional judgement, but many cases were observed in which this was carried out in an unsystematic way, relying as much upon 'gut feelings' as on reasoned argument. The pressure of the high volume of cases dealt with by many panels also made it impossible to give close consideration to all the details relevant to risk assessment in every case.

The above picture clearly raised many questions about the effectiveness and defensibility of risk management decisions. The new MAPPA have attempted to correct this by providing a standard structure and set of procedures for decision-making. Two assessment tools have been formally approved for standard use: Risk Matrix 2000 for sex offenders, and the Offender Assessment System (OASys) for other kinds of offender. It is, however, stressed that these are not intended to be used in a mechanical fashion: professional judgement is required in addition to standard scoring procedures. Although the recent Home Office guidance (2003) focuses on procedural issues, more attention is needed to the quality and consistency of risk assessment decisions, and the integrity with which tools are used has yet to be adequately addressed. There is still a considerable need for more training in this area and for the best of local practice to be consolidated nationally.

In Scotland, the MacLean Committee (Scottish Executive 2000) proposed a Risk Management Authority with responsibility for 'ensuring the effective assessment and minimisation of risk' (s.3(1)). Importantly the Authority is also tasked with the provision of guidance on risk assessment and management, and with setting standards against which risk assessment and management plans can be judged. In this respect, the Scottish Risk Management Authority will have an important regulatory and quality assurance role.

Risk management

The final area identified by Maguire *et al.* (2001) as problematic was that of 'risk management'. As with the other three, this took a range of forms, and practice varied between panels. Agreed best practice was for the panel to draw up a 'risk management plan' (or 'action plan') for those assessed as posing a substantial level of risk, each agency being assigned specific responsibilities. For prisoners under statutory supervision by the probation service – most commonly, those under license on release from prison – the main burden of responsibility was usually accepted by the probation service, which already has statutory duties in such cases and also possesses considerable powers to ensure compliance with licence conditions. In these circumstances, the main potential 'value added' by the multi-agency approach (aside from the acquisition of extra information) was access to additional facilities and services, such as appropriate housing, psychiatric treatment and police surveillance, that were likely to reduce the level of risk. In cases where the offender was not under statutory supervision (or was approaching the end of a period of statutory supervision but was still considered a risk), the main responsibility tended to be taken by the police. Most such cases involved registered sex offenders, and the most common form of risk management practised by police officers was periodic unannounced visits to their homes in order to check that they were actually residing there, to look for any warning signs that they might be planning to offend and, indeed, to act as a deterrent – as one officer put it, 'They get the message that "Big Brother is Watching You").' Again, other agencies could also help with, for example, housing or specialist advice.

Although these methods were considered by practitioners to be effective if implemented systematically (even though valid evidence on effectiveness in this area is extremely hard to obtain), it was clear that practical and resource problems often frustrated the good intentions of the panels. First of all, the high volume of cases dealt with by some panels meant that individual plans tended to be made for only a proportion of offenders, but it was not always clear what basis was used to decide the kind and level of intervention needed. In some areas, for example, high- and medium-risk offenders were automatically made subject to a minimum number of police visits over a set period, or their cases had to be reviewed after a set period of time. Elsewhere, there were no firm rules, plans being made entirely on a case-by-case basis.

Second, in cases where clear plans had been agreed, agencies often had difficulty in implementing them, and several examples of 'slippage' were found. This was exacerbated in some areas by a lack of systematic follow-up of cases at panel meetings, again a consequence of the constant flow of new cases to deal with. It should be noted in this context that such problems were not apparent in cases that clearly posed an exceptionally high risk – these tending to be dealt with very carefully and thoroughly – but emerged mainly in relation to 'medium-risk' cases in which the first few weeks passed without problem and practitioners' attentions began to be directed elsewhere.

The new MAPPA set down basic risk management procedures to be used in the different contexts in which cases are discussed and managed.

'NORMAL AGENCY MANAGEMENT'

First, in low risk cases or cases in which no particular need is identified for the involvement of partners, one agency alone accepts responsibility for the offender, engaging others only if the situation changes or new needs become apparent.

LOCAL RISK MANAGEMENT MEETINGS

Cases that are perceived as likely to benefit from interagency co-operation are referred to Local Risk Management Meetings, comprising representatives from local agencies, at which a 'multi-agency public protection plan' is devised. This assigns specific responsibilities to each agency, as well as clear dates for reviews. It is also considered important that if it becomes clear that the multi-agency input is no longer necessary, the case is redefined as one for 'normal agency management', thus alleviating the pressure on the Local Risk Management Meeting. Equally, if the risk is adjudged exceptionally high, or if extra resources are considered necessary, the case should be referred upwards to a MAPPP.

MULTI-AGENCY PUBLIC PROTECTION PANELS

As noted above, MAPPPs are the highest level of panel, reserved for the management of the 'critical few'. They are thus convened on a case-by-case basis rather than (as is the case with Local Risk Management Meetings) sitting at regular intervals. In terms of the 'ownership' of cases, the normal rule is that the lead agency with core responsibility for ensuring that the plan is properly implemented is the one that called the MAPPP, although all those involved will have particular responsibilities. Reviews of cases at agreed intervals are also very important, and in every case in which re-offending occurs, it is expected that a formal review will be undertaken by a sub-panel of the Strategic Management Board in order to learn any lessons that may become apparent.

Conclusion

The research by Maguire *et al.* (2001) revealed major variations, and a widespread lack of clarity, among MAPPPs about who was responsible for which aspects of the work, which offenders should be included in the process, how risk should be assessed and managed, and how cases should be monitored and followed up. Although there were pockets of excellent practice, and very high-risk cases were generally dealt with effectively, the system overall could not be said to inspire confidence in terms of defensible decision-making, organization or accountability. Part of the problem was that agencies had been obliged, at relatively short notice, to collaborate in what was for some a new area of work, without either clear national guidance or extra resources. These criticisms have, however, since been taken on board at central level, and the MAPPA provide a carefully thought-out framework to overcome most of the obstacles described. The most important aspects of these, apart from the welcome increase in consistency of approach across the country, appear to be the role of the Strategic Management Board, the introduction of the national Violent and Sex Offender Register and the 'gate-keeping' procedures to avoid over-loading panels. These changes may enable MAPPPs to be reserved for the 'critical few': it is in this area that the quality of multi-agency work is most important, and how well MAPPPs engage with the offenders concerned is an urgent topic for future research.

References

Bryan, T. and Payne, W. (2003) 'Developing MAPPA: Multi-Agency Public Protection Arrangements.' *Criminal Justice Matters 51*, Spring, 20–21, 29.

Cobley, C. (1999) 'Keeping Track of Sex Offenders: Part 1 of the Sex Offenders Act 1997.' *Modern Law Review 60*, 690–699.

Cobley, C. (2000) *Sex Offenders: Law, Policy and Practice.* Bristol: Jordans.

Edwards, D. (2003) 'ViSOR – Violent and Sex Offender Register.' *Criminal Justice Matters 51*, Spring, 28.

Expert Panel on Sex Offending (2001) *Reducing the Risk: Improving the Response to Sex Offending.* Edinburgh: Scottish Executive.

Grubin, D. (1998) *Sex Offending Against Children: Understanding the Risk.* Police Research Series Paper No. 99. London: Home Office.

Hanson, R.K. and Thornton, D.M. (2000) *Static 99: Improving Actuarial Risk Assessment for Sex Offenders.* Ottawa: Public Works and Government Services, Canada.

Hebenton, B. and Thomas, T. (1996) 'Tracking Sex Offenders.' *Howard Journal 35*, 2, 97–112.

Hebenton, B. and Thomas, T. (1997) *Keeping Track? Observations on Sex Offender Registrations in the US.* Crime Detection and Prevention Series Paper No. 83. London: Home Office.

Home Office (2001) *Initial Guidance to the Police and Probation Services on Sections 67 and 68 of the Criminal Justice and Court Services Act 2000.* HOC 10/2001. London: Home Office.

Home Office (2002a) *Protecting the Public: Strengthening Protection Against Sex Offenders and Reforming the Law on Sexual Offences.* Cmnd 5668. London: HMSO.

Home Office (2002b) *Multi-agency Public Protection Arrangements: Annual Report 2002.* London: Home Office.

Home Office (2003) *The MAPPA Guidance.* London: National Probation Directorate.

Hughes, B., Parker, H. and Gallagher, B. (1996) *Policing Child Sexual Abuse: The View from Police Practitioners.* London: Home Office.

Hughes, G. (1998) Understanding Crime Prevention: Social Control, Risk and Late Modernity. Buckingham, Open University Press.

Kemshall, H. (1998) *Risk in Probation Practice.* Aldershot: Ashgate.

Kemshall, H. (2001) *Risk Assessment and Management of Known Sexual and Violent Offenders: A Review of Current Issues.* Police Research Series 140. London: Home Office.

Kemshall, H. and Maguire, M. (2001) 'Public Protection, Partnership and Risk Penality: The Multi-agency Risk Management of Sexual and Violent Offenders.' *Punishment and Society 3*, 2, 237–264.

Kemshall, H. and Maguire, M. (2002) 'Community Justice, Risk Management and Multi-Agency Public Protection Panels.' *Community Justice 1*, 1, 11–27.

Kemshall, H. and Maguire, M. (2003) 'Sex Offenders, Risk Penality and the Problem of Disclosure to the Community.' In A. Matravers (ed) *Managing Sex Offenders in the Community: Contexts, Challenges and Responses.* Devon: Willan.

Kitzinger, J. (1999) 'The Ultimate Neighbour from Hell: Media Framing of Paedophiles.' In B. Franklin (ed) *Social Policy, Media and Misrepresentation.* London: Routledge.

McIvor, G. and Barry, M. (1998) *Social Work and Criminal Justice,* Volume 7. *Community-Based Throughcare.* Edinburgh: Stationery Office.

McIvor, G., Kemshall, H. and Levy, G. (2002) *Serious Violent and Sexual Offenders: The Use of Risk Assessment Tools in Scotland.* Edinburgh: Scottish Executive.

Maguire, M., Kemshall, H., Noaks, L., Sharpe, K. and Wincup, E. (2001) *Risk Management of Sexual and Violent Offenders: The Work of Public Protection Panels.* Police Research Series Paper No. 139. London: Home Office.

Plotnikoff, J. and Woolfson, R. (2000) *Where Are They Now? An Evaluation of Sex Offender Registration in England and Wales.* Police Research Series. Paper No. 126. London: Home Office.

Power, H. (1999) 'The Crime Disorder Act, 1998: Sex Offenders, Privacy and the Police.' *Criminal Law Review,* 3–16.

Scottish Executive (2000) *A Report on the Committee on Serious Violent and Sexual Offenders* (The MacLean Report). Edinburgh: Scottish Executive.

Scottish Executive (2002) *Throughcare: Developing the Service.* Report of the Tripartite Group. Edinburgh: Scottish Executive.

Thomas, T. (2001) 'Sex offenders, the Home Office and the Sunday papers.' *Journal of Social Welfare and Family Law 23*, 1, 103–4.

Worrall, A. (1997) *Punishment in the Community: The Future of Criminal Justice.* London: Longman.

CHAPTER 11

Sex Offender Registers and Monitoring

Terry Thomas

Introduction

The Sex Offenders Act 1997 created the UK's sex offender register, which came into being on 1 September 1997. Part One of the Act required those convicted or cautioned for a designated sexual offence to notify the police whenever they changed name or address. The register was never a discrete and separate register as such but simply a sub-category within the complete national collection of criminal records held by the police. Certain names within the national collection were to be annotated to signify that that individual was required to notify changes to the police.

The sex offender register was conceived as a contribution to improving child protection and community safety rather than as a penal sanction. It was an administrative regulatory measure and not any form of additional punishment for the offender. Registration was an automatic 'add-on' when sentence was passed in a criminal court. The distinction between the regulatory role and the punishment role has not always been clearly maintained, but the Home Office and Scottish Executive have recently categorically stated that the 1997 Sex Offenders Act is: 'a measure aimed at helping to protect the community from sex offenders not an additional penalty for the offender' (2001, Ch.3, para. 1).

The purpose of this chapter is to consider the origins of the register, its legal and administrative framework and how it appears to work in practice. It will also examine the question of who, apart from the police, should have access to the register, and in particular whether the sex offender register should be open to any member of the public to see, for example, whether any offenders live in their street.

Early precedents

The idea that sex offenders could help keep their own records up to date was first tried out in the USA. In the 1940s, both California and Arizona are credited with being pioneers of sex offender registers, others following in the 1950s. After a lull in their development, registers found favour again in the late 1980s and early 1990s until, in 1994, a federal statute (the Jacob Wetterling Crimes Against Children and Sexually Violent Offender Registration Act) required all states to create registers of sex offenders and have laws in place putting a duty on those offenders to notify any changes in their circumstances, in particular changes to their name or address (Earl-Hubbard 1996).

The Americans appear to have been driven to create their registers by public opinion and politicians, usually reacting to some terrible, high-profile sex crime:

> contemporary sex offender legislation was fuelled by community outrage at a few highly publicised sex crimes against children. Statutes passed in Washington and New Jersey in response to such crimes began the wave of Sex Offender Registration Acts. (Small 1999)

What was conspicuous by its absence was any kind of research, pilot scheme or evaluation that such registers would make communities safer:

> in reviewing the available published literature (in the USA) on evaluation of registration as an investigative and preventive tool, one is struck by the dearth of good research studies…No substantial effort has been devoted to examining base-rates for offending and the scientific literature on long-term reconviction data, nor even to looking at the career path of offenders and the efficacy of registering all (as opposed to some) sexual offenders. (Hebenton and Thomas 1997)

American experiences of sex offender registers inevitably filtered across the Atlantic to inform UK thinking in this area, but in the meantime the UK had only its police-held criminal record collection and the child protection registers held by local authorities. Child protection registers were started in the early 1970s and were indexed by the names of children 'recognised to be at continuing risk of significant harm' (Department of Health, Home Office and Department for Education and Employment 1999, paras. 5.99–5.104); the child protection register would lead on to the names of adults in the same household who could well be abusers. Individuals convicted of offences against children became familiarly known as 'Schedule One offenders' if their offences included any of the offences against children listed in Schedule One of the Children and Young Persons Act 1933.

The origins of the UK sex offender register

At the 1988 Annual General Meeting of the British Association of Social Workers (BASW), delegates queried why children as victims were on child protection registers but nothing was held in similar fashion for the adult perpetrators of the crimes committed against children. The AGM passed a resolution calling for a sex offender register ('Setting up Registers of Child Abusers Referred to Council.' *Community Care*, 31 March; 'Social Workers Call for Paedophile Register.' *Professional Social Work*, June).

By the mid-1990s, others were calling for some kind of register on adult abusers. The London Borough of Brent Area Child Protection Committee was just one such committee that wondered 'why the police have no Borough based register of (Schedule One) offenders' (DH 1995, para. 23.2), and a new campaign group called Action on Child Exploitation (ACHE) started to lobby for a number of changes, including 'a register of convicted child abusers in the UK, so that they have to notify the authorities of any change in job or address' (ACHE undated; Niven 1996).

Some local authorities had actually started keeping their own informal registers of sex offenders and child abusers, leading to warnings from the Home Office that such lists have 'limitations', not least in terms of data quality (Home Office, DH, Department of Education and Science and Welsh Office 1991, paras. 6.52–6.54). Not much was known about these unofficial compilations, although the Director of Social Services for Manchester was willing to go on record to say 'we are committed to doing this in the interests of protecting children'; the Manchester database was reported to include men who had *not* been convicted (*Manchester Evening News* 1996).

At the University of Manchester, research was carried out among police child protection practitioners that revealed the shortcomings of the existing systems, especially when child sex offenders were mobile:

> Even if local systems are effective in sharing information about the arrival of a Schedule I offender in the locality, there are no clear systems for tracking the individual and monitoring his movements...if convicted offenders know that an effective tracking system is in operation they may be deterred. (Hughes, Parker and Gallagher 1996)

As this critical mass built up among practitioners, two MPs tried unsuccessfully to bring in a Private Members' Bill introducing a register, and the press continued to give coverage to sex offending cases. The 1995 trial of Rose West for sexual crimes and murder committed jointly with her husband in Gloucester received widespread reporting (*The Sun* 1995) as did the 1996 trial of the man who abducted and killed nine-year-old Daniel Handley in East London (*The Guardian* 1996) The trial of the killers of seven-year-old Sophie Hook in North Wales by a local man who had been known to the police for some time led to more direct linkage with a register (*The Independent* 1996)

In 1996, a Home Office consultation paper proposed a series of measures on the sentencing and supervision of sex offenders, including the idea of a register that would 'ensure that the information on convicted sex offenders contained within the police national computer was fully up to date' (Home Office 1996, para. 43).

Apart from improving data quality, it was tentatively suggested that the register would also 'help [the police] identify suspects once a crime had been committed...*possibly* help them to prevent such crimes [and]...*might* also act as a deterrent to potential re-offenders' (Home Office 1996, emphasis added).

Other surveillance measures proposed in the consultation paper included a form of extended supervision of sex offenders by the probation service and extended powers to take DNA samples from sex offenders; the

UK claimed to have created the world's first national DNA database in 1995 (Home Office 1995).

The Home Office received 238 formal responses to its consultation paper proposals, 87 per cent of which were in favour of a register (HC Deb 25 October 1996 WA 965). The civil liberties campaign group Liberty were among those who were hesitant because:

> no evidence is given, however, to support any of the supposed benefits (of a register), nor is there any suggestion of how the proposed register would achieve the claimed objectives. (Liberty 1996, para. 27)

The Sex Offenders Bill was duly published on 18 December 1996. On the political front, a general election was imminent, and within the politics of law and order no one wanted to be seen to be 'soft' on crime – least of all on sex offenders, who were becoming universally the most disliked of criminals. One extra-Parliamentary critic pointed out that 'there is no reason for this Bill. No reason at all. It is simply a piece of electioneering' (Parris 1997).

The bill as published did carry a few departures from the consultation paper, including a reduction in the number of designated offences that would result in registration and the inclusion of police cautions, as well as court convictions, as precursors to registration. The bill also recognized what the consultation paper had overlooked: the need to list designated offences for Scotland and Northern Ireland. The Parliamentary debate looked at making the requirement to notify retrospectively, and include those only *suspected* of offending; the debate also opened up the question of public access to the register. All of these possibilities were defeated in the Committee stages (see Thomas 2000a for a more complete account of the bill's Parliamentary passage).

The Sex Offenders Act 1997

The Sex Offenders Act was implemented from 1 September 1997, Part One of the Act requiring offenders, convicted or cautioned for a designated sexual offence, to notify the police every time they changed their name or address; changes in address had to be for any changes of more than 14 days. The police would note the relevant offenders as being registered – or 'required to notify' changes – on receipt of information from the courts, prisons, hospitals, probation service or their own police colleagues, and the offenders were expected to report to the police initially within 14 days; any changes thereafter also had to be reported within 14 days. Reporting could be in person, by letter or by e-mail.

Offenders had to comply with these requirements for different lengths of time depending on the severity of the original sentence (Table 11.1), and failure to do so could lead to a fine, imprisonment or both. The bill originally set the fine at £1000 and the custodial sentence at a maximum of one month, but the Government amended its own bill to put these sanctions up to £5000 and six months' custody 'after receiving further representations from the police' (Home Office, 1997a). The act said nothing on how the police were to ensure compliance or verification of no changes (Cobley 1997).

Young offenders (under 18) were to have a duty to notify for time periods that were half as long as for adults and penalties for non-compliance were to be a fine but no custodial sanction; the youth court could order someone with parental responsibility to comply on behalf of the young person, although no such similar arrangements existed if the young person was cautioned (National Association for the Care and Resettlement of Offenders 2002).

Schedule One of the act listed the designated offences that would lead to registration; in effect, this was to be three separate lists for Scotland, Northern Ireland, and England and Wales. The courts were to have no discretion in the matter, and registration was an automatic add-on to conviction for the various listed offences.

At the time of the register's launch, the Home Office was not over-triumphalist about its introduction, and the Minister responsible was quite circumspect in his choice of words:

> there is no magic wand – so we will be open to new ideas and initiatives…I want to see how the sex offenders register operates and if changes are necessary then I will look at how it can be developed and improved. (Home Office 1997b)

Table 11.1 Sex offender register notification periods	
Sentence	*Notification period*
Life imprisonment	Indefinite
Admitted to Hospital subject to a restriction	Indefinite
30 months' or more imprisonment	Indefinite
Imprisonment for less than 30 months but more than 6 months	10 years
6 months' or less imprisonment	7 years
Admitted to a hospital not subject to a restriction order	7 years
A non-custodial sentence (including guardianship under the Mental Health Act 1983) *or* a caution	5 years

Other observers were even more cautious in wondering whether the register was actually going to be a poisoned chalice (Soothill and Francis 1998).

The register in practice

The Home Office produced guidance for the police and other agencies who would be implementing the 1997 act from 1 September in England, Wales and Northern Ireland (Home Office 1997c), and the Scottish Office did the same for Scotland (Scottish Office 1997); the Northern Ireland Office also produced its own separate guidance (Northern Ireland Office 1997), as did the Association of Chief Officers of Police for its members (1997a).

It is arguable that the proponents of the act had underestimated the amount of work and resources the police would need to put into maintaining the register, and in strictly legal terms the act only places a new duty on offenders with regard to 'notifying changes' or 'registering'. The reality was that the police had to start deploying officers to oversee the register and to train others at the public desks of police stations to deal with registrants calling in. Other agencies, such as prisons, hospitals and courts, had to ensure the police were alerted to the fact that a certain individual would have to call in to notify the police of changes in their circumstances.

Hospital managers appear to have been somewhat 'difficult' in their interpretation of the act, not seeing why they should have to notify the police of offenders due to register. The act placed no duty on the hospital, and medical confidentiality arguments were used to deflect any ideas of automatic disclosure to the police. ACPO reported that this matter had 'been the subject of considerable debate' (1997a, para. 15) and lamented that 'it therefore seems unlikely that the release of patients in this category will be notified to the police' (para. 18). In practice, there has been little manifest difficulty in this area.

By the end of December 1997, some 3365 names were reportedly on the register out of a possible 4524, giving a national compliance rate of 88 per cent (*Sunday Telegraph* 1997). By February 1999 this number had risen to 8161 (HC Deb 12 May 1995 Col. 159 WA) and by March 2001 the figure was put at 'about 15,000' and with 'a further 2000 offenders join[ing] the register every six months' (Home Office 2001a: Ch. 3, para. 2); the compliance rate was now 97 per cent (Ch. 3, para. 4).

In 1998, the Government introduced Sex Offender Orders, which could be made on convicted sex offenders who had offended *before* 1 September 1997 and who were therefore ineligible for inclusion on the register. The Crime and Disorder Act 1998 ss. 2–4 empowered courts to place these orders on individuals acting suspiciously (so-called 'trigger' behaviour) and known to have old convictions for sexual offences. The Sex Offender Order is a civil order placing prohibitions on the activities of individuals to prevent possible crimes and also permitting their names to go on the register; any breach of the order could result in criminal proceedings. The Home Office always intended these orders – originally called Community Protection

Orders – to partly compensate for the fact that the register was not retrospective (see Home Office 1997d, para. 2). In fact, only 170 Sex Offender Orders had been made by the summer of 2002 (Home Office 2002a), which made little impact on the reported 110,000 convicted – but unregistered – sex offenders out in the community (see, for example, Marshall 1997).

The Crime and Disorder Act also re-named police cautions as 'reprimands' and 'final warnings' for young offenders. The police were supposed to tell any young sex offenders dealt with in this way that they would automatically go on the register. When two police forces failed to do this, the High Court ruled that this was incompatible with Article 6 of the European Convention on Human Rights, which guarantees the right to a fair hearing (*Daily Telegraph* 1998)

After one year's experience of the register, a survey of social workers commissioned by the journal *Community Care* found that 60 per cent of social workers felt the register fell short of expectations, not least because it was not retrospective. Sixty per cent also believed that there should be a separate register for individuals suspected of abuse or found 'guilty' of abuse through civil proceedings even if there had been no criminal proceedings. Overall, only 23 per cent of social workers thought the register had made their work with sex offenders any easier (Valios 1998).

'Every parent's nightmare'

Over the summer of 2000, a fierce media-led debate was entered into that would have direct implications for the sex offender register. To unravel what happened, a short chronology of events has to be followed:

26 June –   Home Office announces its intention to review the register, which it describes as having been 'enormously successful' (Home Office 2000a).

1 July –   Eight-year-old Sarah Payne is abducted in Sussex, and a major police hunt begins, under the spotlight of the media.

17 July –   Sarah Payne's body is found in a field by a farm-worker.

23 July –   The Sunday newspaper the *News of the World* starts its 'For Sarah' campaign to get the register opened to the public; the newspaper says it will publish the photographs and names of

sex offenders in lieu of any government activity (*News of the World* 2000a).

- A MORI poll carried out for the *News of the World* finds that 30 per cent of adults in the general population thought the register had been 'fairly effective' and 31 per cent thought it had been 'not very effective'. Only 4 per cent of those surveyed thought the register was 'very effective', compared with 18 per cent who thought it was 'not at all effective' (*News of the World*/MORI 2000a).

26 July – The Home Office publishes the proceedings of its Inter-departmental steering group that has been reviewing all the law relating to sexual offending (Home Office 2000b).

29 July – Demonstrations against sex offenders – with some accompanying violence – start in Paulsgrove, Portsmouth, and continue for a week (*The Guardian* 2000a). Other attacks are made on individual offenders around the country (e.g. *The Independent* 2000b).

30 July – The *News of the World* continues its 'For Sarah' campaign, inviting readers to complete a form and send it to the Home Secretary demanding open access to the register. The newspaper also publishes more photographs (*News of the World* 2000) and other newspapers join the clamour (*Sunday People* 2000).

2 August – The Home Office publishes its formal evaluation of the register (Plotnikoff and Woolfson 2000).

4 August – The *News of the World* agrees to suspend its campaign following a meeting with the National Society for the Prevention of Cruelty to Children (NSPCC), ACPO, the National Association for the Care and Resettlement of Offenders (NACRO) and the Association of Chief Officers of Probation.

Sex offenders who targeted children had, for a few weeks, found themselves at the centre of a media 'feeding frenzy' (see Thomas 2001). More than a year later, Roy Whiting would be convicted for Sarah Payne's murder; the sentencing judge described him as 'every parent's nightmare'.

Where Are They Now?

The Home Office-commissioned evaluation of the sex offender register published in the summer of 2000 was entitled *Where Are They Now?* All 43 police forces in England and Wales were subject to a survey completed by telephone, six forces receiving follow-up interviews in person (Plotnikoff and Woolfson 2000).

The police reported that the register had resulted in improved data quality and improved multi-agency work, especially when it came to risk assessment work. On the other hand, the maintenance of the register was considered low-status work within forces and was hampered by a lack of resources, despite the ever-growing workload it entailed. Home visits in the interests of verification and compliance work were made in 70 per cent of the forces surveyed, and this in turn created more work and produced more information.

The compliance rate among registrants was put at 94.7 per cent, but whether or not the register was effective the picture is less clear. No figures had been kept on re-conviction rates among registrants, and the picture was further muddled because the definition of sexual offence within the Home Office Criminal Statistics did not match the offences that led to register requirements. As for the question of greater community safety being achieved, the evaluators lamented that:

> forces had no agreed way of quantifying the contribution of sex offender monitoring to improving community safety…no single measure of effectiveness emerged from this study as suitable for performance measurement. Rates of registration compliance and re-conviction needed careful interpretation. (Plotnikoff and Woofson 2000)

The Government's response to *Where Are They Now?*

The Government was now faced with making changes to the sex offender register based on either the considered tones of its evaluation report or the more strident tones of the media storm. It would later freely admit that it had chosen the latter path:

> following the tragic death of Sarah Payne, widespread public concern was expressed about the dangers posed by sex offenders. In response, the Government introduced, in Autumn 2000, a number of amendments to the then Criminal Justice and Court Services Bill to strengthen the Sex Offenders Act. (Home Office 2002b)

Schedule Five of the Criminal Justice and Court Services Act 2000 brought in the main changes to the register by amending the 1997 Sex Offenders Act. The changes were implemented from 1 June 2001 but did *not* include any public right of access to the register. In summary, the changes included the following:

- New offenders had to make their initial reporting to the police within 3 days, rather than 14 as before.

- This first report had to be in person, and offenders no longer had the option of writing in or e-mailing.

- First reports and subsequent reports of changes had to be to a prescribed police station rather than to any police station.

- The police were given new powers to photograph and fingerprint offenders on first registration.

- The sanction for non-compliance rose from a maximum six months' imprisonment to a possible five years.

- Registrants had to notify the police if they were going abroad for more than eight days. (For further details, see Home Office 2001a.)

Apart from these changes, the Criminal Justice and Court Services Act also put Multi-Agency Public Protection Panels (MAPPPs) on to a statutory footing (see Maguire and Kemshall, this volume), made non-compliance with register requirements an arrestable offence and banned any one going on to the register from having early release from prison by being electronically tagged (Home Detention Curfew).

The evaluation report *Where Are They Now?* had not recommended any of these changes. The report had pointed out that agencies hardly had time to tell the police to expect a new registrant coming in within the existing 14 days – let alone 3 days – and had reported that 'sometimes [the police] first

heard about a registration requirement from the offender himself'
(Plotnikoff and Woolfson 2000). The report also said that 75 per cent of
offenders already turned up in person rather than wrote in and that some
police forces were already taking fingerprints and photographs; to that
degree, the changes were only legitimizing existing practices. As for the
need to increase the sanction for non-compliance when compliance was
lying at 94 per cent, the evaluation report was again silent.

As the Government would later say, these changes were a response to
public concerns and a possible 'trade-off' to avert demands for public access
to the register. The changes do reflect a *News of the World*-commissioned
MORI poll reporting that 84 per cent of the public wanted tougher
sanctions for non-compliance with the register and 93 per cent wanted the
'requirement to notify' to be within three days rather than 14 (*News of the
World*/MORI 2000b).

Reviewing the Sex Offenders Act

In the summer of 2001, the Home Office published a consultation paper to
initiate its promised review of the sex offender register. In his introduction
to this consultation paper, Home Secretary David Blunkett stated his belief
that 'the Sex Offenders Act has proved a valuable tool in helping protect the
public' but that 'experience in implementing it has suggested that aspects
could be strengthened' (Home Office/Scottish Executive 2001). The question of wider access to the information on registered sex offenders was specifically excluded from the review (Home Office/Scottish Executive 2001).

The compliance rate for registration was now cited as 97 per cent, a rate
that was described as 'steadily improving' (Home Office/Scottish Executive
2001). Not only that, but 'despite what one might assume to be the case,
nearly all registered offenders co- operated with the police when they made
home visits, although they were not required to do so' (Home
Office/Scottish Executive 2001).

In terms of procedural arrangements, this all seemed like a success story,
but the consultation paper now recommended a further tightening up of the
register:

- The 14 days allowed for notifying changes should fall to 8 days. The review team considered reducing this time limit to 3 days but concluded that 'this period is too short…and would make unreasonably high demands on police resources':

  it should be recognised that any period chosen is *to some extent arbitrary* but eight days is a significant tightening of the current arrangements by almost halving the current time allowed. (Home Office/Scottish Executive 2001, emphasis added)

- All changes – not just initial reporting – should be given in person, e-mails and letters no longer being acceptable.

- Verification exercises should become annual events, and a duty to report annually should be placed on the offender rather than leaving the onus on the police to make home visits.

- More offences should be designated as leading to registration (e.g. burglary with intent to rape).

- Relevant offences committed abroad should lead to registration at home whether the offender was a UK or a foreign national. Protests had been provoked by the Home Secretary's decision to allow the boxer Mike Tyson into the country despite his conviction for rape in America (*The Independent* 2000a).

- Cautions and conditional discharges should only lead to registration if the victim was under 18 and the offender aged over 20, and length of registration in these circumstances should be reduced from 5 years to 12 months; absolute discharges should not require registration. This recommendation recognized confusion over whether a discharge counted as a conviction; the Powers of Criminal Courts (Sentencing) Act 2000 suggested that it did not and that registration should therefore not follow.

The situation became more anomalous when it was remembered that cautions in England and Wales *did* result in registration:

  a caution means that the matter has not gone before the courts and so one could argue that it is less serious than a discharge which is a sentence handed down by a court. Why should it be that a less serious matter attracts potentially more serious repercussions than a sentence of a court? (Gillespie 2002)

Any recommendations the review made that appeared to be 'tightening' the register had to be balanced against the possibility that too much tightening could change the very nature of the register and move it from being a regulatory form of achieving community safety – which it was intended to be – to becoming a punishment in its own right. The review team reminded itself that:

> Challenges to the Sex Offenders Act on human rights grounds have been successfully resisted because the registration requirement has been seen as an administrative consequence of a sentence passed by the court, rather than being a separate sentence in its own right. Were the registration requirement to become more onerous, there could come a point at which the Act could no longer be seen as an administrative requirement. (Home Office/Scottish Executive 2001)

The review ran into deeper waters over the registration of young sex offenders and reported findings of 'considerable concern' and a lack of consensus on the way forward. The questions now posed included whether or not registration was even appropriate for the under-18's, who were more open to change at that age than when older and in any event might have been guilty only of youthful experimentation with people their own age.

The review asked for comments on five options:

1. leaving the system unchanged

2. registering only those aged over 16, unless there had been a custodial sentence or hospital order

3. having different custodians of the register other than the police and requiring a greater therapeutic input

4. introducing more judicial discretion into the registration decision

5. leaving the system unchanged but allowing de-registration at age 18 if assessment showed no further risk of offending.

All of these options reflected a long-standing concern that the register was not really appropriate for young sex offenders. The NSPCC had voiced its concerns when the register first came into being (NSPCC 1997). The options offered the possibilities of a more welfare-orientated approach that were countered only by the review team's suggestions that there should also be a heavier sanction for non-compliance; it was proposed that the existing fine arrangements be supplemented by a maximum sanction of two years in custody for non-compliance (Home Office/Scottish Executive 2001). This clash of welfare and penal sanctions for young offenders is not unique to the position of young sex offenders (e.g. Goldson 2002).

The Government's response to the review

The Government's response to the review did not emerge in the midst of any public/media furore comparable to that met by *Where Are They Now?* The conviction and sentencing of Roy Whiting in December 2001 for the murder of Sarah Payne led to some further calls for open access to the register (see below), but in general terms the response was received in measured terms.

The Home Secretary trailed some of the response in his speech to the Labour Party Conference of October 2002 (Home Office 2002c), but the full picture of future directions came with publication of the White Paper announcing the proposed changes to be made overall to the law on sexual offending (Home Office 2002b). Changes to the register included proposals to:

- reduce the 14 days allowed for notifying changes to three days

- make verification exercises annual events with the onus on the offender to report in, in person (no letters or e-mails);

- make any change of address for over 7 days notifiable, rather than keeping the existing period of 14 days

- extend the power to photograph and fingerprint to all verification exercises rather than just the initial reporting to the police

- extend the number of offences that would lead to registration

- introduce a new order to enable offenders to be registered when the offences had been committed abroad; the order would be applicable to UK and foreign nationals.

Some of these White Paper proposals ignore the review recommendations, which recommended, for example, reducing the 14 days allowed for notifying changes to 8, because 3 days 'would make unreasonably high demands on police resources'. The White Paper also came up with proposals never mentioned in the review, such as requiring notification for any changes longer than 7 days rather than the existing 14, or extending the power to photograph and fingerprint at every verification contact.

As for the review's options significantly to change the register for young offenders, the White Paper says nothing at all. Proposals are made to reduce the penalties for young people engaged in 'consensual and experimental' sex below appropriate ages (Home Office 2002b, para. 52), but no changes are proposed regarding registration.

The Government does make a more-clear cut statement on this subject in its summary of the 50 or so submissions it received from organizations responding to the review. This summary has only been published online at www.sexualoffencesbill.homeoffice.gov.uk and therein the Government states that:

> Registration will continue to apply to offenders above the age of criminal re-sponsibility (10). We are introducing sentence and age thresholds for some of the offences which will mean that a young offender is only required to register where the seriousness of the offence warrants it.

All of the more liberal options in the review are thereby dismissed despite 18 respondents wanting judicial discretion, 15 wanting de-registration at 18, 13 wanting a non-police agency to take over the register for young offenders and only 6 respondents suggesting that the present regime continue. The online summary says that the Government will be bringing forward a maximum two-year custodial sanction for non-compliance by young offenders – only 4 out of 26 respondents opposed this proposal.

A public right of access to the register

A continuing debate on the register has been the question of the public's right of access to it. As noted earlier, the suggestion had been made during the 1997 Parliamentary discussion on the Bill that something akin to the American 'Megan's Law' was needed. Megan Kanka was a seven-year-old girl from New Jersey assaulted and killed by a man living in the same street who had previous convictions. At that time, ACPO was among those who believed that the register should remain 'closed' (*The Times* 1997) and subsequent Home Secretaries have held this line. As noted above, the review consultation paper went out of its way to say that 'the issue of wider access to the information on registered sex offenders is not further dealt with in this review' (Home Office/Scottish Executive 2001), and at the Labour Party

Annual Conference the following year, Home Secretary David Blunkett was again categorical that 'we cannot open the register to the vigilantes who do not understand the difference between paediatricians and paedophiles' (Blunkett 2002). Blunkett was referring to an incident where vigilantes had confused the two and vandalized the home of a paediatrician (*The Guardian* 2000b).

Before the sex offender register had come into being, the disclosure of police-held information was already occurring on a limited scale (ACPO 1997b). When the North Wales Police disclosed information on two known sex offenders to a local community in the summer of 1997, however, the two people concerned sought a judicial review of the police decision. The High Court ruled that the police had acted properly because of the possible risk to the public but added that such disclosures should not be routine and should be undertaken only when the risk was demonstrable. As a general principle, and in terms of good public administration, the police should keep criminal record histories confidential (*R* v *Chief Constable of North Wales Police* ex parte *AB* 1997). The Appeal Court supported this view, adding that the police had to adopt 'a proactive rather than a reactive policy for dealing with offenders who had committed offences against children in the past' (*R* v *Chief Constable of North Wales Police* ex parte *Thorpe* 1998). The Home Office would now allow what was termed 'controlled disclosure' rather than any right of access. The police would decide when to disclose and to whom. Any risk assessment would be made jointly with other agencies.

Apart from the North Wales decision, other precedents for police disclosures of information have been cited. Since the mid-1980s, the police have disclosed criminal records to local authorities for purposes of pre-employment screening of child care workers; in 2002, the Criminal Record Bureau took over this work. Section 115 of The Crime and Disorder Act 1998 also permits a free exchange of personal information held by the police and other agencies in the interests of crime reduction; the exchange has to be with other agencies rather than the public (see Justice 2000 for a critique of these arrangements).

In 1999, the Home Office issued further guidance on the 'controlled disclosure' of sex offender register information in 1999 and the circumstances in which information on individuals likely to pose a particular risk could be given to housing officials, an offender's place of work, schools and playgroups, youth groups and sometimes immediate members of a household:

> The person making the disclosure should explain that it is made in confidence and ensure that the recipient understands the reasons for having been given the information; what use they are to make of it; and any restrictions applying to its further dissemination. (Home Office 1999)

This guidance was described as 'draft' guidance, but at the time of writing no further finalized version has been produced 'due to competing work pressures' (Home Office, 5 November 2002, personal correspondence).

This resolve to not allow a wider public access to the register has not stopped the public and parts of the media from continuing to press for a new open policy. Put simply, the rationale for access was that 'if you – the professionals – know where these people are living, then we – the public – also want to know, in order to better protect ourselves and our children'. In particular, the *News of the World* started its 'name and shame' campaign in the wake of the Sarah Payne murder (see above).

Over a year later, Roy Whiting was convicted for Sarah Payne's murder and it was revealed that Whiting was a known sex offender, although his offences had been committed in 1995, thereby allowing him to not have to register (*Daily Express* 2001). It was enough to start the *News of the World's* second campaign for a Sarah's Law (*News of the World* 2001). But this was again resisted by the Home Office, although the concession was made that there might in future be a local lay representative on the MAPPPs deciding on the risk that sex offenders posed:

> This is an important way of ensuring the local area feels they have a voice and a representative in the process who can help agree the best way to manage an offender's presence in the community. (Home Office 2001b)

The editor of the *News of the World* reportedly believed that this did not go far enough and made veiled threats to return to the campaign at a later date (*The Guardian* 2001); for the time being, the campaign for a Sarah's Law was put on hold.

What research there is on the effectiveness of open access to the sex offender register is ambivalent in its findings. In the US State of Wisconsin, for example, residents attending 'community notification' meetings at which they were given details of a sex offender resident in their area were found to be confused by what it all meant and sometimes went away more anxious than when they had arrived (Zevitz and Farkas 1999). Research commissioned by the UK's NSPCC to ask the question 'Does Megan's Law work?' in the USA concluded that 'the majority of states have little, if any, understanding of the impact of community notification in their jurisdictions' (Lovell 2001).

Conclusion

In Europe, only the UK and the Republic of Ireland have sex offender registers; Ireland's was implemented by its Sex Offender Act 2001 and, like that of the UK, has provisions for 'controlled disclosure' (Thomas 2000b).

The rest of Europe seems more ambivalent about registers. In 1997, the European Union adopted a Joint Action on the protection of children from sexual exploitation (97/1 54 JHA), and in 2001 it produced an updated and revised version as a Council Framework Decision (COM (2000) 854 final). These documents called for the stronger and more effective policing and punishment of child sex offenders by Member States, more encompassing laws and a better use of techniques such as DNA analysis as a means of detection. Neither document suggested a need for sex offender registers.

Whether or not registers actually make a difference and improve community safety remains an open question. The lack of good research studies on registers in America was noted earlier (Hebenton and Thomas 1997), and research commissioned by the Home Office found 'no single measure of effectiveness emerged from this study as suitable for performance measurement' (Plotnikoff and Woolfson 2000). What the study did show was the emergence of an efficient implementation of the Sex Offender Act and a compliance rate of 94 per cent, which a year later had risen to 97 per cent. On that level, the register is successful, but high compliance rates are not the same as being able to demonstrate that we have safer communities.

The Home Office has described the register as being 'enormously successful' (Home Office 2000a) and a 'valuable tool in helping protect the public' (Home Office/Scottish Executive 2001). Most police officers engaged in register work have found that its' 'contribution to policing justified the extra work involved', especially in terms of better data quality and multi-agency work (Plotnikoff and Woolfson 2000). Once again, however, such statements are more about the process of implementation rather than any evaluation of the effectiveness of the register in terms of improving community safety.

Forms of surveillance, and a knowledge that offenders are where we can see them, have long been guiding principles of crime prevention and forms of punishment. The sex offender register *per se* keeps offenders visible by registering their whereabouts for professionals, if not – in the UK – for the wider community. The problem appears to be that there is no certain way of measuring the effectiveness of registers actually to make a difference to community safety, and to that extent they remain an act of faith or merely a means of creating a false sense of security. Others have suggested that the register just performs a function by excluding sex offenders as 'the other' against which the communities' sense of self can be identified (Kleinhaus 2002).

In the UK, there has since 1997 been a gradual 'tightening' of the sex offender register as requirements on offenders have become slowly more onerous and sanctions for non-compliance have increased. Much of this 'tightening' has arguably been in response to public concerns, including the demand for public access, and for political reasons rather than in response to evaluations, research on 'What Works' or the considered responses of practitioners in the field. Although policy-makers might be clear in their own minds that the register is still a community safety mechanism, the feelings of registrants might be that at best it is turning them into 'second-class citizens' and at worst the register is slowly becoming a punishment in its own right, a possibility that the Home Office has already recognized – 'there could come a point at which the (Sex Offenders) Act could no longer be seen as an administrative requirement' (Home Office/Scottish Executive 2001, Ch. 3, para. 7).

References

ACHE (Action on Child Exploitation) (undated) Explanatory Leaflet. Birmingham: ACHE.

ACPO (Association of Chief Officers of Police) (1997a) *Sex Offenders Act 1997 – Implementation Guidelines.* ACPO Crime Committee. London: ACPO.

ACPO (Association of Chief Officers of Police) (1997b) *Disclosure of Information – Sex Offenders: Results of a Survey of Police Forces in England and Wales.* ACPO Crime Committee. London: ACPO.

Blunkett, D. (2002) 'Fighting Crime and Disorder at Core of Social Justice.' Speech to the Labour Party Conference, Blackpool, 2 October.

Cobley, C. (1997) 'Keeping Track of Sex Offenders – Part 1 of the Sex Offenders Act 1997.' Modern Law Review September, 690–699.

Daily Express (2001) 'He's Done it Before'. 13 December, 1.

Daily Telegraph (1998) 'Boys, 15, Win Fight to get Names off Sex Offender List.' 30 November, 10.

Department of Health (1995) *Annual Reports of Area Child Protection Committees 1993–4.* London: HMSO.

Department of Health, Home Office, Department for Education and Employment (1999) *Working Together To Safeguard Children: A Guide to Inter-agency Working To Safeguard and Promote the Welfare of Children.* London: HMSO.

Earl-Hubbard, M. (1996) 'The Child Sex Offender Registration Law.' *Northwestern Law Review 902,* 788–862.

The Guardian (1996) 'Daniel Handley's Killers Told they Must Die in Prison' 17 May, 1.

The Guardian (2000a) 'Vigilantes Defy Calls to End Paedophile Protests'.10 August, 1.

The Guardian (2000b) 'Doctor Driven out of Home by Vigilantes'. 30 August, 1.

The Guardian (2001) 'Parents to Get Seat on Paedophile Panels'. 17 December, 2

Gillespie, A. (2002) 'Discharging Sex Offenders.' *Criminal Law Review 00,* 53–55.

Goldson, B. (2002) 'New Labour, Social Justice and Children: Political Calculation and the Deserving–Undeserving Schism.' *British Journal of Social Work 32,* 683–695.

Hebenton, B. and Thomas, T. (1997) 'Keeping Track? Observations on Sex Offender Registers in the US.' Crime Detection and Prevention Series Paper No. 83. London: Police Research Group, Home Office.

Home Office (1995) 'Boost for Crime Fighters as New Powers Come into Force.' Press realease, 10 April.

Home Office (1996) *Sentencing and Supervision of Sex Offenders: A Consultation Document.* Cm 3304. London: HMSO.

Home Office (1997a) 'Sex Offenders to Face Tougher Penalties – Maclean.' Press release, 27 January.

Home Office (1997b) 'Sex Offenders Register Comes into Effect.' Press release, 31 August.

Home Office (1997c) 'Sex Offenders Act 1997.' Home Office Circular 39/1997. London: HMSO

Home Office (1997d) *Community Protection Order: A Consultation Paper.* London: HMSO.

Home Office (1999) 'Draft Guidance on the Disclosure of Information about Sex Offenders Who May Present a Risk to Children and Vulnerable Adults.' London: Police Science and Technology Unit.

Home Office (2000a) 'Sex Offenders Register To Be Reviewed.' Press release, 26 June.

Home Office (2000b) 'Setting the Boundaries: Reforming the Law on Sex Offences.' London: HMSO.

Home Office (2001a) 'Criminal Justice and Court Services Act 2000: Amendments to the Sex Offenders Act 1997.' Home Office Circular 20/2001. London: HMSO.

Home Office (2001b) 'Statement from the Home Secretary.' Press release, 18 December.

Home Office (2002a) 'Research into Sex Offender Orders Published.' Press release, 19 June.

Home Office (2002b) *Protecting the Public: Strengthening Protection Against Sex Offenders and Reforming the Law on Sexual Offences.* Cm 5668. London: HMSO.

Home Office (2002c) 'New Moves to Tighten Sex Offender Register.' Press release, 2 October.

Home Office/Scottish Executive (2001) *Consultation Paper on the Review of Part One of the Sex Offenders Act 1997.* London: HMSO.

Home Office, Department of Health, Department of Education and Science, and Welsh Office (1991) *Working Together: A guide to Arrangements for Inter-agency Co-operation for the Protection of Children from Abuse.* London: HMSO.

Hughes, B., Parker, H. and Gallagher, B. (1996) *Policing Child Sexual Abuse: The View from Police Practitioners.* London: Police Research Group.

The Independent (1996) 'Murdered Girl's Father Supports Register Plans'.20 July, 5.

The Independent (2000a) 'Anger as Tyson is Granted Visa for Glasgow Fight'. 19 May, 4.

The Independent (2000b) 'Man Accused of Paedophile Offences Kills Himself after Vigilante Attack.' 9 August, 4.

Justice (2000) *Disclosure of Crime Prevention Data and Privacy Rights.* London: Justice.

Kleinhaus M.M. (2002) 'Criminal Justice Approaches to Paedophilic Sex Offences.' *Social and Legal Studies 11*, 2, 235–255

Liberty (1996) *Response to the Home Office Consultation Paper on Sentencing and Supervision of Sex Offenders.* London: Liberty.

Lovell, E. (2001) *Megan's Law: Does it Protect Children?* London: NSPCC.

Manchester Evening News (1996) 'City Aims for Sex Fiend File.' 5 September 1.

Marshall, P. (1997) *The Prevalence of Convictions for Sexual Offending.* Research Finding No.55. London: Research and Statistics Directorate, Home Office.

NACRO (National Association for the Care and Resettlement of Offenders) (2002) *Young People and the Sex Offenders Register.* London: NACRO.

News of the World (2000a) 'Named, Shamed.' 23 July, 1.

News of the World (2000b) 'Sign Here for Sarah.' 30 July, 1.

News of the World (2001) 'Named, Shamed'.16 December, 1.

News of the World/MORI (2000a) 'Crime and Sentencing Poll.' 23 July.

News of the World/MORI (2000b) 'Naming and Shaming Poll.' 20 August.

Niven, D. (1996) 'Suffer the Little Children.' *The Guardian.* 16 October.

NIO (Northern Ireland Office) (1997) *The Sex Offenders Act 1997 – Introductory Guide for Northern Ireland.* Belfast: NIO.

NSPCC (National Society for the Prevention of Cruelty to Children) (1997) 'NSPCC Concerned re Inclusion of Juvenile Offenders on Sex Offenders Register.' October 24.

Parris, M. (1997) 'All-party Witch-Hunt.' *The Times,* 24 January.

Plotnikoff, J. and Woolfson, R. (2000) *Where Are They Now? An Evaluation of Sex Offender Registration in England and Wales.* Police Research Series Paper No.126, London: Home Office.

R v Chief Constable of North Wales Police ex parte *AB. The Times,* 14 July.

R v Chief Constable of North Wales Police ex parte *Thorpe. The Times,* 28 March.

Scottish Office (1997) 'Sex Offenders Act 1997 Guidance on Implementation.' Circular HD 12/1997 2154. Edinburgh: Scottish Office.

Small, J. A. (1999) 'Who are the people in your neighbourhood? Due Process, Public Protection and Sex Offender Notification Laws.' *New York University Law Review 74,* 1451–1494.

Soothill, K. and Francis, B. (1998) 'Poisoned Chalice or Just Deserts? (The Sex Offenders Act 1997).' *Journal of Forensic Psychiatry 9,* 2, 281–293.

The Sun (1995) 'Burn in Hell.' 23 November, 1.

Sunday People (2000) 'Hang Them.' 30 July, 1.

Sunday Telegraph (1997) 'Hundreds of Violent Sex Offenders Go to Ground.' 28 December, 1.

The Times (1997) 'Police Chiefs Oppose Plan to Advertise Paedophiles'. 15 February, 2

Thomas, T. (2000a) *Sex Crime: Sex Offending and Society.* Cullompton: Willan.

Thomas, T. (2000b) 'Protecting the Public: Some Observations on the Sex Offender Bill 2000.' *Irish Criminal Law Journal 10,* 2, 12–15.

Thomas, T. (2001) 'Sex offenders, the Home Office and the Sunday Papers.' *Journal of Social Welfare and Family Law 23,* 1, 103–108.

Valios, N. (1998) 'Social Workers Warn Register is Flawed.' *Community Care,* 27 August – 2 September 00.

Zevitz, R. and Farkas, M. (1999) *Sex Offender Community Notification: Assessing the Impact in Wisconsin.* Washington DC: National Institute of Justice.

The Contributors

Anthony Beech is a Reader in Criminological Psychology at the University of Birmingham and a Fellow of the British Psychological Society. Over the past eight years, he has been the lead researcher of the STEP (Sex Offender Treatment Evaluation Project) team. Here, he has been involved in treatment evaluation and the development of systems to look at treatment need and treatment change in sex offenders, specifically child abusers. He has taken a keen interest in process issues in sex offender therapy. This work is regarded as having a major influence on assessment and treatment in the UK. He has written widely on the topics of assessment and treatment of sexual offenders and other related subjects.

Grant Devilly is currently a Professorial Research Fellow at Swinburne University, Victoria, Australia. His research interests include treatment models of post-traumatic stress disorder and other anxiety disorders, iatrogenesis in clinical practice, psychometric measurement within the clinical domain and pseudoscience within mental health practice.

Dawn Fisher, Consultant Clinical and Forensic Psychologist, is Head of Psychology at Llanarth Court Hospital, Wales. She is also an Honorary Senior Research Fellow at the University of Birmingham. She was a member of the Joint Prison–Probation Panel between 1999 and 2002. She has been extensively involved in sexual offender assessment and treatment for around 20 years and has recently co-written one of three probation-based sex offender treatment programmes running in the UK. In addition, she is currently involved in developing the Healthy Sexual Functioning programme of the National Probation Directorate and Offender Behaviour Programmes Unit of the UK prison service. She has also written extensively on the assessment and treatment of sexual offenders.

Don Grubin is Professor of Forensic Psychiatry, University of Newcastle and (Honorary) Consultant Forensic Psychiatrist, Newcastle, North Tyneside and Northumbria Mental Health Trust. Trained at the Maudsley Hospital, Institute of Psychiatry and Broadmoor Hospital, he is a member of the Home Office Correctional Services Accreditation Panel for Offending Behaviour Programmes and a national trainer for the police in the use of risk assessment instruments.

Hazel Kemshall is currently Professor of Community and Criminal Justice at DeMontfort University, Leicester. She has research interests in the risk assessment and management of offenders, effective work in multi-agency public protection, and implementing effective practice with offenders. She has completed research for the Economic and Social Research

Council, the Home Office and the Scottish Office. She is the author of the Home Office risk training materials for probation officers and the Scottish Office materials for social workers, and has written numerous publications on risk. She has recently completed a literature review on risk assessment tools for violent and dangerous offenders and an evaluation of Multi-Agency Public Protection Panels for the Home Office and Scottish Executive, as well as an audit of risk tools in Scotland with Gill McIvor.

Andrew Kendrick is Professor of Residential Child Care in the Department of Social Work, University of Strathclyde, and linked to the Scottish Institute for Residential Child Care. He has carried out a range of research on services for children and young people, including studies of reviews of children in care, outcomes of residential and foster care, and interagency working both for children and young people in care and those at risk of exclusion from mainstream schooling. His current research focuses on residential child care and includes evaluations of a residential unit for sexually aggressive young men and secure care. He is the editor of the *Scottish Journal of Residential Child Care.*

Gill McIvor is Professor and Director of the Social Work Research Centre at the University of Stirling. Her previous research has focused primarily upon community penalties, young people and crime, and women's experience of community sentences. She has also undertaken research on risk assessment of serious violent and sexual offenders and is currently evaluating the pilot Drug Courts in Scotland. She has written and edited several books, including *Sentenced to Serve* (Avebury, 1992), *Working with Offenders* (Research Highlights in Social Work No. 26, Jessica Kingsley Publishers, 1995), *Understanding Offending Among Young People* (Stationery Office, 1999, with Janet Jamieson and Cathy Murray) and *Women who Offend* (Research Highlights in Social Work No. 44, Jessica Kingsley Publishers, 2003).

Mike Maguire is Professor of Criminology and Criminal Justice at Cardiff University, where he has worked since 1989, having previously been a research fellow at the Centre for Criminological Research, Oxford University. He has conducted research and written books and articles over many years on aspects of crime and criminal justice, particularly in the areas of policing, probation, prisons and criminal statistics. He and Hazel Kemshall were principal researchers in a recent study of the work of Multi-Agency Public Protection Panels. He is a co-editor of a major textbook, *The Oxford Handbook of Criminology*, now in its third edition. He is currently a senior adviser to the Crime Reduction Director for Wales and a member of the Correctional Services Accreditation Panel.

Bill Marshall is Emeritus Professor of Psychology and Psychiatry at Queens University and Director of Rockwood Psychological Services, Kingston, Ontario, Canada. He has been working with sexual offenders for 34 years and has over 280 publications, including 16 books, to his name. In 1993, he received the Lifetime Achievement Award from the Association for the Treatment of Sexual Abusers, and in 1999 he was awarded the Santiago

Grisolia Prize from the Queen Sophia Centre in Spain for his worldwide contribution to the reduction of violence. In 2000, he was elected a Fellow of the Royal Society of Canada.

Helen Masson is a Reader in Social Work at the University of Huddersfield. She teaches on a range of undergraduate and postgraduate programmes for social workers and other welfare professionals, and is a founder member of the University's Centre for Applied Childhood Studies. Since 1994, she has been researching policy and practice developments in relation to children and young people with sexual behaviour problems, and she is the author of a number of book chapters and journal articles on this and related subjects. She is also the current co-editor, with Marcus Erooga, of the *Journal of Sexual Aggression*, the academic journal of NOTA, the National Organisation for the Treatment of Abusers.

Heather Moulden is a doctoral student at the University of Ottawa and a part- time therapist with Rockwood Psychological Services, where she has worked with sexual offenders for the past four years. Heather's present research interests concern the relationship between empathy and social intelligence, as well as the relevance of hope theory for understanding and treating sexual offenders.

Mayumi Purvis is a postgraduate PhD forensic psychology student at the University of Melbourne researching the relationship between human needs, goals and sexual offending. Her additional research interests in the sexual offending area include cognitive distortions, cultural factors and offender rehabilitation.

Gerris Serran is a doctoral student at the University of Ottawa and a Senior Therapist with Rockwood Psychological Services. She has been involved in research and treatment of sexual offenders for the past 5 years and has written 15 publications. Her current interests concern the influence of the therapist in sexual offender treatment and the capacity of sexual offenders to cope with stress.

Terry Thomas is Reader in Social Work in the School of Health and Community Care, Leeds Metropolitan University. He is the author of *Sex Crime: Sex Offending and Society* (Willan, 2002) and 'The Collection and Use of Information on Child Sex Offenders Across Europe' in M. Herczog and C. Wattam (eds) *Child Sexual Abuse in Europe* (Council of Europe, 0000). In 2002, he was awarded a six-month Leverhulme Trust Study Abroad Fellowship to the University of Minnesota, USA, on the project 'Protecting the Public from Sex Offenders'.

Tony Ward is Professor of Psychology at Victoria University of Wellington, New Zealand and was co-ordinator of the forensic psychology doctoral programme at the University of Melbourne. His research interests include the area of social competency in offenders, theories of sexual offending, cognitive distortions and forensic treatment models.

Subject Index

Author Index